Bringing the Civic Back In

In the series *Urban Life, Landscape, and Policy*, edited by
DAVID STRADLING, LARRY BENNETT, and DAVARIAN BALDWIN.
Founding editor, ZANE L. MILLER.

Henry C. Binford, *From Improvement to City Planning: Spatial Management in Cincinnati from the Early Republic through the Civil War Decade*

Dennis E. Gale, *The Misunderstood History of Gentrification: People, Planning, Preservation, and Urban Renewal, 1915–2020*

Amy D. Finstein, *Modern Mobility Aloft: Elevated Highways, Architecture, and Urban Change in Pre-Interstate America*

Mark Shiel, ed., *Architectures of Revolt: The Cinematic City circa 1968*

Maureen Donaghy, *Democratizing Urban Development: Community Organizations for Housing across the United States and Brazil*

Maureen A. Flanagan, *Constructing the Patriarchal City: Gender and the Built Environments of London, Dublin, Toronto, and Chicago, 1870s into the 1940s*

Harold L. Platt, *Sinking Chicago: Climate Change and the Remaking of a Flood-Prone Environment*

Pamela Wilcox, Francis T. Cullen, and Ben Feldmeyer, *Communities and Crime: An Enduring American Challenge*

J. Mark Souther, *Believing in Cleveland: Managing Decline in "The Best Location in the Nation"*

Nathanael Lauster, *The Death and Life of the Single-Family House: Lessons from Vancouver on Building a Livable City*

Aaron Cowan, *A Nice Place to Visit: Tourism and Urban Revitalization in the Postwar Rustbelt*

Carolyn Gallaher, *The Politics of Staying Put: Condo Conversion and Tenant Right-to-Buy in Washington, DC*

Evrick Brown and Timothy Shortell, eds., *Walking in Cities: Quotidian Mobility as Urban Theory, Method, and Practice*

Michael T. Maly and Heather Dalmage, *Vanishing Eden: White Construction of Memory, Meaning, and Identity in a Racially Changing City*

Harold L. Platt, *Building the Urban Environment: Visions of the Organic City in the United States, Europe, and Latin America*

Kristin M. Szylvian, *The Mutual Housing Experiment: New Deal Communities for the Urban Middle Class*

Kathryn Wilson, *Ethnic Renewal in Philadelphia's Chinatown: Space, Place, and Struggle*

A list of additional titles in this series appears at the back of this book.

Bringing the Civic Back In

ZANE L. MILLER and American Urban History

Edited by LARRY BENNETT, JOHN D. FAIRFIELD, *and* PATRICIA MOONEY-MELVIN

With a foreword by DAVID STRADLING

TEMPLE UNIVERSITY PRESS
Philadelphia • *Rome* • *Tokyo*

TEMPLE UNIVERSITY PRESS
Philadelphia, Pennsylvania 19122
tupress.temple.edu

Copyright © 2022 by Temple University—Of The Commonwealth System
of Higher Education
All rights reserved
Published 2022

Library of Congress Cataloging-in-Publication Data
Names: Bennett, Larry, 1950– editor. | Fairfield, John D., 1955– editor. | Mooney-Melvin, Patricia, editor. | Stradling, David, writer of foreword. | Miller, Zane L. Works. Selections.
Title: Bringing the civic back in : Zane L. Miller and American urban history / edited by Larry Bennett, John D. Fairfield, and Patricia Mooney-Melvin ; with a foreword by David Stradling.
Other titles: Zane L. Miller and American urban history | Urban life, landscape, and policy.
Description: Philadelphia : Temple University Press, 2022. | Series: Urban life, landscape, and policy | Includes bibliographical references and index. | Summary: "Commemorates the legacy of the late urban historian Zane L. Miller"— Provided by publisher.
Identifiers: LCCN 2022002753 (print) | LCCN 2022002754 (ebook) | ISBN 9781439922422 (cloth) | ISBN 9781439922439 (paperback) | ISBN 9781439922446 (pdf)
Subjects: LCSH: Miller, Zane L. | Cities and towns—United States—History. | Urbanization—United States—History.
Classification: LCC HT123 .B737 2022 (print) | LCC HT123 (ebook) | DDC 307.760973—dc23/eng/20220521
LC record available at https://lccn.loc.gov/2022002753
LC ebook record available at https://lccn.loc.gov/2022002754

♾ The paper used in this publication meets the requirements of
the American National Standard for Information Sciences—Permanence of Paper
for Printed Library Materials, ANSI Z39.48-1992

Printed in the United States of America

9 8 7 6 5 4 3 2 1

To Janet Miller and in memory of Henry Shapiro

Contents

Foreword: Of Community and Scholarship:
The Zane L. Miller Process / David Stradling — ix

Preface and Acknowledgments — xvii

Part I: On Civic Nationalism

Introduction to Part I — 3

1 From Istanbul to Philadelphia: Ideas and the Urban Origins of the United States / Zane L. Miller — 9

2 The Resiliency of Cities and the Uncertain Future of American Civic Nationalism / Zane L. Miller — 22

3 Cities, American Civic Nationalism, and Fundamentalism / Zane L. Miller — 43

Part II: Urban Life as Urban History

4 "The *Metropolitan* Mode of Thought": Zane L. Miller and the History of Ideas / John D. Fairfield — 55

5 Creating Cities in the Post–World War II Southwest: The Arlington, Texas and Mesa, Arizona Experiences / Robert B. Fairbanks — 90

6 Claiming Space: Petrified Ethnics, Identity, and
   Civic Space / PATRICIA MOONEY-MELVIN   127

Part III: Reflections on Zane Miller

7 "I See My Job as Helping You": Zane L. Miller the Scholar,
   Mentor, and Friend / CHARLES LESTER   155

8 Working with Zane Miller / LARRY BENNETT   181

Appendix: A Zane L. Miller Timeline and Selective
Bibliography   187

List of Contributors   193

Index   195

Foreword

*Of Community and Scholarship:
The Zane L. Miller Process*

DAVID STRADLING

At first glance this volume appears to be an odd assemblage. Consisting of prose meant to introduce an urban history textbook, autobiographical essays reflecting on relationships with an urban historian, and original essays on urban history itself, this collection mixes genres around one unifying theme: the work of Zane L. Miller. A book is a fitting form for honoring one of the most important practitioners of urban history, one who had faith in the power of books to shape ideas and, in turn, the power of ideas to shape history. By offering fragments of his last and uncompleted work, combining it with contributions from a few of his students, and offering thoughts on how much his work as mentor and editor shaped individual careers and the field as a whole, this assemblage makes the case for Zane's lasting influence. But it accomplishes more, by demonstrating how Zane achieved his success: through the creation of a community of scholars that crossed generational, ideological, and disciplinary boundaries.

Zane was committed to the process of scholarship and engaged in it up to the moment of his passing. As all good scholars do, he read widely, absorbing and learning from good writing regardless of genre. He was particularly keen on anything that might help him refine his thinking on how cities worked, although that placed little restriction on his reading list. As a researcher, his engagement with primary documents meant not just fact finding but interrogation, the identification of the ideas that structured the details that populated the pages. He was a prolific writer, the author of five monographs, a textbook, and dozens of articles, introductions, and essays, all of which reveal his attention to the clarity of prose as much as to scholarly contribution. In these ways, Zane was a typical, if highly successful, scholar.

What set Zane apart, what made him truly exceptional, was the depth and range of his correspondences. During his thirty-five years at the University of Cincinnati (1965–1999), Zane had extensive communications with colleagues, students, prospective authors for his book series, and the authors who had already appeared in his series. He wrote long, detailed letters in the early decades of his career. He typed up memos to his students, capturing what otherwise would have been fleeting thoughts on their work. (I was the beneficiary of many of these famed Zane-O-Grams, as we called them). In recent decades he wrote thousands of emails, even in retirement. It wasn't just the volume of these communications that mattered. They were seldom chatty, and although they could contain references to college basketball, the weather in Florida, or his golf game, they were mostly serious in tone and in purpose. They formed the basis of important intellectual relationships, including with me and my coeditor Larry Bennett from the Urban Life, Landscape, and Policy series at Temple University Press. They also created a community of scholars, as Zane commonly connected us with each other by sharing historiography, ideas, and (when he figured out how to use it) through the cc function in email. Indeed, this is the phase of scholarship, so often ignored in the academy, in which Zane thrived: the discussion and formation of ideas outside published venues.

This volume perfectly captures the result of Zane's scholarly method. A collective work with distinctive voices, it comes out of the scholarly community Zane knit together with his ideas, his curiosity, and his goodwill. Among the authors are Zane's students and mentees, including Patty Mooney-Melvin, Robert Fairbanks, and Charlie Lester; and his colleagues, including John Fairfield, who teaches at neighboring Xavier University in Cincinnati, and Larry Bennett.

I too am a part of this community of scholars. For nearly a decade, I worked with Zane and Larry Bennett as coeditor of the Urban Life, Landscape, and Policy book series. Nearly the entirety of this work—annually hundreds of hours for each of us—occurred at a distance. Zane and Larry never did meet in person, as Larry describes in his remembrance of Zane, and although I knew Zane from our time together in Cincinnati, I saw him only once in the nine years we coedited. Oddly, I don't think the lack of physical meetings slowed us down, and in fact, I suspect Zane preferred it. Indeed, as many of his colleagues at the University of Cincinnati have told me, Zane preferred to write rather than speak, especially about important matters. This should not be mistaken for a lack of interest in personal connections—far from it. Zane was among the most congenial colleagues I have ever had. I shared hundreds if not thousands of conversations with him over the years, nearly all of them in writing.

I was quite honored when Zane asked me to join him as coeditor when his Urban Life and Urban Landscape book series moved to Temple University Press. At the same time, Zane added "Policy" to the series title and a third editor, the political scientist Larry Bennett. The three of us developed prose about the series, attempting to articulate a vision that would shape and limit our list, a statement that could be used to attract prospective authors. After much editing, our statement fittingly began: "Ideas about what cities have been, are becoming, or might yet become have always been of interest to urban scholars and policy makers." Like Zane's work, the series list would feature books that "examine urban and regional planning, environmental issues, and urban policy studies, thus contributing to ongoing debates." It was essential to Zane that scholarship—his own and that appearing in his series—contribute to the never-ending task of improving cities.

We began work on the series with a flurry of activity in the early months of 2007, as Zane contacted seemingly every urbanist he had come to know over the course of his long career. Book writing is always a community project. For Zane, the community aspect was particularly strong, as he developed early partnerships with authors that lasted through publication, even when that publication happened outside the series Zane was editing. Often, he began conversations by proposing book ideas. Some of these ideas were little more than conceptions of books that he had imagined reading, or even writing, if he had the time. Sometimes he merely sent a note asking an old acquaintance what they were up to, when their next book might appear, and where it might find a home. Some of these scholars had published in one of Zane's earlier series, including John Fairfield, who had published in the Ohio State University Press series. Others were simply scholars whose past work he had admired, including Frank Cullen, a well-known criminologist at the University of Cincinnati. Some of these early projects failed to materialize or failed to come to Temple, but most are now published, the surest sign of success.

Zane had a very democratic sense of knowledge. Scholarship, he thought, should be accessible to everyone, inside and outside the academy. Zane believed that essentially everyone could understand complex ideas, and accessible scholarship need not simplify the past to reach a broad audience, to influence the public. Effective scholarship merely required accessible prose, devoid of jargon. Just as Zane believed anyone could read good scholarship, he also believed nearly anyone could write it. Zane acted as though anyone could write a book, and more generally, he welcomed any serious thinker into his scholarly community. In 2011, he sent me an email letting me know he had received the program for our graduate student conference, which I had sent by mail. He read through the titles of our graduate students' work with interest and asked, "Can you when you get a chance tell Ross, David, Yeager, Hewitt, Bailey, and Keys that I'm interested in their work as potential contributions to our urban series (I've been in touch with McGee)." He had listed nearly half the participants! Most of them were master's students at the time, but, according to Zane, they should have been thinking about publishing a book. To Zane, all the process required was a seriousness about ideas and a faith in your own perspective, your own voice. Both of these characteristics could be cultivated. That's what Zane did, as a mentor and editor.

Unsurprisingly, Zane's own scholarship followed this ideal. Much of his published work focused on his adopted home, Cincinnati, and its surrounding neighborhoods. As John Fairfield describes so well in the historiographical review contained in this volume, Zane wrote book-length treatments of seemingly unimportant places, like Forest

Park, a planned and integrated postwar suburb of Cincinnati, and Clifton, the in-city suburb he called home for more than thirty years. As Zane demonstrated with these works, however, all places are worthy of study, and no place can hide from the trends of the day. Zane divined broader meaning from the telling of seemingly narrow stories. As Fairfield notes, from the publication of *Boss Cox's Cincinnati* in 1968 through his last essays, included here, Zane demonstrated how taxonomies of social reality shaped—and especially impeded—change over time.

The final essays of Zane's career expanded on his theory of "liberation history," in which Zane emphasized human agency rather than broad social forces in explaining human events. He also continued to focus on cities, for in them he found hope for democracy, the civic nationalism that forms the core of his interest toward the end of his career. His essay "From Istanbul to Philadelphia" is a retelling of the founding of the United States around the ideas that would shape the urbanization of the nation. The positive tenor of the essay—in tone, reminiscent of old Whiggish interpretations of American exceptionalism—comes not from Zane's dismissal of inequality, racism, and the other forces that fractured the American experience but rather from his belief that at its founding the United States established a culture of participatory politics (civic nationalism) that would be necessary for the creation of a "more perfect union." From that founding era, the actions of individuals—informed and circumscribed by dominant modes of thinking certainly but not merely the result of faceless social forces (racism, capitalism, individualism)—have driven positive change across two centuries. This is empowering history, empowering both the subjects of the narrative and the readers. It moves us beyond the chaos, crisis, and conflict that dominate today's urban historiography. A half decade into the era of postfactual politics catalyzed by Trumpism, Zane's faith in empathy and civility may seem quaint to many readers, but his reading of urban history reminds us that these traits have always been present, and they have indeed shaped our cities at least as much as have conflict and crisis.

This collection also contains two essays of urban history that model and explain how Zane's influence continues to affect practitioners. Robert Fairbanks, professor of history at the University of Texas at Arlington, presses Zane's theory on taxonomies of social reality. He follows

Zane's example of studying smaller, understudied cities as a means of learning something new about urban America. Here Fairbanks describes post–World War II suburbanization and the creation of a new type of suburban city. His two case studies—Mesa, Arizona, and Arlington, Texas—rapidly climbed the list of largest American cities not because automobiles or federal policy demanded that they spring to life but because an increasing number of Americans thought suburban-style, isolated communities were the new urban ideal. These individual actors, following a common ethos of the day, had little sense of civic obligation. Their suburban cities would be built by and for individuals who thought of themselves as apart from and irresponsible for the problems of older, sometimes nearby cities.

In her contribution to this volume, Patricia Mooney-Melvin, of Loyola University Chicago's History Department, who like Fairbanks completed her dissertation working with Zane at the University of Cincinnati, reminds us of Zane's own sense of civic responsibility. In describing how ethnic communities staked a claim to the built environment of Chicago through the creation and installation of celebratory statues, she emphasizes the tolerance necessary for the development of cosmopolitanism in American cities and the diversity at the core of urban vitality. At the same time, Mooney-Melvin describes how Zane gave her the tools she needed to interpret the actors in her work, allowing her to create a deeper history of urban statuary in which the actors were not just celebrating their ethnic identity but claiming a place in the broader society. Perhaps ironically, then, the installation of ethnic statuary cemented a civic unity, a unity that affirms the diversity of contributions to it.

The durability of the statuary—literal embodiments of ideas in urban space—poses interesting challenges to scholars, given the changing interpretations of their purpose. Indeed, new modes of thought, ushered in by new realities, call into question the seeming permanence of these monuments. Today, these pleas for inclusion might be read as assertions of separateness, physical representations of the conflicts that ran through urban America. Of course, current debates about Confederate statuary remind us that meaning can also persist into new eras of thinking. Rebel soldiers placed to honor the sacrifice made in defense of white supremacy still remind us of the Jim Crow era's reestablishment of a racist regime and the imperfect dismantling of this regime in the decades since the civil rights movement began. Finally, Mooney-Melvin makes the case for Zane's early contributions to the analysis of urban space as a container of ideas. Indeed, in this way Zane's work has influenced my own thinking about how to write and teach urban history. In one formative year, I studied with Zane and his many students at the University of Cincinnati, taking a seminar he boldly called Frontiers of Urban Research. If Zane had his way, all of us in that class would be urbanists; all of us would feel empowered to write books about cities. Much more than the specific ideas he imparted, Zane gave me and his other students a philosophy of how to work. We were engaged in a community project. Zane showed us how to improve our work by improving our community of scholars.

Preface and Acknowledgments

The city as an arena for action and its dynamic interaction with the nation as a whole is the bedrock upon which Zane L. Miller approached his understanding of the city. Whether in the classroom or in his research, he focused on what he saw as the inside and the outside of the urban experience. This synergistic relationship shaped his beliefs about ideas, place, and civic activism. As the United States entered the twenty-first century, Miller characterized the content of these relationships as civic nationalism.

The inside/outside interaction defined Miller's approach to understanding the city. The inside view rested on the examination of particular places during specific periods. The outside view assessed the role of urban centers in American civilization over time. The synergy between the inside and outside approaches represented the strengths as well as the challenges facing urban dwellers as they addressed issues important to the larger national polity.

The ties among problem-solving, locality, and action also reflected Miller's belief in urban centers as crucibles of change—for good or ill. As the nation continues to grapple with the legacy of racism, for example, Miller would expect urban areas simultaneously to expose the problems associated with power and privilege and to serve as laboratories for finding solutions. "Civic activity," as Miller wrote in the fall/winter 1996 edition of *McMicken*, "makes democracy tick." The city as a site of action and the arena for problem-solving constitutes the focal point for citizen engagement.

The contributed essays in this volume as well as Miller's final reflections on the state of the urban enterprise illustrate his commitment to ideas, action, and civic engagement. As with all scholarly enterprises, this has been a cooperative venture. It draws not only on the energies of our contributors but also on the support of others. Janet Miller encouraged the completion of Zane's final work and has been supportive of its reshaping over the course of the project. We especially appreciate that she trusted our vision in shaping this work. Judith Sprawl-Schmidt provided invaluable information from Zane's archival collection. Perhaps more importantly, she reminded us of his commitment to community engagement and the responsibility of the scholar to work collegially with multiple constituencies. At Temple University Press, the anonymous reviewers provided useful suggestions that helped us improve the final version. We also thank Aaron Javsicas for believing in this project. We are indebted to the Taft Research Center at the University of Cincinnati for a grant to defray the costs of publication.

Zane dedicated his life to making knowledge work in the world. We hope our readers accept his challenge in their own lives and work.

Bringing the Civic Back In

PART I
On Civic Nationalism

Introduction to Part I

The three excerpts that follow come from the survey of American urban history that Zane L. Miller was writing, in collaboration with Patricia Mooney-Melvin and Larry Bennett, at the time of his death in 2016. We chose these pieces as the most distinctive parts of the manuscript. We have only lightly edited them, and they appear here largely in the form Miller left them. They well represent Miller's lifelong effort to rethink the American urban past and to influence its future.

These essays also suggest Miller's central role in inspiring a Cincinnati school of urban history. Emphasizing the importance of ideas in social change, the Cincinnati school examines how conceptions of the city, citizenship, and democracy shaped, and continue to shape, the development of American society. Miller argued that these conceptions, what he called "taxonomies of social reality," provided the agreed-upon ground on which debate about the future of American society proceeded. As these excerpts show, Miller's interests ranged widely in time and space. But much of his work focused on Cincinnati in the belief that local histories could reveal the taxonomy of social reality operating in a given period. This is what he meant by symptomatic history, using local stories to illuminate larger national trends and developments.[1]

Beneath Miller's interest in taxonomies of social reality stood his curiosity about how communities held together as they changed over time. He shared this interest with the famous Chicago school of urban sociology, whose treatment of the city as laboratory shaped Miller's thinking. But unlike the Chicago sociologists, who explained urban development in terms of impersonal processes, Miller placed human thought and action at the center of urban life. He much admired the early-twentieth-century "metropolitan mode of thought" for its emphasis on the organic, interdependent nature of human society and its call for citizens to transcend their narrow interests. He also worried about the eclipse of the metropolitan mode in the mid-twentieth century with the rise of "communities of limited liability," a term he borrowed from the Chicago school. Miller warned that an excessive form of cultural individualism produced footloose, self-interested residents who lost sight of any greater public good.[2]

Miller's lament for the decline of the metropolitan mode of thought and the rise of communities of limited liability shaped much of his later work. In the essays that follow, Miller invoked "civic nationalism" as the best hope for twenty-first-century urbanism. Even as he traced civic nationalism back to the European Enlightenment and the American Revolution, Miller found it most active in the diverse settings of urban life, where it offered an alternative to ethnic, racial, and religious nationalisms. The idea of civic nationalism thus reflected Miller's lifelong concern for the public interest, his belief that ideas and human agency could secure it, and his conviction that cities played a leading role in the shaping of American civilization. These convictions provided the umbrella under which an eclectic group of scholars formed a Cincinnati school of urban history.

Miller's introductory essay, "From Istanbul to Philadelphia: Ideas and the Urban Origins of the United States," offers his vision for how a survey of American urban history ought to proceed and what it ought to include. Ideas stand first and foremost as Miller ranges widely through time and space. Although the term does not appear, his interest in taxonomies of social reality is also evident. Old "modes of thought" do not survive intact, Miller wrote, but survive in fragments that influence subsequent events. Creative "outsiders" who do not share the dominant mode of thought retain the capacity to upset the status quo and initiate radical change (see Chapter 1). The activist bent in Miller's thinking and writing is also prominent. This is a book, he tells us, for people who care about ideas and about cities and who want to be better prepared to act.

Miller's lifelong interest in the construction of community also shapes this essay, especially in his praise of boosterism. He defines boosterism as a form of patriotism that "links personal striving and fulfillment to civic pride" and helps to bridge ethnic, racial, and other social divides (see Chapter 1). His concern about the atrophy of civic capacity drives Miller's periodization of urban history, as he laments our own age of cultural individualism in which politics revolves around self-expression rather than the public good. Above all, this essay introduces Miller's overriding theme of civic nationalism, an urban-based quality that he believed spoke to the best and most distinctive qualities of the American experiment in self-government and that accounts for his obvious love for cities.

Miller's planned epilogue, "The Resiliency of Cities and the Uncertain Future of American Civic Nationalism," sketches out a future in which city-states play a greater role on the global stage. Synthesizing the work of his students and the authors in the Temple University Press series he coedited, Miller finds plenty to worry about, particularly the continuation of racial segregation that has been exacerbated in an era of cultural individualism. But he also finds reasons for hope, both in the history of urban resilience and in contemporary efforts to enhance metropolitan and regional governance and reestablish leagues of cities and city-states. He does not, however, take the resiliency and durability of American civic nationalism for granted, treating it instead as a still-recent experiment whose future cannot be known. He finds it threatened by the rise of ethnically, racially, and religiously based nationalisms, not just abroad but, as he recognized with the presidential campaign of 2016 heating up, at home as well.

In the final, free-swinging pages of "The Resiliency of Cities," Miller takes dead aim at the era of cultural individualism that he believed blighted American politics. Here Miller's passion and vehemence, his devotion to things civic and urbane, stand out. So, too, do his eclectic reading habits as he marshals writers as disparate as the journalists Gail Sheehy and Hunter Thompson and the psychologist

Abraham Maslow to make his points. His love of jazz is evidenced in his use of a Billy Strayhorn / Duke Ellington composition as a leitmotif for these pages.

In an appendix that Miller drafted, "Cities, American Civic Nationalism, and Fundamentalism," he left behind his reflections on those topics. Dispensing with the "we" of the earlier essays, Miller speaks of his own deepest hopes and worst fears. Invoking the central thesis of his beloved mentor Richard Wade's seminal work, *The Urban Frontier* (1959), Miller advances an urban interpretation of American history, a history driven by cities as the animating source and organizing force of a continental, federated republic. He celebrates this "American civic nationalism, a secular and tribal-less creed that rejected monarchial dynasty, genetic aristocracy, theocracy, and the possibility of establishing a polity based on ethnic, racial, or socioeconomic class ideology" (see Chapter 1). But he finds this vision on the defensive in a world of rising fundamentalism and ethnic hatreds.[3]

Miller took heart that these latest threats to civic nationalism have not been the first, as our history has been punctuated by threats of secession, calls for violent suppression of political foes, and programs for religious rule or ethnic domination. But he offers no guarantee for the success and continuation of civic nationalism and further insists that history provides none either. The future remains in doubt, subject to our own choices, virtue, and vigilance. The spread of civic illiteracy causes him special concern. Above all, he fears a cultural pessimism arising on both sides of the Atlantic, a disappointment with expansive and purportedly outdated promises of human freedom, and a nostalgia for an imagined time of greater certainty and order. That pessimism and disappointment have fueled various fundamentalisms eager to extinguish civic nationalism. The contest between civic nationalism and fundamentalism, Miller concludes, will be waged in our cities, long the "breeding places of both authoritarian and democratic movements" (see Chapter 3). As the readers/editors of Zane's final writings, we of course know on which side he stood.

NOTES

1. David Stradling, "Zane L. Miller and the Cincinnati School of History," *Ohio Valley History* 19, no. 1 (Spring 2019): 3–5; Robert B. Fairbanks and Patricia

Mooney-Melvin, eds., *Making Sense of the City: Local Government, Civic Culture, and Community Life* (Columbus: Ohio State University Press, 2001).

2. The Cincinnati school thus offers a less deterministic, more hopeful urban theory than the more celebrated Chicago and Los Angeles schools of urban thought (the latter tending to depict cities as at the mercy of global economic forces). Robert E. Park, Ernest Burgess, and Roderick McKenzie, *The City* (Chicago: University of Chicago Press, 2010). On "communities of limited liability," Morris Janowitz, *The Community Press in an Urban Setting* (Chicago: University of Chicago Press, 1952). On the Chicago and Los Angeles schools of urban theory, one might start with Michael J. Dear, ed., *From Chicago to L.A.: Making Sense of Urban Theory* (Thousand Oaks, CA: Sage, 2002).

3. Richard C. Wade, *The Urban Frontier: The Rise of Western Cities, 1790–1830*, 8th ed. (Urbana: University of Illinois Press, 1996).

1

From Istanbul to Philadelphia

*Ideas and the Urban Origins
of the United States*

ZANE L. MILLER

We think of this book as an unconventional interpretation of American urban history, in which we pay more attention to the role of ideas than to such social categories as racial, ethnic, class, or gender groups or such impersonal social forces as the capitalist economic system. We of course discuss social groups and social forces, but we do so in a way that starts with ideas. We prefer this "ideas approach" for two major reasons. It assigns to actual human beings, not social forces, the role of defining problems, trends, and policies, the changing configuration of which from time to time divides one chronological era from the next. In contrast to the social groups / social forces approach, our approach pays more attention to ideas that most people take quite seriously and feel passionately about: religious ideologies and sectarian zeal, nationalism and patriotic enthusiasm. We call our approach *liberation history*, a genre unshackled by social scientific prescriptions about what to study and how to study it, an analytic device that attributes to human agency, not social forces, the construction of the boundaries of chronological eras characterized by distinctive modes of thought and action.[1]

So we've written an ideas book, one designed especially but not exclusively for people with an interest in cities, what makes them tick, and what makes them flourish, stagnate, or decline in political and cultural influence. We like to think that, in addition, the book will appeal to others, including people less concerned with cities and more interested in ordinary human beings who worry about their rights and liberties, especially their civil rights, and their health, welfare, status, and influence or lack thereof on social, economic, political, and cultural affairs. Similarly, we think the book might appeal to people who identify with various forms of "association," whose members worry about the status and influence of their group, whether it is a civic association or racial, ethnic, gender, class, or religious group. For in this ideas book about cities, we do indeed deal with the ideas that underlie the activities and interaction of groups, the vital human elements of cities that enliven and complicate urban life on a daily basis.

In developing this focus on ideas and cities, we have been interested in changing ideas about what American urban culture is, is becoming, or ought to become, particularly the interplay of varying conceptions of reality, the clash of which periodically leads to turning points ushering in new periods in urban history. We argue that people during each of the periods we discuss have shared a dominant mode of thought shaping their conception of the culture in which they live and how they define problems and design solutions to those problems. Not everyone in each period shares the dominant mode of thought, so members of the mainstream categorize them as outsiders, who may be ignored or treated as someone else's problem or regarded as amusing exceptions to the rule but who, in some instances, have been incarcerated as criminals or insane people. Some of these outsiders have seemed troublesome to mainstreamers in another way, as rational but radical thinkers and opponents of the status quo eager and capable of rallying others to their cause, people such as John Brown and Frederick Douglass, ardent slavery abolitionists; Julia Ward Howe, a leader in the feminist movement; Eugene Debs and other critics of incorporated wealth; or Marcus Garvey and Malcolm X, influential twentieth-century proponents of Black nationalism.

Civic Nationalism

In our thinking about the urban origins of the United States, we became interested in the idea of civic nationalism—an antiaristocratic, antimonarchical conception of citizenship and governance—and the distinctive forms it took at the various turning points in American urban history. This idea took shape in European philosophical circles and caught on among British North Americans during the middle of the eighteenth century. Its adherents consisted of a broad range of individuals, including women, soldiers, sailors, artisans, and mechanics (slave and free) as well as rich and powerful merchants and owners of large plantations. These people, like enlightened thinkers in aristocratic Europe, not only thought systematically and rationally about how the world worked. They also cultivated an interest in unknown or little-known places, including not only the East Indies and Asia but also the western portions of the North American continent, places, according to Europeans and diverse colonial American thinkers, that contained people who adhered to "alien" habits and customs. These antiaristocratic and antimonarchical ideas and this interest in "different" people and places formed the basis for an American experiment in civic nationalism inaugurated in Britain's North American coastal colonies as the eighteenth century ebbed. The individuals who launched this experiment came from every colony and every social class yet managed to set aside their particular interests and unite in a revolution that rejected monarchical and aristocratic forms of government and created a federal union based on the separation of state and religion. In the most important and perhaps least anticipated consequences of this civic nationalism, backers of this form of federalism laid the groundwork for the eventual extension of the franchise and citizenship status to all individuals, regardless of their race, ethnic affiliation, or gender.

In our analysis of the origins of American civic nationalism, we conceive of cities and urbanization as people then and since have conceived of them. City builders and improvers from time immemorial have thought of cities as policy agencies containing social, economic, political, educational, financial, and cultural institutions that in both a competitive and cooperative way generate agendas for the construction of regional, national, and imperial cultures. City builders and improvers regarded cities not only as bases of operation in the passive sense. They saw cities—each of them, large, medium, and small—as dynamic factors in two ways: first as sources of ideas and the political, financial, and cultural resources to shape developmental programs and secondly as sources of the energy, will, and means to implement their agendas. The city builders and improvers typically have expected that their policy solution would last indefinitely. But in retrospect, we can see that their aims and implementation techniques derived from the mode of thought characteristic of their particular era. These aims and implementation techniques have not survived intact in subsequent eras. On an ongoing basis—and across eras—cities have generated developmental strategies and means specific to particular periods, which have produced distinctive urban cultures within the units of time historians call ages, eras, or epochs.

The United States now ranks as one of the world's most successful city-building civilizations, ancient or modern. In just over two and a half centuries, its polyglot population has created a great number and variety of urban places in a vast, heterogeneous, and lightly settled realm stretching from the Atlantic to the Pacific Ocean and from the Great Lakes to the Gulf of Mexico. This book focuses on the origins and development of those cities and their role in the making of the United States. But the story starts well before the adoption of the Declaration of Independence and the Constitution. It begins with the early modern European settlers of North, Central, and South America. Here, between the 1450s and the 1750s, they encountered the descendants of earlier travelers to this enormous terrain, people who had designed, from a European perspective, a premodern landscape, even though it contained cities and even urban empires. The European intruders regarded these "Indian" urban societies as intriguing but backward and therefore set out both to modernize them and to establish new, European-style cities as the building blocks of European-style empires, which Europeans saw as progenitors of superior urban civilizations.

From this angle of vision, the urbanization of what became the United States begins with the establishment of European cities as rivals to the Indigenous centers of civilization. The stimulus for this process can be traced to Istanbul, in the fifteenth century the seat of the powerful and expansive Ottoman Empire, which dominated the Mediterranean region, including large chunks of Spain and smaller parts of Portugal. Indeed, the aggressiveness of Ottoman imperialism threatened both the dominance of Christianity in Europe and the commercial interests and wealth of its cities. European governments therefore not only resisted but sought to turn back the Ottoman-driven Islamic incursion, a resolve that set off an expensive and often violent contest for economic prosperity, political autonomy, and religious dominance. In the course of that struggle, the besieged European powers decided to outflank the Turks by planting urban-centered Christian colonies in the Americas in the hope that the urbanization of the Americas would forge trading links to the wealth of the Far East and generate the resources necessary to counter the Islamic threat in Europe.

Despite some shaky starts and setbacks, these urban outposts of the Old World survived and grew. By the 1750s the European outposts in North America included an important string of cities draped around the rim of North America, places such as Boston, New York City, Philadelphia, Baltimore, Williamsburg, Charleston, Savannah, and New Orleans. Far from isolated, residents of these North American cities kept in close touch with intellectual, social, economic, political, and religious developments in the Old World cities of Europe, Africa, and Asia, as well as with the other cities of the English, Dutch, French, and Spanish colonies of the Caribbean and in Central and South America. Indeed, by the 1750s the European colonies in North America contained sophisticated, cosmopolitan urban elites who regarded their cities as just as modern as—and more virtuous than— those in Europe and Central and South America. Though smaller and less opulent than London, Paris, Madrid, Amsterdam, Mexico City, or Lima, these North American cities, like their older urban counterparts, contained diverse populations with very particular ethnic and religious mixes.

In general, these distinctions among North American cities, like those among cities elsewhere, amounted to particularities rather than peculiarities, for the North American cities otherwise strongly resembled one another. Slavery existed in all of them and flourished in most. All of them offered lively intellectual and cultural amenities amid thriving commercial economies. All of them relied on artisans and craftsmen for manufactured products and depended on merchants and mariners for the distribution and trade of goods with ports around the globe. To their residents, then, these North American cities seemed quite up-to-date and therefore deserving of respect and the chance to compete on an equal footing with each other and with cities around the world in the race for a higher standing in the urban hierarchy of prospering and enlightened places.

In the 1750s, moreover, a diverse cadre of these ambitious and restless urbanites in thirteen of the English colonies of North America began to think of their cities as foundations for the making of an independent civilization. They pictured that civilization as an "empire of liberty," as Thomas Jefferson called it during the American Revolution, a place with no military emperors or self-declared dictators, no czars or czarinas, no kings or queens, no dukes or duchesses, and with no governmentally mandated religious orthodoxy, neither Muslim nor Christian, Catholic, Anglican, or Protestant. Having imagined such a polity, revolutionary generation activists in the late eighteenth and early nineteenth centuries tried to institutionalize their civic ideal and did so in a manner that added two other legacies to their conception of an empire of liberty and its possibilities. Legislatures eliminated slavery in some states, banned it in American territories, while unprecedented numbers of slaveholders, both in the North and elsewhere, emancipated large numbers of slaves. Federal and state politicians also seriously considered and took a few small steps toward the extension of property rights to married women and the right to vote to all women, married or not.

The first steps in the creation of this empire of liberty came in the 1770s and 1780s. During the summer of 1776, advocates of the new cause—almost all of them full- or part-time city residents, the people most directly, regularly, and adversely affected by British economic, military, political, and religious policies—decided to discuss and address their grievances. They met in Pennsylvania's colonial capital building (known today as Independence Hall), which occupied a generous lot in the center of Philadelphia, one of the busiest ports and the largest of the North American colonial cities. There they adopted a Declaration of Independence from Great Britain that also asserted the essential equality of humankind. Then, just over a decade later, the most persistent of the empire-of-freedom proponents reconvened in the same Philadelphia building, this time to devise and agree upon a stronger central government. After lengthy debates and many compromises, the founders, as we now call them, wrote and signed the Constitution of the United States (1787).

The adoption of the U.S. Constitution and its first ten amendments (1791) both launched a "more perfect Union" and played a crucial role in the joint project of modernizing and urbanizing North America. Those documents broke emphatically from the European past by setting down new rules for a federalist adventure in an American form of civic nationalism, envisioning a politically pluralist entity, not a unified state. This kind of nationalism involved shared sovereignty between the federal government and its constituent states, a global political rarity and, strictly speaking, a logical contradiction. So here the practical necessity of cobbling together expedient compromises overshadowed the rational temptation to promote efficiency by crafting a simpler, tidier political structure.[2]

The Constitution set down additional ground rules for the American experiment in civic nationalism. It established a federal compact that defined patriotism as a voluntary commitment by citizens to support democracy and pursue equality. The Constitution, in effect, both enabled citizens to use federal, state, and local governmental institutions to promote the general welfare of the union and encouraged them to be politically, civically, and socially responsible by participating in the task of shaping the nature and course of American society. So in this instance, pluralism overshadowed uniformity in a place with no supreme central government that might adopt other means of civilization building, such as by adopting a religious, racial, ethnic, or class foundation or ordaining an official secular ideology.

Here too there would be no Paris, London, Rome, Berlin, Moscow, or Beijing, capital cities that exercised unmatched political, economic, social, and cultural influence over their nations. The founders' establishment of Washington, DC, as both a new city and the country's political capital prevented any other American city from acquiring the four-dimensional dominance that characterized the primate capital cities of Europe and China. Washington started out as and remained an essentially single-function town, an urban head of state, so to speak, while New York City and other major cities competed for economic, social, and cultural influence over broad hinterlands. In this contest New York City soon secured the upper hand while other places settled in as "second cities" without descending to the status of "provincial" cities. As a consequence, the United States developed a pluralistic rather than unilineal urban hierarchy. It became a nation in which diverse regional centers—such second cities as Boston, Philadelphia, New Orleans, Chicago, Detroit, Los Angeles, Houston, and Seattle—carved out, developed, and maintained spheres of influence over a terrain of multiple and overlapping hinterlands, a prime source of America's global influence in entrepreneurship, technology, and the arts.

To be sure, the economic and cultural ascent of urban America benefitted from its distinctive and benign setting in a large and lightly populated continent endowed with spectacular landscapes and a rich lode of natural resources. But its natural resources consisted not only of forests, fisheries, fertile soils, minerals, and fossil fuels. Its pool of resources also included an abundant and heterogeneous population of city builders who came by voluntary or involuntary means from all over the world and supplied the American urban scene with an innovative and varied cultural endowment. These polyglot peoples, like urbanites in ancient, medieval, and early modern times, built and used their cities as spearheads in the making of a new civilization. In the chapters that follow, we provide a history of the American experiment in civic nationalism that begins in Istanbul, makes stops at Philadelphia and at other cities of the East, West, and South, and ends in the early twenty-first century with the experiment intact but facing an uncertain future in a world still rife with rival ethnic- and religion-based movements and increasingly threatened by environmental overload.

Boosterism Reconsidered

In our view, the participatory politics characteristic of American civic nationalism is rooted in cities, drawing its vitality from boosterism, an idea and practice that links personal striving and fulfillment to civic pride. Most American city dwellers, for instance, admire and support local recreational and cultural attractions that invite regional or even national attention. They brag about *their* sports teams and heroes, *their* visual and performing arts organizations and stars, *their* architecturally showy downtowns, *their* national public radio and television stations, and *their* city's historic sites and historic neighborhoods. And the boosters' touting of these icons of local pride as regional and national treasures not only prompts a sense of their self-importance but also connects them to a civic enthusiasm bridging neighborhood, ethnic, racial, social class, religious, gender, sexual orientation, and political party divisions.

American urbanites are a pluralistic people who identify with their localities—neighborhoods, suburban towns, cities, and metropolises—and they take pride in what they make of their local worlds. This book takes boosterism seriously in another way, through the intersection between local civic pride and the demands of making a living. At that intersection lay the multiple occupational crafts and skills that yield city building, an economic skill that we dub the *city-improving specialty*. This of course is not a peculiarly modern or American phenomenon. Even in ancient times the world's first cities regarded administrative, occupational, intellectual, and spiritual specialists, artisans, mechanics, and even laborers as "the creators, sustainers, and organizers of civilized life."[3] In American history these city-building and improving specialists have included persons of every race, class, ethnicity, gender, sexual orientation, and national affiliation, and they have pursued an incalculable array of communal activities. In the twenty-first century, such urban specialists include the board members of public, private, and nonprofit corporations and bureaucrats in business corporations and in local, state, and federal government agencies. But the roster of city-sustaining and enlivening specialists also contains a vast range of other actors: political consultants, candidates, and pundits, artisans and mechanics (especially in the building trades), artists and academics, musicians and writers, moral and social crusaders, revolutionaries, reformers, and reactionaries, entrepreneurs, financiers, merchants, and labor unionists, inventors, philosophers, and philanthropists; as well as the broad range of occupational callings closely connected to civic coherence, pride, and welfare, such as priests, preachers, rabbis, mullahs, major and minor league sports figures, nurses, doctors, lawyers, teachers, scientists, engineers, firefighters, emergency rescue teams, and those quintessentially urban characters, cops and private eyes, gangsters and vice lords.

We provide this lengthy list of urban occupational specialists to drive home the point that the people, not merely elites, build cities and the societies that are shaped by their urban cultures. Every city in every epoch, past and present, and every class and social group in those cities have contained the dreamers, thinkers, and organizers whose ideas and energies contribute to the tone and texture of urban life. Most of these urban specialists operate within the law, but some of them operate above it or outside it. But it is the mix of the progressive and the conservative, the proper and the improper, that gives urban life its zest and its resilience and the capacity of cities to function as centers for creating, sustaining, and sometimes transforming whole societies, often by dismantling empires, ousting royal dynasties, or revolutionizing nation-states.

The idea of such varied specialists as city builders and organizers of civilizations also provides the foundation for a multidimensional definition of the city as "a cultural focus, a social resort, a political center, but before all—though not above all—[as] a place where people earn a living."[4] This terse but telling observation identifies precisely the enduring genius of the urban mystique, for city life yokes not only the economic but also the social, cultural, and political aspirations of individuals to the flourishing of a particular place. And it is that confluence of interests that forms the basis for urban imperialism, another ancient and persisting aspect of the history of cities. After all, one's city cannot flourish except in competition with other cities, a conception of social reality that drives the urban sweepstakes, a contest among cities in which strivers in each place seek to spread their own and their communities' economic, social, cultural, and political influence over ever larger hinterlands.

Cities Observed from Two Angles, across Three Eras

This book offers its readers two ways of thinking about the city and its relationship to other cities that they may construe as "theirs." In one dimension, we offer an analysis of how cities have grown. This *internal* view of city building concentrates on describing and analyzing the changing shapes and physical size of cities, the shifts in the location of populations and commercial and manufacturing facilities, and the evolution of urban politics and government. The second, *external* dimension offers an assessment of the role of urban specialists and city representatives in initiating, defining, and responding to trends, problems, and issues in American society generally. This second dimension therefore contains discussions of cities and national political episodes, such as the American Revolution, the Civil War, and the New Deal; such processes as industrialization and its seeming aftermath, postindustrialization; and modes of thinking about American society as a whole, such as the rise of cultural individualism in the middle of the twentieth century.

One might classify this synthesis of internal and external approaches to urban history as ecological, an approach to human experiences in which everything is connected to everything else. Our treatment of the urban social and physical environment as a complex of intensely interdependent individuals and groups provides a useful basis for examining the way individuals imagine and deploy cities and use their social, economic, political, and cultural institutions to shape and reshape their societies as vehicles for confronting the future. It also provides a way to make sense out of events that, at first glance, seem utterly chaotic. American cities at any given point in time look astonishingly diverse. They possess varying populations and economic profiles; they differ in age, size, regional settings, and growth rates. But by focusing on common patterns of internal growth and on the relationship between cities and the larger society, we can organize American history into three periods: the preindustrial city of the seventeenth, eighteenth, and early nineteenth centuries; the industrial city of the late nineteenth and first half of the twentieth centuries; and the contemporary postindustrial city.

We further identify three parallel phases in the discourse of thought and action about American urban culture and what it might become. Before the 1830s, American city boosters pursued an agenda intended to create in America an improved version of Old World modes of urban life. Then, in the mid-nineteenth century, the focus shifted to defining and establishing a distinctively American urban culture as a national, socially diverse yet coherent way of living, a discourse that construed social groups, the city, and the metropolis as the fundamental elements of urban life. The third and final phase, the age of cultural individualism, emerged in the mid-twentieth century, during which political leaders, experts, and the public at large have tended to think of urban life in terms of individual values, neighborhoods, and suburbs as the basic units of American urbanism and urbanization.

Across this tripartite chronological division, we also analyze geographic patterns of urban dominance. In the first period, a string of cities along the Atlantic coast challenged London and Paris, the seats of immense Old World empires, for control of the trans-Appalachian

West. In the second era, the center of gravity in the new United States shifted to the urban heartland, anchored in New York City but stretching along the Great Lakes corridor and Ohio River valley to St. Louis on the Mississippi River. In the most recent era, the rate of urbanization on the periphery of the heartland soared, and the upstart cities of the South, Southwest, and trans-Mississippi West challenged the heartland for economic, cultural, and political leadership.

We hope that this vision of our urban past provides a persuasive antidote to the current view of our past as chaotic and serves to counter the idea of perpetual urban crisis, the idea that city dwellers confront such irremediable problems as interracial strife, crime, environmental devastation, and political ineptitude. Certainly, American cities have had to confront a multitude of challenges, but the preoccupation with problems and conflict has unfortunately led to the neglect of another crucial aspect of cities' role in the life of America. This is the underreported story of civic engagement and problem-solving. In our times, such stories include the essential virtue embodied by the vast majority of city residents as they navigate their daily lives, obeying prevailing laws and cooperating with their fellow citizens. More profoundly, there are the many acts of positive empathy performed by the residents of our cities and suburbs: individuals respecting the peculiar circumstances, eccentricities, or, as contemporary academics often put it, the *difference* of their fellow urbanites. In respect to collective action, we also observe numerous political leaders and municipal officials who are committed to understanding their constituencies and improving the quality of urban governance. Likewise, there are countless nonprofit organizations across urban America offering emergency assistance to their fellow citizens and in various ways seeking to uplift socially marginalized or economically disadvantaged groups.

Such acts can be viewed as late-in-the-day (and rare) efforts to hold on to viable and livable urban communities, but similar acts of civility go back a long way and, in our view, derive from a particular civic temperament. This civic temperament can be summed up as our compact with comity,[5] the origins of which may be traced to the adoption of the Declaration of Independence and the hammering out of the compromises that structured the Constitution and its first ten amendments. Those documents foresaw the utility within a democracy of a willingness to live and let live (more or less) and to make adjustments necessary for smoothing over the inevitable differences that would emerge in an extraordinarily pluralistic society. Today, the cultivation of our civic temperament also plays a cohering role in urban and national affairs. It helps keep the peace among disparate individuals and social groups. It also supports the development of civic, governmental, and business organizations whose members willingly (more or less) and self-consciously make compromises in the interest of sustaining both our cities and one of the world's most diverse and complex societies. Our neglected civic temperament ranks as one of our most important cultural attributes, one that contributes to the resiliency of our cities, the coherence of American society, and the effectiveness of American civic nationalism.

NOTES

1. For more information about "liberation history," see Zane L. Miller, *Visions of Place: The City, Neighborhoods, Suburbs, and Cincinnati's Clifton, 1850–2000* (Columbus: Ohio State University Press, 2001), 167–168.

2. For a useful, readable, and arresting introduction to the concept of civic nationalism with special emphasis on the late twentieth century, see Michael Ignatieff, *Blood and Belonging: Journeys into the New Nationalism* (New York: Farrar, Straus and Giroux, 1994). For a well-received study of cities as policy tools, see Jerome I. Hodos, *Second Cities: Globalization and Local Politics in Manchester and Philadelphia* (Philadelphia: Temple University Press, 2011).

3. William H. McNeill, *The Rise of the West: A History of the Human Community* (Chicago: University of Chicago Press, 1963), 36.

4. Richard C. Wade, *The Urban Frontier: The Rise of Western Cities, 1790–1830*, 8th ed. (Urbana: University of Illinois Press, 1996), 39.

5. On the compact with comity see Richard Hofstadter, *The Progressive Historians* (New York: Alfred A. Knopf, 1969), 440–454. For our "more or less" on the compact with comity, see Daniel J. Monti Jr., *Engaging Strangers: Civic Rites, Civic Capitalism, and Public Order in Boston* (Madison, NJ: Fairleigh Dickinson University Press, 2012), xxii–xv, xvii–xviii; and less optimistically from a religious stance, Jacques Ellul, *The Meaning of the City* (Grand Rapids, MI: Wm B. Erdmans, 1970).

2

The Resiliency of Cities and the Uncertain Future of American Civic Nationalism

ZANE L. MILLER

A sage and ironically minded historian of world civilizations once described "chronic warfare" as "one of the painful but powerful mainsprings of the West's vitality."[1] That vitality arose from the resiliency of cities, their astonishing capacity not only to survive their martial mauling, maiming, and incineration but also the tendency of such ravaged places to bounce back and to forge new identities and roles for themselves. European examples of this phenomenon abound, in ancient times and modern—Byzantium/Constantinople/Istanbul and Rome, for example, or more recently, in the World War II era, Dresden, Stalingrad/Volgograd, and Coventry, England. In the United States, Atlanta presents one of America's most spectacular examples of urban destruction by war and postbellum reincarnation. A third-rate but militarily important town burned by Yankees during the Civil War, Atlanta's battered boosters rebuilt it by 1900 as one of the top cities in the southern urban hierarchy, and their successors elevated it by 2000 into one of the major cities in the national urban sweepstakes. Indeed, some urban analysts ranked it in 2011 as an international "second city," a rating inferior only to the few truly "global" cities, places such as New York, whose worldwide fame and envy derived from its enormous financial and cultural influence.

The testament to the resiliency of American cities may be expressed in two other ways. The prospect of the death of the city haunted the American discourse of thought and action among urban political and civic leaders during the last half of the twentieth century. These postindustrial activists worried that runaway suburbanization would debilitate the core cities of metropolitan areas, impoverish them economically and fiscally, drain them of their best and brightest citizens, and undermine their status as centers of social, artistic, civic, and intellectual innovation. This dimension of the so-called urban crisis set off a drive for the creation of an urban renaissance, an intense and extended effort to restore the vitality of metropolitan core cities as part of a larger effort to keep the nation competitive, first with the Soviet Union and then with such formerly "third world" nation-states as India and China.

A similar sense of despair about the vitality of American cities in the late nineteenth century had ignited an intense and extended effort to restore their health as the nation elbowed its way into the crowded imperial circle of world powers. Some of the people concerned with the apparent inability of city leaders to staunch the deterioration of the contemporary urban social, political, and physical environment turned to the past to find out what had gone wrong, and they found their answer in medieval Europe during the golden age of urban government, when myriad city-states challenged nations and empires for economic dominance and military superiority. We like to call these Americans "medievalist" urban reformers, because they both admired the European city-states and mourned their death.[2]

The medievalist urban reformers admired the city-states for two reasons. First, they embraced democracy and eschewed bossism. That is, the city-states did not suffer from the rule of undemocratic and corrupt bosses more interested in the welfare of their political parties than in the welfare of their cities. Instead, guilds, overtly economic but essentially civic associations composed of bankers, merchants, artisans, and craftsmen, set the agenda for the administration of municipal government based on their agreement on how to advance the welfare of the city. Second, the city-states, as the name suggests, operated as sovereign powers beyond the control or regulation of monarchs, emperors, or nation-states. They could do whatever they wanted.

Unfortunately (in the eyes of our American medievalist urban reformers), the European city-states in the fifteenth and sixteenth centuries traded their independence for protection by the armies of monarchs and emperors. And to the American medievalist reformers, a similar fate had befallen the cities of the United States due to a flaw in the founding fathers' constitutional framework for American civic nationalism, the states' rights fetish embedded in the Tenth Amendment. That concession to the mourners of the Articles of Confederation led in the mid-nineteenth century to secession and Civil War and then to the Reconstruction-era Thirteenth, Fourteenth, and Fifteenth Amendments, designed to rein in the states' rights zealots without paralyzing them. Those measures established the ultimate sovereignty of the federal government on many issues but fell short of the municipal reformers' medieval vision of autonomous city governments. Those amendments, like the body of the Constitution itself, left the creation and regulation of city governments where the founding fathers had lodged it, in the hands of state legislators, who continued in the late nineteenth century their mid-nineteenth-century practice of exercising their sovereignty over municipalities by telling city governments what they could and could not do and in some cases by enacting state laws for the direct control of some aspect of city life, often the creation and management of city police forces.[3]

This medievalist analysis of the impotence of American city government led the municipal reformers in the late nineteenth and early twentieth centuries to demand and gradually to secure from state governments the right of city home rule. Home rule provided cities the power to draft their own charters of incorporation (their constitutions, essentially), so long as their provisions did not contravene state constitutions. The municipal reformers of the late nineteenth and early twentieth centuries, with the saga of secession and Civil War still fresh in their memories, sought by the home rule device to restore a shadow of the lost independence of medieval city-states and thereby to recast the mold of American civic nationalism. Instead of a dualistic bipartite sharing of self-rule between the federal and state governments, they saw it in pluralistic terms as a tripartite system of interdependent, cooperative, and sometimes competing parts—the federal tier, the state tier, and the city tier.

The pluralistic home rule coup laid the basis for the extraordinary expansion of municipal activities during the first half of the twentieth century, especially during the New Deal's federal/urban partnership.

Under this alliance the federal government provided funds and general guidelines for *national* programs, offered those programs as nonmandated options that state and city governments might adopt or ignore, and ceded to states and cities the authority to implement and administer them. Unfortunately, the arrangement essentially localized the programs and handed to racial segregationists a tool for perpetuating the separation of white and African American neighborhoods. This federal-state-city compromise popularized various mid-twentieth-century urban decongestion policies, including not only public housing and urban-redevelopment / slum-clearance programs but also urban renewal and core city neighborhood conservation, all of which intended to shore up and revitalize core cities of metropolitan areas. Indeed, these expensive and complicated programs caught on even among politicians wary about federal meddling in their constituents' way of life. As a result, public housing, urban redevelopment, and urban renewal programs more often than not perpetuated or created new racially distinct neighborhoods. This occurred not only in the Jim Crow South but also in northern cities, where anti–African American sentiments had in the late nineteenth century established a ubiquitous practice of isolating African Americans in particular parts of core cities, a pattern many whites vowed to uphold even as the civil rights movement gained force during the 1940s and 1950s.

A string of racial clashes and a rash of racially motivated neighborhood turf wars ensued. The death of the city specter rose once more and focused attention on the plight of core cities in debates over urban policies throughout the last half of the twentieth century. This took place, moreover, at the onset of the age of cultural individualism and a mode of thought that held that not only people but also urban neighborhoods and core cities should be able to reincarnate themselves with new identities and roles. Yet the actualization of this participatory ideal proved difficult, for the decongestion urban agenda, including the expressway legislation adopted during the Eisenhower administration, both failed to stop the deterioration of core cities and accelerated suburbanization, which among other things eroded the fiscal integrity of core cities in metropolitan areas across the country. New York City flirted with bankruptcy in the 1970s, Detroit went over that cliff in 2013, and across that span of years, luckier core cities pursued stability and revivification and managed to survive on austerity budgets. As these cities struggled in their competition with one another to keep afloat in the national urban sweepstakes, most avoided a descent into the nadir occupied by places like Detroit, where bankruptcy proceedings followed a state takeover of the city's finances and the appointment by the state's governor of an "emergency manager."

But by then the urban scene had changed, and for the worse in the eyes of some. To be sure, New York City had recovered from its fiscal crisis and resumed its place as one of the world's booming global cities. But most other core cities still struggled not merely to maintain their second- or third-class status but to keep from slipping even farther down the slippery slope of the national and global urban hierarchies. These places included Philadelphia, which in the late eighteenth and early nineteenth century held global city status but whose civic and political leaders since the mid-nineteenth century had scuffled to retain for it the less noble but still honorable rank as one of America's second-class urban centers, what some now call second cities.

Into this struggle for core-city survival stepped a small, intellectually agile band of twenty-first-century urban reformers, policy analysts we like to call neomedievalist in their vision of the urban future. Like the late nineteenth-century medievalist urban reformers, the neomedievalists also looked for guidance to the golden age of the medieval city-states. But unlike their predecessors, the neomedievalists focused less on home rule than on the establishment by particular medieval city-states of a foreign policy commercially and militarily favorable to the fortunes of the cities and their network of guilds, the medieval version of civic associations. And the neomedievalists from this angle noticed the tendency of medieval city-states to band together in leagues as agencies for the manipulation of foreign affairs in ways useful to league members, a strategy pursued most effectively by the Hanseatic League, which during its heyday consisted of some two hundred northern European cities. And the neomedievalists also noticed, this time with regret, that the city-states lost control both of their sovereignty and foreign policies to monarchs, emperors, and nation-states by trading their political sovereignty for military protection during the commercial and religious warfare that racked early modern Europe.

The moral seemed clear to the neomedievalists. In the mid- and late twentieth century, the federal government both shaped national urban policy and directed foreign policy for the entire nation, and sometimes in ways not entirely satisfactory to core cities. To be sure, core-city civic and political leaders lobbied Washington more or less successfully on behalf of the welfare of particular or groups of core cities. But the neomedievalists thought such efforts would benefit from a new form of inter-core-city coordination by reincarnating themselves in internationally independent pacts analogous to the medieval Hanseatic League as a way of acquiring more direct power in both the national and the global urban sweepstakes.

The neomedievalists' strategy for doing this included several items. First, core cities should develop metropolitan "regimes"—coalitions of metropolitan-area economic and cultural interest groups sharing a common set of goals—that should first establish their hegemony in their hinterlands ("provinces" in the neomedievalist lexicon). These regimes, the neomedievalists proposed, should then establish associations for transnational activity, leagues that would circumvent or use their clout to amend foreign policies flowing from Washington to establish policies more favorable to the American urban regimes. And at least one neomedievalist presented this option not as a theory but as an extension of a trend already established abroad, the Eurocities organization. Founded in 1986, this Hanseatic-like league adopted a charter that envisaged what this neomedievalist called "a world of cities," ushering in "a future in which cities" rather than nation-states provided "the main locus of citizenship and policy making."[4]

No such organization existed in the United States, but the neomedievalist analysis contended that such an American association would be useful and rest upon the basic tenets of American civic nationalism, democracy, religious tolerance, socioeconomic diversity, and cultural comity. Establishing such a league would not set off power struggles between it and the American or other nation-states. After all, the argument ran, nation-states remained powerful and "unlikely to concede direct challenges to their authority by other territorial organizations. No nation state has yet dissolved, no city-state has yet declared independence, and a wave of urban revolutions and secessions is certainly not in the cards." Beyond that, this neomedievalist contended, "most cities" lacked both "the leadership" and "the political capacity to agitate for such a world-historical shift."[5]

Having domesticated the beast, so to speak, this neomedievalist put together a list of six American second cities most capable of "global integration": Atlanta, Denver, Philadelphia, Phoenix, San Jose, and Seattle. They could be joined, according to a study by the Globalization and World Cities Project, by sixty-seven other non-American second cities, including Barcelona, Birmingham, Dusseldorf, Glasgow, Hamburg, Leeds, Lisbon, Lyon, Melbourne, Montreal, Osaka, Rotterdam, Stuttgart, Tel Aviv, Turin, and Vancouver. Among these, the neomedievalist cited Barcelona as "probably the most prominent second city in the late twentieth century." Barcelona used its hosting of the 1992 Summer Olympics "to redefine itself and enhance its global position," an aspect of its larger "revitalization planning that has been studied and emulated by dozens of cities across the globe."[6]

The attractiveness and efficacy of this neomedievalist Hanseatic prescription will remain moot until tested by time, but the above list and related discussion of established and potential global and globalizing second cities contained some interesting shortcomings suggesting a Western civic nationalist blind spot. It left out the city-states of Singapore and Vatican City, the latter of which in medieval times, as part of its global religious mission, promoted the establishment of the Lombard League[7] as a military alliance for the conduct of warfare, defensive and offensive. In the postmodern world, Vatican City used peaceful means of exerting its moral influence around the world. The second city list and accompanying analysis of "global integration" also ignored the second city potential of certain other sacred cities, such as Jerusalem and Mecca. In the distant past, these cities generated evangelical zeal and warfare between Muslims and Christians and in the twentieth and the early twenty-first centuries also inspired militant Muslim jihadists to attack and occupy cities as bases from which to perpetuate both their international Sunni/Shia sectarian conflict and their postmodern version of the Islamic jihadist assault on Western civilization.

The American and global urban future thus must be seen both as promising and as less than serene. But the neomedieval, Hanseatic-like vision reminds us of how far urban thought, politics, and policy have traveled in the short time after the first half of the twentieth century, a trip from social politics and social planning to identity politics and identity planning. In the early twenty-first century, the focus of concern fell on the acquisition of urban notoriety and respect in a status contest among cities on a national and global scale of celebrity. By this calculus, first-class global cities—the mega stars of the planetary urban scene—represented the ideal, and second-city urban reformers took on the task of helping second cities to retain and capitalize on their second city-ness, not on how to become bone fide world-class global cities. That left the lower tier cities the option of scrambling for roles as supporting actors, bit players, or stagehands. Some tried this by establishing an annual film festival, while others strove for fifteen minutes of fame by making a cameo appearance in the global urban sweepstakes, by supporting and celebrating a World Cup soccer team, by hosting the Winter Olympics, or by pulling off some other one-shot event capable of generating global publicity.

The early twenty-first-century strategy for improving the image of cities differed sharply from that pursued by political and civic planners and political policy makers in the first half of the twentieth century. To be sure, the home rule medievalist reformers, like the boosters of that period, worried about the reputation of their cities in their competition for respectability. But they measured urban progress by the ability of cities to retain their distinctive identities while coping with social problems that seemed serious threats to the welfare of the whole because of their effect not only on individuals but on what the home rulers saw as systematically interacting and interrelated groups of people. These problems consisted of particular "evils" related to the megaproblem: urban congestion. The list of evils included tenements and the lack of family privacy, disease, vice, crime, cancerous slums, ethnic and religious intolerance,[8] low working-class wages, debilitating working conditions in factories and retail stores, the demoralizing influence of visual blight, and the democratic disgrace of boss rule and political corruption,[9] which together created the professional planning movement's quest for both the city beautiful and the city efficient, a search for socially and aesthetically pleasing architectural and urban designs that yielded plans aimed at both the beautification and efficiency objectives.[10]

Unlike these earlier urban reformers, the neomedievalists of the early twenty-first century placed a low priority on elimination of core-city social and physical problems. Their critics, however, laid out a long and unfinished agenda of overdue improvements. The list included ineffective schools, income inequality, joblessness, persisting poverty (despite the war on it started by President Lyndon Johnson in 1964),[11] lagging rates of social mobility for white and Black core-city inhabitants, gun violence, drug abuse and drug dealing (which persisted despite the war on drugs started by President Richard Nixon in 1971), crumbling sewers, roads, bridges, public transit facilities, especially bus service, and fiscal shortfalls and partisan wrangling that stalled action on these issues.

But that unfinished agenda did not include one matter, an old problem that most political and civic leaders all but ignored as a tractable public question. Congress in 1968 passed the Fair Housing Act as part of the effort to provide African Americans an unfettered choice of residence, a chance to move out of core-city "ghettos" if they so desired. Fifty years later, despite the best efforts of fair housing organizations, such as Housing Opportunities Made Equal and a belated effort by the Obama administration in 2015 to apply new rules, guidelines, and pressures on local governments, 60 percent of African Americans lived in segregated urban neighborhoods. Though seldom noticed in the media, these ghettos, like the ones that took shape in the late nineteenth century, contained a varied population that included not only unemployed people but low- and middle-income workers and a variety of occupational categories, including clergymen (Baptists and Methodists mostly but also some Muslims and a few Catholics and Episcopalians), doctors, lawyers, and a variety of businesspeople (such as real estate and insurance agents as well as retail, grocery, restaurant, and other entrepreneurs). Some pundits argued that the existence and persistence of these ghettos generated interracial resentments and fears that corroded the political system by encouraging many city, state, and federal politicians and political activists, liberals and conservatives alike, to play the "race" card.[12] As often as not, this ideological ploy contributed to governmental gridlocks that blocked or deferred action not only on civil rights legislation but also on other issues and cast doubt on the ability of the managers of American civic nationalism to make the system work.

In any event, America's urban future remains predictable but unknowable, a subject of conjecture but a problem beyond the reach of human rationality. Yet this history provides a reason for hope. No other country in the early twenty-first century contained such a large collection of cosmopolitan and influential global and second-city metropolitan areas. Based on the long-run record of urbanization and urbanism, the resiliency and durability of America's metropolises may be taken for granted, but not the resiliency and durability of American civic nationalism. This idea and institution, after all, is not very old in the annals of civilizations. It remains, in that light, as Abraham Lincoln said at Gettysburg, an extraordinary experiment. Established in the late eighteenth century, it served for three centuries as an admirable and sturdy device for city founding and city building. Along the way it survived a bloody Civil War that strengthened northern cities for their lurch into the urban industrial age but retarded for a generation the growth of southern cities and their liberation from the prison of King Cotton. American civic nationalists in the first half of the twentieth century also spurned the international lure of right and left dictatorships and the slaughterhouse era those political monstrosities generated, two grisly world wars, the massive destruction of European and Asian cities, and the murder of uncounted millions of civilian residents of totalitarian states. Somehow from this nightmare of annihilation the American civic nationalist state emerged as the world's chief financial power and most admired cultural icon, due in large part to the vitality of its metropolitan areas, despite the persistent difficulties confronting their core cities.

Exactly why and how the American civic nationalist experiment and its urban foundation lasted into the twenty-first century remains an intriguing and unresolvable question.[13] But its record of city building and improvement provides a secular source of solace to those anxious souls who, in the wake of 9/11, fret about the future of American civic nationalism and the cities on which its pliability and perpetuation rests. Time and again, from ancient Sumer to early modern Istanbul, and from late eighteenth-century Philadelphia into the twenty-first century, ordinary but mentally adroit and energetic city dwellers, civic and political activists, and intellectuals of various stripes have demonstrated the human ability to reject the cultural legacy of the past and to think and act in new ways. By the cultivation and exercise of that ingenuity, they kept alive or reincarnated their cities and, through them, the civilizations that sustained the human drama of urban adaptation and innovation.

So too may the next generations of urbanites, if they choose. But those American civic nationalists, like their predecessors in the Civil War and World War II eras, will face a challenge then and ever since associated with nationalism. "What's wrong," wrote one civic nationalist, "is not nationalism itself. Every people must have a home.... What's wrong is the kind of nation.... A struggle is going on between those who still believe that a nation should be a home to all, and race, color, religion, and creed should be no bar to belonging, and those who want their nation to be home only to their own. It's the battle between the civic and the ethnic nation. I know which side I'm on. I also know," he concluded gloomily, "which side, right now, happens to be winning."[14]

Michael Ignatieff, a scholar, novelist, and self-styled cosmopolitan, wrote those words in 1993 after taking a survey of a spasm of ethnic nationalism in the former Soviet Union, Northern Ireland, and the Canadian province of Quebec. His prediction of its spread seemed accurate. In the early twenty-first century, Vladimir Putin's nationalistic Russian government vowed to protect Russian-speaking blocs wherever they might live, and several western European countries cracked down on immigration, particularly the influx of ethnics from eastern Europe and northern Africa, amid persistent cries that such people belonged in some other country, in their own home. Meanwhile, Islamic terrorists continued their attacks as part of a larger campaign to strengthen states friendly to the jihadist antimodern idea and to create new ones.

So Ignatieff's late twentieth-century sense of the other side winning sounds feasible. Yet his concern may underestimate the resilience of civic nationalism, especially in light of the American experiment with it, which survived under preindustrial, industrial, and postindustrial conditions. This book treats American civic nationalism as an ideal that goes back to the late eighteenth century, well before the invention of ethnic nationalism. It links urban cosmopolitanism not just to gigantic global cities but also to second, third, and lower tier urban areas, all of them pluralistic culturally, all of them the historic homes, as Ignatieff put it, of "expatriates, exiles, migrants, and transients of all kinds."[15] It treats urban cosmopolitanism and its practice as a majority rather than a minority phenomenon and as the principal source and progenitor of the American civic nationalist idea as laid out in Declaration of Independence, the Continental Congress's regulations of 1787 for the governance of the first U.S. territories, and the Constitution of 1789 and its Bill of Rights. Generations since then have striven not only to preserve the United States as a polity but also to make it "a more perfect Union," and with considerable success, including the election and reelection to the presidency of an African American, Barack Hussein Obama, a former (and innovative) Chicago community organizer. So in the United States, the "other side," so far, has lost and seems unlikely to win, as long as American voters embrace and nurture their legacy of urban cosmopolitanism.

The outcome of the cosmopolitan challenge, in this view, depends on those urban specialists who choose political and civic leadership as their contribution to American civilization. According to some observers, they should continue to recognize and insist upon the flourishing of political and civic organizations on the grounds that every social organization, "be it a political party or a kennel club, must follow a governance structure that is, in essence, a school of democracy." Together, such leaders might sustain a kind of civic spirit that could "infect the country's political culture with the ... sense of responsibility for the public good ... that is still democracy's best hope."[16]

But in the age of cultural individualism, it has not been easy to imbue the residents of American cities and the nation with a compelling sense of responsibility for the common good, and it seems unlikely to get any easier. A turning inward from the public to the private sphere stands as a chief hallmark of that era, and a symptom of its primacy and staying power may be found in the enormous popularity of the smart, relentlessly energetic, courageous, and compassionate Gail Sheehy, the author of dozens of magazine articles and sixteen books. A protege of Margaret Mead, the anthropologist who became a celebrity intellectual by virtue of the popularity of her first book, *Coming of Age in Samoa* (1928), Sheehy's work appealed to a broad audience of millions of people in the same way and for the same reasons as the work of Mead, Tennessee Williams, Norman Mailer, Tom Wolfe, and Truman Capote. All of these writers specialized in the intensive exploration of private lives (including their own) and the artfully spectacular, even flashy examination of the vogue for self-defined identity, the response to identity crises, and the metamorphoses of personalities as individuals picked and chose their way through identity options as they navigated and negotiated their passages through the stages of life, from childhood to adolescence, adulthood, midlife, old age, and on to terminal illness. To juice up their stories, the celebrity journalists utilized fictional devices to personalize their prose, the obverse of the conventional reportage in the *New Yorker*. Indeed, the books of Sheehy and the others read more like novels than detached analyses.

Sheehy's particular journalistic forte rested in the construction of compelling character sketches, none of which, even those of such major political figures as Margaret Thatcher and Mikhail Gorbachev, dealt with the problems and possibilities of democracy or with the public policy question of how to define and nurture the public good. Instead, they focused on the interpersonal relationships of their interview subjects. This journalistic approach ranked not as civic but as individual identity journalism, a genre that treats cities not as schools of democracy and the public interest but as career infrastructure, collections of buildings, places, spaces, institutions, and social organizations useful as instruments for launching ambitious people to ascendancy and stardom in the national and international celebrity sweepstakes. Individual identity journalists, in short, focused their reporting not on their subjects' roles as public servants or public enemies but on the psychodrama of interpersonal experiences that shaped their characters and on their adaptability and their mesmeric attraction (Thatcher, Sheehy reported, had sexy legs, lips, and terrifying eyes) as keys to their ability (or inability) to draw attention to and sustain curiosity about themselves.

We all, of course, are interested in and care about such things—children and adolescents with characters shaped by their experience in imperfect families, corrosive sibling rivalries, for example, and parental peccadilloes and worse, such as sexism, racism, wife and child abuse, under- or overexaggerated career expectations, gambling, alcoholism, philandering, divorces, occupational failure, inertia. But, as the popular song says about life, is that all there is? Are there additional things of interest that we might and should care about? That question—is that all there is?—is the title of a popular tune from the 1960s about the widespread disillusionment with and the futility of idealism, a lament that appealed to the existentialist angst among those disappointed by the seeming meaningless of life, which reduced to triviality supposedly important and uniquely important events, such as the burning of one's home or a first trip of a child to the circus or even death. And if "that's all there is, my friend" according to the song's lyrics, "let's keep on dancing. Let's break out the booze and have a ball." The "is that all there is" song delivered in a haunting melody a sobering moral message. Those afflicted with this malaise, it suggested, had turned inward, preferring sybaritic pursuits to civic commitment for the building of a better, more fulfilling future for themselves and others. Indeed, "is that all there is" posited a disenchanted urban population of prosperous and educated individuals suffering from what the Germans call Weltschmerz (world weariness), a debilitating sense of ennui, melancholy and despair that prompted an urge to escape from the meaninglessness of freedom and the discipline of civic, religious, and ethical obligations by recourse to drink, carousing, and the distractions of a lush life (the title of a slow, bluesy Billy Strayhorn / Duke Ellington musical lamentation for a lost ideal involving jazz and "twelve o'clocktails"). The "is that all there is" song evoked not an image of the city on a hill but rather of even older biblical cities, Sodom and Gomorrah. Or, and equally ominous, in the twentieth century, the ambience of Berlin in the 1920s as depicted in the stage and screen hit of the 1960s and 1970s, *Cabaret*, which juxtaposed lush life decadence and civic numbness with the rise of right-wing political extremism. In this context, lush lifers didn't give a damn about the future of the city or civic nationalism (the term *lush life* is also the title of Richard Price's book about drugs, vice, crime, and cops in Manhattan's Lower East Side in 2003, which features as its protagonist an unfulfilled, unmoored, and directionless habitué of an identityless, directionless, anomic, and civically indifferent neighborhood).

Sheehy, in the final reckoning, did not think that this is all there is and eschewed cynicism and the sybaritic route and a capitulation to a static existence devoted to an "escape from freedom" (the title of a 1941 book by the German-born psychologist Erich Fromm). The fundamental virtue of the political figures she interviewed and wrote about—a list that included such disparate figures as Robert Kennedy, Ronald Reagan, and Anwar Sadat as well as Thatcher and Gorbachev— consisted of the strength of character and grit that drove them to keep on going, to break with the past and seek a new future. But she praised them without reference to the political salience of their particular vision for safeguarding the public interest.

Sheehy also included on that list of worthies Hillary Rodham Clinton, a well-informed and talented figure, in Sheehy's view, who spent far too much of her life helping others instead of going it alone by inventing some other role for herself. Hillary Clinton's wasted years, so to speak, included especially, Sheehy emphasized, the devotion of her time and energies exclusively to molding and managing Bill Clinton's political career. So Sheehy applauded with a characteristically Sheehy bravo when Hillary Clinton emerged as a powerful political figure in her own right by announcing her intention to become a senator representing New York State. Now, Sheehy wrote, after Hillary Clinton had come through "the little death of midlife" and a career of standing "up against shame and scorn," she had finally chosen to follow her own lights on a mission to "alter the direction of the planet by dreaming of a different direction that we can take in our own lives." A few years later, when Clinton announced her run for the Democratic Party presidential nomination, Sheehy repeated her bravo. But once more Sheehy did not express an admiration for or specify Clinton's public policy positions or commitment to the public good, which she might have done by analyzing Clinton's communitarian book *It Takes a Village* (1990). Sheehy described Clinton instead as, in a sense, just more of the same, a standard-issue candidate, "ruthless, nakedly aggressive, hawkish, and often tone deaf—qualities common among politicians who dare to compete at this level." But, wrote Sheehy, Clinton "was also extraordinary: killer smart, empathetic, unsparing of her energy and commitment, and so resilient she could eat scandal for breakfast."[17]

Journalists in Sheehy's genre seldom addressed the city directly as a way of assessing the state of American culture, but one did, and in a book that attracted enough attention that movie makers tuned it into a popular film. Hunter Thompson's *Fear and Loathing in Las Vegas: A Savage Journey into the Heart of the American Dream* (1971) lamented the political failure of the countercultural ("hippie") participatory democracy and peace-and-love movement of the 1960s and launched his career as a celebrity journalist, one notorious for expressing his support for a drug-free version of this idealistic cause (see pp. 178–180, for example) in intentionally shocking irreverent and "vulgar" prose, including sexually explicit slang. The book recounts in fictionalized, ribald, and satiric form the trip of two socially, civically, and morally irresponsible protagonists on a search for the American Dream, which they find in Las Vegas. The book, originally a journalistic piece for *Rolling Stone* magazine (est. 1967), focused on their drugged-out, gambling spree on maxed-out credit cards in the casinos and hotels in the city of greed, a place they depicted as catering exclusively to the single-minded pursuit of wealth and its perquisites, power and ego gratification. But the book treated the city not as a place in which to analyze the resiliency of cities or as a school for the democratic buttressing of the public interest or as a way of assessing the prospects for the future of American civic nationalism. Instead, the book depicted the city, as Sheehy had, as a setting for a nonurban, noncivic story, a deliberately shocking satire of American hypereconomic and decadent cultural individualism, a setting useful in the hands of a moralizing celebrity journalist.

Both Sheehy and Thompson, then, reached for a large audience of Americans by advocating a particular kind of enlightened (in their view) idea of cultural individualism, and neither of them did so by making a systematic, coherent case for civic and political literacy and a commitment to the public interest as a necessary intellectual superstructure to support the cosmopolitan promise of American cities and American civic nationalism. Sheehy replaced social determinism with a form of psychological determinism but thought that people should and could, with proper mentoring and counseling, throw off their psychic thralldom and escape to the freedom of self-creation through identity manipulation. Like Sheehy, Thompson also eschewed social determinism and replaced it with a form of psychological determinism with which to overcome the failure of the drug-ridden counterculture and eliminate the bane of American cultural individualism, its rejection of peace and love in favor of economic individualism as the American Dream. For him Las Vegas seemed an ideal tool for use as a last-ditch effort to repoliticize the ideas of a just political economy and foreign policy by exaggerating the excesses of American capitalism in a moralizing rant about a city of greed awash in sexism, racism, violence, middle- to low-brow taste in the arts and entertainment, a place oblivious to the carnage of the war in Vietnam but so frightened by the allegedly violent drug culture that it happily (and profitably) hosted the National District Attorney's Association and its Third National Institute on Narcotics and Dangerous Drugs.

To both Sheehy and Thompson, then, the redemption of "the city" rested upon the self-redemption of individuals, which to both of them seemed possible. Sheehy thought that people could be "cured" by inspiring them to overcome their childhood maltreatment and take control of their own lives, from adulthood to death. Thompson, like Sheehy, thought people could be saved, could exorcise the demon of hypereconomic individualism with the assistance of mentors and counselors adept in the inspirational sermonizing of a modern-day Jeremiah, the guru of the drug-free counterculture. Both Sheehy and Thompson, then, hoped, in their own way, to counter the malaise of the lush life singer, a sense of the meaninglessness of existence that left no recourse, as Strayhorn's lyrics had it, except a lush life "in some small dive," a place of profound, existential melancholy, a place in which to escape "with the rest of those whose lives are lonely too."

But the public appetite for self-invention as the path to a meaningful life and its lack of interest in civic analysis and the public good in the age of cultural individualism not only enriched and made celebrities of journalists; it also rewarded in the same way like-minded professional academics, especially psychologists, and most notably Abraham Maslow, author of the hugely successful book *Motivation and Personality* (1954). This widely read and quoted volume laid out his anti-Freudian and antisocial deterministic theory, which contended that humans, regardless of race, ethnicity, religion, class, or gender, possessed an innate system of motivational needs that led them level by level up a hierarchy of needs. The hierarchy's bottom consisted of physiological needs, such as air, drink, shelter, warmth, and sex, and then proceeded through safety, love and belongingness, and self-esteem needs. At the apex of the hierarchy stood the loftiest of needs, self-actualization (self-fulfillment), the quest for realizing one's personal potential, an innate special talent (to become all that one can become, as the army's twenty-first-century recruiting TV ad expressed it), the realization and exercise of which led to "peak experiences," the exhilaration of self-satisfying accomplishments. According to this theory, the human genetic endowment includes an urge to strive toward a level of personal autonomy and identity flexibility that prompted individuals to strive toward self-fulfillment regardless of their race, religion, ethnicity, or socioeconomic class and regardless of the governmental system in which they lived—tribal, authoritarian, or democratic. Such a strictly psychological approach to well-being and the meaning of life treated as immaterial an examination of character structure and the problems of the public good and civic and political illiteracy and the future of cities and American civic nationalism.[18]

Maslow, of course, like most contemporary American intellectuals, worried about the future of American and global politics, and especially deplored the rise of Nazi Germany, the Soviet Union, and the anti–Vietnam War countercultural movement. And he also, like many of his intellectual contemporaries, thought that the study of history, properly construed, could buttress liberal democracy as a sensible way of fending off both authoritarian and antiauthoritarian radicalism of the mid-twentieth century. He even entertained the idea of developing a political theory compatible with his hierarchy of needs. He died before he could write such a work, but what we know of his political ideas indicate that such a book would have been more psychological than civic, more concerned with establishing for individuals a universal motivational ideal, like a psychological Declaration of Independence, than with laying out public good policies for particular problems and issues in particular national and cultural contexts.[19]

But is that all there is? Is the neglect of the public good and a preoccupation with personal self-fulfillment enough, especially in the face of the temptation to bask in the comfort of and relish the empowering sense of religious, class, racial, or ethnic ideological and communal exclusiveness? Such extremist movements represent a threat to urban diversity, the bedrock of the resiliency of a nation dedicated to the cosmopolitan political proposition that places the public welfare above the interests of particular social groups. In the beginning, the United States, a nation "conceived in Liberty," as Lincoln put in his Gettysburg address, took shape after 1776 from a series of civic and political choices and compromises over the issue of the welfare of the whole—the striving for a more perfect union—that yielded fifteen years later a government of, by, and for the people, as prescribed in the Constitution and its first ten amendments. That conception of liberty seemed at the time a daring experiment, virtually unprecedented. And now, in the age of cultural individualism, it stands as a major challenge for defenders of American civic nationalism and the public interest who define their task as completing the unfinished work of Revolutionary War and Civil War generations, an effort to see whether "a nation so conceived and so dedicated, can long endure." It remains to be seen if the carriers of that legacy can put the state of our cities and American civic nationalism rather than individuals in pursuit of personal self-fulfillment at the center of our concern about the uncertain American future, a self-restraining stance quite compatible with twenty-first century environmentalist concern about our uncertain global future.[20]

NOTES

1. William H. McNeill, The *Rise of the West: A History of the Human Community* (Chicago: University of Chicago Press, 1963), 545. For the martial origins of the national state, see Charles Tilly, *Coercion, Capital, and European States: AD 900–1990* (London: Basil Blackwell, 1990), which in its preface also draws useful distinctions between city-states, the national states, and nation-states and points to the possible, even likely, eclipse of the latter two.

2   Alan I Marcus, "The Medieval Image in the Modern Mind: History, Democracy, and Turn-of-the-Century American Municipal Governance," in *Making Sense of the City: Local Government, Civic Culture, and Community Life in Urban America*, ed. Robert B. Fairbanks and Patricia Mooney-Melvin (Columbus: Ohio State University Press, 2001), 34–56.

3. An important essay on the legal standing of municipalities in the nineteenth century is Judith Spraul-Schmidt, "Reconstituting City Government: Midcentury State Constitution Making, Defining the Municipal Corporation, and the Public Welfare," in Fairbanks and Mooney-Melvin, *Making Sense*, 11–33.

4. Jerome I. Hodos, *Second Cities: Globalization and Local Politics in Manchester and Philadelphia* (Philadelphia: Temple University Press, 2011), 188.

5. Hodos, *Second Cities*, 189. Hodos's neomedievalism encompasses "the growth of a global civil society and movement toward the institutionalization of global civic action." This trend includes nongovernmental organizations, such as Global Urban Development (GUD). Founded in 2001, GUD became by 2015 a policy organization and professional network involving five hundred civic leaders and urban strategies experts in sixty countries who put cities at the center of promoting environmentally responsible growth and regulatory programs. GUD set up and operated offices in fourteen cities: Barcelona, Beijing, Belo Horizonte, Curitiba, Hong Kong, Istanbul, London, Prague, Rehoboth Beach (Delaware), San Francisco, Singapore, Sydney, Toronto, and Washington, DC.

6. Hodos, 183

7. The standard history of this league is Philip Jones, *The Italian City-State: From Commune to Signoria* (London: Clarendon, 1997).

8. On an important and neglected aspect of the role of municipal government in promoting cosmopolitanism, see Andrea Tuttle Kornbluh, "Playing with

Democracy: Municipal Recreation, Community Organizing, and Citizenship," in Fairbanks and Mooney-Melvin, *Making Sense*, 119–137.

9. On the two phases of the battle against political corruption and boss rule, see Robert A. Burnham, "The Boss Becomes a Manager: Executive Authority and City Charter Reform," in Fairbanks and Mooney-Melvin, *Making Sense*, 75–94; on social scientists and the second phase of urban reform, see Alan I Marcus, "When Numbers Failed: Social Scientists, Modernity, and the New City of the 1930s," in *The Great Depression: People and Perspectives*, ed. Hamilton Cravens (Santa Barbara, CA: ABC-CLIO, 2009), 165–148. On the origins of the assault on urban problems during the first half of the twentieth century by neighborhood associations, see Patricia Mooney-Melvin, "Before the Neighborhood Organization Revolution: Cincinnati's Neighborhood Improvement Associations, 1890–1940," in Fairbanks and Mooney-Melvin, *Making Sense*, 95–118.

10. For an underappreciated aspect of the movement to legitimize city planning as a municipal responsibility, see Robert B. Fairbanks, "Advocating City Planning in the Public Schools: The Chicago and Dallas Experiences, 1911–1928," in Fairbanks and Mooney-Melvin, *Making Sense*, 57–74.

11. On the switch in the 1950s and 1960s from a communalistic war on slums to an individualistic war on poverty, see Robert B. Fairbanks, *The War on Slums in the Southwest: Public Housing and Slum Clearance in Texas, Arizona, and New Mexico* (Philadelphia: Temple University Press, 2014), appendix A. On the politically corrosive consequences of that same switch for the post–World War II, desegregationist fair housing movement, see Charles F. Casey-Leininger, "Giving Meaning to Democracy: The Development of the Fair Housing Movement in Cincinnati, 1945–1970," in Fairbanks and Mooney-Melvin, *Making Sense*, 156–174.

12. Liberals, but not conservatives, tended to emphasize white discrimination as the chief factor in creating and sustaining African American ghettos.

13. For an introduction to the discussion of this enigma, see Daniel J. Boorstin, *The Genius of American Politics* (Chicago: University of Chicago Press, 1953); David Runciman, *The Confidence Trap: A History of Democracy in Crisis from World War I to the Present* (Princeton, NJ: Princeton University Press, 2013); and the review of Runciman's book by John Gray, "The Dangers of Democracy," *New York Review of Books*, March 20, 2014, 42–44. Boorstin, for his part, suggested (3), as a "rule-of-thumb," that "our national well-being is in inverse proportion to the sharpness and extent of the theoretical differences between our political parties." Not a bad point from which to start a discussion.

14. Michael Ignatieff, *Blood and Belonging: Journeys into the New Nationalism* (New York: Farrar, Straus and Giroux, 1994), 249.

15. Ignatieff, *Blood and Belonging*, 11.

16. Paul Wilson, "Vaclav Havel: What He Inspired," *New York Review of Books*, April 23, 2015, 27.

17. Gail Sheehy, *Daring: My Passage* (New York: Harper Collins, 2014), 212. This book also introduces us to what Sheehy calls the clubby world of New York City

journalism (235), including especially, it's worth noting, the claque devoted to Clay Felker, the founding editor of *New York* magazine memorialized in his *New York Times* obituary as "a visionary editor... widely credited with inventing the formula for the modern magazine, giving it energetic expression in a glossy weekly named for and devoted to the boisterous city that fascinated him—New York" (447). Felker gave Sheehy her start toward journalistic celebrity by selecting her to write stories for *New York* magazine, and they became long-standing lovers and eventually husband and wife. The book contains heart-wrenching segments about his illnesses and Sheehy as a consummate caregiver to the very end. The "alter the direction of the planet" quote may be found in Gail Sheehy, *Hillary's Choice* (New York: Random House, 1999), 353.

18. A friendly biographer concluded that Maslow seems to have regarded liberal democracy as the best political environment for self-actualizers. But he did not divide self-actualizers into conservative and liberal types, for he regarded both the hero of Ayn Rand's *The Fountainhead* and Eleanor Roosevelt as representative self-actualizing types. He also considered self-actualized people as rare human beings, leaders in their fields of endeavor. As he once put it, "Apparently, every baby has possibilities for self-actualization, but most get it kicked out of them.... The average man is a human being with dampened and inhibited powers." For the quote, see Edward Hoffman, *The Right to be Human: A Biography of Abraham Maslow* (Los Angeles: Jeremy P. Tarcher, 1988), 173–174.

19. See, for example, Hoffman, *Right to be Human*, 311, 318–319, 322, 324, 329.

20. On twentieth- and twenty-first-century environmentalism, see, for example, Nathaniel Rich, "The Very Great Alexander von Humboldt," *New York Review of Books*, October 22, 2015, 39.

3
Cities, American Civic Nationalism, and Fundamentalism

ZANE L. MILLER

Perhaps half our people . . . have come from Europe. . . . If they look back through this history to trace their connection with those days by blood, they find they have none, they cannot carry themselves back into that glorious epoch and make themselves feel that they are part of us, but when they look through that old Declaration of Independence they find . . . that moral sentiment taught in that day evidences their relation to those men, that it is the father of all moral principle in them, and that they have a right to claim it as though they were blood of the blood, and flesh of the flesh of the men who wrote that Declaration, and so they are. That is the electric cord in that Declaration that links the hearts of patriotic and liberty-loving men together, that will link those patriotic hearts as long as the love of freedom exists in the minds of men throughout the world.[1]

—ABRAHAM LINCOLN, Chicago, July 10, 1858

It is my contention that the United States ranks as one of the world's most successful city-building civilizations. This accomplishment derives essentially from the founding documents of the United States, the Declaration of Independence and the Constitution, the nature of which facilitated the spread and growth of cities as the dynamic factors in forging of what I call American civic nationalism. The authors and signers of those documents saw themselves, like the ancient Roman builders who were their heroes, as residents of the easternmost edge of what could become a continental, republican empire, the cities of which would serve as the anchors and progenitors of a rational, urban, and urbane civilization.[2] The founders anticipated that this citified republican empire would "civilize" the sparsely populated, undertilled lands and underexploited natural resources of the western and southwestern sectors of the continent by turning these vast areas into populous hinterlands connected to eastern cities in a myriad of ways.

The promoters of this urban imperial vision thought of the new nation as consisting of two societies: one urban, one rural, each with "its own institutions, habits, and living patterns" and each supporting the other. "The rural regions," as a premier historian of the early republic put it, "supplied the cities with raw materials for their mills and packinghouses, and offered an expanding market for their shops and factories. In turn, urban centers serviced the surrounding areas by providing both the necessities and comforts of life as well as new opportunity for ambitious farm youths." But the cities "represented the more aggressive and dynamic force." They spread "the fruits of civilization across the mountains and by insinuating their ways into the countryside" spearheaded the creation of an urbanized empire of continental scale.[3]

This republican vision of the American "empire of liberty," as Thomas Jefferson described it, imagined it as a federated national state, an experiment in political economy, not an American nation-state but rather a sociocultural organization. To be sure, the founders of this entity forbade the establishment of religion by either the federal or state and local governments, hobbled the extension of slavery into some territories and states, and put the importation of African slaves on the road to extinction. But they did not otherwise use federal authority to tinker with the habits and customs of the residents of the United States. They gave that question to decision makers in state and local government agencies, who also, until the mid-nineteenth century, thought of their responsibilities in terms of political economy. The founders of the federal government, that is, left to state and municipal governments the future of slavery where it existed, the distribution of voting rights to men and women, the regulation of immigration and of schools and schooling (including medical, legal, religious, and liberal arts institutions), the treatment of crime, vice, filth, noxious manufactures, disease, gambling, dueling, popular entertainment, and mentally or physically disabled individuals, and the passage of laws regarding marriage and divorce.

To put it another way, this vision of an empire composed of a republican federal government and democratic states and municipalities derived from and depended upon the idea of American civic nationalism, a secular and tribal-less creed that rejected monarchial dynasty, genetic aristocracy, theocracy, and the possibility of establishing a polity based on ethnic, racial, or socioeconomic class ideology. The founders instead held that American patriotism should be fundamentally political and voluntary, a matter of rational choice, not a question of blood, ethnic culture, race, religious faith, or socioeconomic class, an ethos transcending but not extinguishing social, economic, and religious interests. And the logic of this proposition called for the spread and proliferation of republican territorial, state, and municipal governmental bodies across the continent. In this way, participants in republican self-government on both the eastern seaboard and in the westerly states would multiply and collectively practice civic nationalism and reap the economic and cultural benefits of their loyalty to the civic ideal and its incarnation in America.

The device for fulfilling this mission emerged from a series of compromises at the Philadelphia Constitutional convention via the new U.S. Constitution and its quickly adopted first ten amendments. From this bedrock of American civic nationalism emerged a profusion of republican governments and governmentally established institutions and agencies, each one located in a city of some sort, whether large or small. The Constitution, that is, established not only a federal government in Washington, DC, but also structured states and territories containing federal offices and installations, including military bases, and a broad and varied range of civilian services, such as post offices, weather observatories, customhouses, federal courthouses, agricultural experiment stations, and land grant universities for agriculturists and mechanics in particular.

The Constitution, in addition, established territorial and state governments, which themselves established headquarters in capital cities, which were endowed with state agencies and other governmental institutions. And from the outset, those territorial and state legislatures created mazes of local governments, including villages, cities, townships, counties, special purpose districts, and semiautonomous nonmunicipal corporations (serving commercial, religious, educational, cultural, and charitable purposes), almost all of which were situated in cities. These developmental and disciplinary operations offered jobs to city dwellers and spent money on projects in both urban and rural settings, including, to mention just a few, the construction of city halls, courthouses, roads, bridges, water and sewerage lines, jails, and prisons, as well as the broad range of economic and beneficent structures managed by nonmunicipal corporations or other agencies.

This form of federalism,[4] in short, functioned in the new nation as a potent city-building mechanism, one supported by citizens as voters and taxpayers and managed by political and civic activists from the bottom up. Excepting for business enterprises, the proliferating federal, state, and local institutions of development and discipline did not pay real estate taxes. But their civic-minded and socially responsible employees supported the federal governmental architecture by endowing public treasuries with the financial sinew to advance the general welfare. And during the nineteenth and early twentieth centuries, the number of federal, state, and local governmental city-building agencies grew rapidly as the nation gained new territories and states. By 1920, town and city dwellers composed half the population of the country, while the other half lived in urban-inflected rural areas shaped by and closely connected to the most dynamic cities. During the decades after 1920, moreover, the creation of city-building governmental services and developmental corporations persisted, a process that eventually came to be seen, ironically, as both a boon to and blight on the social, economic, political, and cultural aspirations of residents in the world's most wealthy and individualistic society.

The ultimate outcome of this long experiment in American civic nationalism is situated beyond the vision of even the wisest of prophets and pundits, but the record to date seems clear. The Declaration of Independence and the Constitution set in motion a powerful urbanizing tendency, one that provided more than a federal structure fostering a proliferation of municipalities. Both the federal and the state governments seeded those municipalities with agencies, institutions, and services that yielded cities, not merely places of local coherence and identity but cities as centers of social, economic, and cultural influence as well as of political vitality. From this perspective, the country's founding documents prescribed a federated governmental framework promoting cities as the primary foundations for and generators of an American urban way of life built on civic and political participation by an expanding range of citizens, a capitalist economy, and a constitutionally mandated separation of church and state.

However, there is nothing inevitable about the durability of civic nationalism in America, no magic embedded in the founding documents that assures its perpetuation or prevents the union's dissolution or the erosion of American civil nationalism as the founders envisaged it. Secession and threats of secession form a minor but persistent theme in American politics, and not only in the early nineteenth century, when Boston and other New England ports, disenchanted with President's Jefferson's embargo of 1807, sincerely considered it; or in 1860, when Southern nationalists actually tried it. Along another track, many mid-nineteenth-century political economists expected in the near future the creation of a socialist American civic nationalism because of the rise of that quintessential urban class, the bourgeoisie, the financiers and the owners of the means of production, both rural and urban. As Karl Marx expressed it, the hegemony of the bourgeoisie has "subjected the country to the rule of the towns. It has created enormous cities, has greatly increased the urban population as compared with the rural, and has thus rescued a considerable part of the population from the idiocy of rural life. Just as it has made the country dependent on the towns, so it has made barbarian and semi-barbarian countries dependent on the civilized ones, nations of peasants on nations of bourgeois, the East on the West."[5]

Marx and Engels wrote that passionate passage, of course, not to praise the bourgeoisie but as a call for its destruction by artisans and mechanics, intellectuals and artists, and unskilled workers. And they issued this "Manifesto of the Communist Party" in 1848, during the early stages of the mid-nineteenth-century municipal and industrial revolutions that reshaped American cities and society, yielding a sinister and disorienting urbanism that provoked strong socialist movements in both Europe and the United States. In the American late nineteenth and early twentieth century, citizens in several cities favored socialist city governments; socialist political parties regularly ran candidates for Congress—with many winning election—and several socialist presidential candidates mounted strong though unsuccessful campaigns. In continental Europe, urban politicians, political organizers, and publicists persuaded voters to install enduring socialist regimes. And in Great Britain, urban voters after World War II backed the Labor Party as it set up a socialist-inflected government and remained a viable alternative to conservative rule over the subsequent decades.

But civic nationalism—peoples united by their commitment to elected political systems—has fostered not only strong socialist movements and governments but also varieties of religious rule or dominance. In 1924 and 1934 (though in the latter year, voting rights were limited and tilted toward Fascist sympathizers), the Italian electorate voted to retain Mussolini's dictatorial government, which struck a deal in 1929 with the Catholic church to make Catholicism the state religion in return for the pope's relinquishing temporal rule in Rome and other territories in Italy. The Church of England still receives financial support from the government, and some of its bishops hold seats in Parliament. Elsewhere in the twenty-first century, moreover, religion-proselytizing politicians have had great electoral success in such polities as Lebanon, the Palestinian territories, and Egypt. And Israel, whose founders in the 1940s included a strong contingent of resolute secularists, has become, by democratic means, a de facto Jewish state with a decidedly religious inflection.

The Indian experience resembles the Israeli case. Jawaharlal Nehru, India's first prime minister, sought to nurture a strictly secular state that would restrain if not eliminate the influence of religious fundamentalists seeking the comfort of a religious state. His expectation was that tolerance extended to Muslims would prove his point. Instead, Nehru's commitment to an inclusive secular state enraged Hindu supremacists and set off a vicious round of sectarian violence culminating in a Hindu extremist's assassination of Mahatma Gandhi, a Hindu, religious pluralist, and leader of India's independence movement. Even today the memory of this act haunts the ruling Hindu nationalist party. It, like Nehru's administration, seeks to govern inclusively, much to the continued disgust of Hindu nationalists, whose longing for a religiously oriented state still runs strong.

And of course there is the tragic playing out of Adolph Hitler's rise to power, a champion of racial superiority in one of the world's leading urban-industrial countries. Hitler became Germany's leader under civic nationalist auspices at the end of the Weimar Republic, a democratic government created in the 1920s with a constitution establishing universal suffrage, proportional representation, and a two-house legislature, one composed of regional representatives and the other representatives of the people. This parliamentary, multiparty arrangement was led by a prime minister as head of government (the chancellor) assisted by a president as head of state (in lieu of a monarch). When that system deadlocked in 1932–1933, the president, Paul von Hindenburg, quite legally appointed Hitler chancellor.

These various democratic experiments remind us that civic nationalism comes with no guarantees. It might in the future produce some American-style democracies in other places, but they may not last. One might assume that the continued American commitment to civic nationalism is beyond doubt, but it too may not last. As with all cases of democratic nationalism, the survival of American civic nationalism comes down to a matter of choice and the exercise of political vigilance and persistence in keeping at bay the prophets of extremist, "purified" democracy and undemocratic alternatives that are religiously, racially, ethnically, or socioeconomically based. This task seems particularly daunting in light of the appallingly high level of adult illiteracy in the United States. The federal government, in fact, responded to that problem in 1991 with the passage of a National Literacy Act, which, among other things, set up a National Institute for Literacy. Yet, by 2015, the rate of adult literacy showed no increase from ten years earlier.

Meanwhile, concern for civic illiteracy—the ignorance of the basic documents and principles of American civic nationalism and a superficial understanding of American political history and its compact with comity—has become a separate but related issue for critics concerned about the dismally low turnout of voters in national, state, and local elections, which gives disproportionate influence to nonmainstream candidates and self-interested initiative and referendum petitioners. This concern has provoked the American Bar Association and some state legislators to advocate the teaching of civics in public schools. As of 2015 only nine states mandated such tests for high school students, and a civic education curriculum reaching from kindergarten through the twelfth grade, a Bar Association favorite, has proved even rarer.[6]

But the root problem may be more severe and intractable than civic illiteracy, and it may be both a European and an American problem, an aspect of what Mark Lilla has called "cultural pessimism" in an essay about France and its rising Muslim population. Lilla describes this malaise as a phenomenon "as old as human culture" and one with "a long history in Europe," the "persistent European worry that the single-minded pursuit of freedom—freedom from tradition and authority, freedom to pursue one's own ends—must inevitably lead to disaster." This, he adds, leads to a nostalgia for an imagined past that never existed, "a pre-modern Christendom" of "strong families, moral education, social order, a sense of place, a meaningful death, and, above all, the will to persist as a culture."

So from Lilla's perspective, the threat to American civic nationalism may stem from its successes, a wager made two centuries ago not only in France but also by Americans, a bet that "the more they extended human freedom the happier they would be." But "that wager has been lost," for unhappiness abounds here also, and it has yielded a reaction both similar to and different from the Gallic malaise. Like the French, we live with the fear that our country "is adrift, and susceptible to a much older temptation to submit to those claiming to speak for God." But here the potential contenders worship not one but many Gods, some of them supported by powerful and rabid followers, Catholic, Protestant, Jewish, of course, but also Mormons, Muslims, Buddhists, Hindus, and Sikhs. And in America the sense of drift also nourishes nostalgia for an imagined lost past that afflicts people on both the right and left of the political spectrum, including those who favor ethnic or racial or gender and sexual-orientation "orthodoxy." In light of our spectacular diversity, the test for Americans in the twenty-first century may be our willingness and ability to sustain both cultural pluralism and democratic social coherence, the resilience characteristic so far of American civic nationalism, which embraced from the outset not cultural nationalism but the idea and practice of theological, social, and cultural cosmopolitanism as the keystone of the national edifice.[7]

Similarly, the principal global threat to American civic nationalism may reside in religious fundamentalism, which seems unlikely to go away. "Fundamentalists of all kinds," as Michael Ignatieff has put it, object to "the epistemology of democracy itself, to the idea that political truth is contestable and is arrived at through public debate." Beyond that, they also object to "the fundamental moral norm of democratic debate, that there are no enemies in a free politics, only opponents. For a true fundamentalist, truth is divinely received and when a political opponent denies it, he becomes an enemy, to be dealt with, if necessary, by the sword."

That leaves twenty-first-century democracies with a dilemma. Civic nationalist supporters deplore but would not ban religious fundamentalism, and the many and varied fundamentalists who oppose civic nationalism not only yearn for its downfall but will also try to overthrow it. In the face of this dilemma, Ignatieff says, "Only a pessimist would believe that the ultimate outcome is a foregone conclusion, and only a dogmatist would want a final crushing victory for either side."[8] But whatever the outcomes of the conflict between fundamentalism and civic democracy, it will be decided in cities, the breeding places of both authoritarian and democratic movements, including American civic nationalism.

NOTES

1. Roy P. Basler, ed., *The Collected Works of Abraham Lincoln* (New Brunswick, NJ: Rutgers University Press, 1953–1955), 2:499–500.

2. The founders' fascination with the ancient Roman republic made them leery of "savage" hordes of hunters and herders who descended from their villages to sack, pillage, and sometimes conquer cities, which the founders, like the Romans, regarded as the bases and progenitor of "civilized" life. On the threat of herders and hunters, see William McNeill, *The Rise of the West: A History of the Human Community* (Chicago: University of Chicago Press, 1963), 102–107, 232–245, 361–416 (esp. 385–412), 484–486. The founders also regarded as inevitable the cyclical rise and fall of civilizations as exemplified in Roman imperial history and, therefore, in the preamble to the Constitution, pledged the establishment of a "more perfect," not a permanent, union and viewed the United States as an "experiment" to see how long it might endure as a republic.

3. Richard C. Wade, *The Urban Frontier: The Rise of Western Cities, 1790–1830*, 8th ed. (Urbana: University of Illinois Press, 1996), 341–342.

4. Reno, Nevada, provides an amusing illustration of the federal urban sweepstakes and urbanization process. Nevada entered the union with an abundance of land (it contained more acreage than the combined areas of Maine, New Jersey, Vermont, Connecticut, Massachusetts, Maryland, Delaware, West Virginia, New Hampshire, and Rhode Island). Its first important town, Virginia City, rose on top of the Comstock Lode of gold and silver, and from 1859 into

the 1880s, Nevada produced almost half the silver minted in the United States. But the mines soon ran dry, and the Nevada legislature sought to jump-start the growth of cities by adopting a loose divorce law, the chief source of the early affluence of Reno. The divorce market flourished into the 1930s, when Nevada legislators decided to counteract the economic doldrums by legalizing gambling, and an enterprising gambling entrepreneur revived Reno by advertising it nationally as a gambling mecca, a gaming center for popular public rather than furtively clandestine entertainment, the first of a series of openly seductive sin cities, many of them suburbs, such as Newport and Covington, Kentucky, of major big cities. On Reno, see Daniel J. Boorstin, *The Americans: The Democratic Experience* (New York: Vintage Books, 1974), 64–76.

5. Lewis S. Feuer, ed., *Marx and Engels: Basic Writings on Philosophy and Politics* (Garden City, NY: Anchor Books, 1959), 111–112.

6. For a concise introduction to the view that adult illiteracy coupled with a remarkably high level of civic illiteracy poses a prime threat to the viability of American civic nationalism, the wellspring of the American Dream, see Michael F. Ford, *The American Dream, or What's a Heaven For?* (Cincinnati: Cincinnati Book Publishing, 2015), chap. 8 and the afterword.

7. Mark Lilla, "Slouching toward Mecca," *New York Review of Books*, April 2, 2015, 42.

8. Michael Ignatieff, "The Religious Specter Haunting Revolution," *New York Review of Books*, June 4, 2015, 68.

PART II
Urban Life as Urban History

4

"The *Metropolitan* Mode of Thought"

Zane L. Miller and the History of Ideas

JOHN D. FAIRFIELD

One of the founders of the new urban history, Zane L. Miller celebrated the city as the center of creative thought and civic vision. He never doubted the capacity of urbanites to define the problems and possibilities facing their cities and to use public powers to address them. The new urban history emerged in the midst of, and in part in response to, the urban crises and civil disturbances of the 1960s. Sam Bass Warner's masterful *The Private City* (1968) traced the "endlessly repeated failures" to "create a humane environment" to what he called "privatism." What the "private market did well American cities have done well," Warner explained. "What the private market did badly, or neglected, our cities have been unable to overcome," and the "public dimensions of urban life suffered accordingly." Yet much of the new urban history also neglected those public dimensions. Eager to recapture the lives of the common people and aided by new quantitative and ethnographic methods, the new urban historians explored rates of social mobility, ethnic and racial identities, changing gender roles, leisure time activities, and other aspects of private life.[1]

Miller's work pushed in a different direction. His explorations of the public and political dimensions of urban life provided an essential, hopeful complement to the indictment of privatism and the excavation of private experience. Miller's interest in civic life reached back to his high school education and found expression in his dissertation and first book, *Boss Cox's Cincinnati: Urban Politics in the Progressive Era* (1968). Ostensibly about the contest between machine and reform politics, Miller's study highlighted the development of energetic, positive governance aided by both machine and reform forces. Over a long and productive life of scholarship, teaching, and civic engagement, Miller continued to champion the civic capacity of American cities. At the end of his life, he was writing a new survey of urban history with the working title *Urbanism as a Way of Life: The City and American Civic Nationalism*. Organized around cities as the carriers of what he called "civic nationalism," the project highlighted the creativity, imagination, and capacity for compromise that made for successful and resilient cities.[2]

But Miller always tempered his hopefulness with concern about the deteriorating civic capacity of cities. In a series of books and articles in the late 1970s and early 1980s, Miller lamented the decline of "the public interest," which he defined as "a civic interest above and beyond individual and group interests—for the advancement of which individuals and groups ought to be willing to sacrifice, by volunteering time to work on a 'community' project, for example, or by approving tax increases." He linked the decline of the public interest with the eclipse of "the *metropolitan* mode of thought" that had emerged in the early decades of the twentieth century.[3]

The Metropolitan Mode of Thought and Its Demise

The metropolitan mode of thought treated the city as an organic, interdependent community and encouraged citizens to look beyond their narrow interests and to cooperate and compromise for the greater good. In the 1950s, however, the metropolitan mode of thought gave way. The new view, Miller argued, held that "individuals constituted the fundamental units of society and thus comprised the only 'real' and therefore appropriate entities of study and objects of concern." The city "seemed almost an illusory construct which veiled the greater and real process of interaction among classes, institutions, and organizations." Instead of an organic, interdependent metropolitan community, the city devolved into a collection of "communities of limited liability" to which mobile and self-interested individuals gave only provisional allegiance.[4]

Miller's embrace of the metropolitan mode of thought goes back to the work that made his mark as a leading urban historian, *Boss Cox's Cincinnati*. Writing during the long, hot summers of the 1960s when Americans looked anxiously at the state of their cities, Miller examined an earlier period of urban anxiety at the turn of the twentieth century. The explosive growth of cities in the late nineteenth century overwhelmed the old walking city and gave rise to a new, enlarged, and reorganized metropolis. As Miller might have put it some years later when he began to articulate a more ambitious philosophy of history, an older conception of the city clashed with the real city of people's immediate perceptions. The resolution of this cognitive dissonance would only come with (in his later words) "the establishment of a new taxonomy of reality and the dominant conception of what society is, is becoming, or ought to be."[5]

The metropolitan mode of thought provided that new taxonomy of reality, a set of assumptions that shaped perception and the identification of problems to be addressed. Even as the specialization of land use and the differentiation of city districts created a more divided city (central business district, tenement districts, suburban neighborhoods, and industrial satellites), a recognition of the interdependence of the city's parts enabled Cincinnatians to bring order and coherence to their growing city. While Miller argued that residence provided the "touchstone" to political experience in the city, he also showed how first the Cox machine and then its reform opponents managed to unite citizens across the city to address metropolitan-level issues. Recognizing the choice between efficient management of growth or disorder and decline, the bosses and reformers mediated conflicts between the city's affluent hilltops and its impoverished basin, promoted cultural pluralism in an ethnically and religiously diverse city, and secured annexation of outlying neighborhoods. Beginning in the 1890s and continuing into the first two decades of the new century, Boss Cox and his antagonists acted upon—and helped to spread—a belief in the interdependent metropolis as the basic unit of society.[6]

Given his reputation as a corrupt manipulator of elections and legislatures, the saloonkeeper George B. Cox might seem an unlikely proponent of the idea of the metropolis as a delicate organism in need of careful management. But as Miller explained, Cox "had grown up with the new city and received a liberal education in its ways." Young Cox worked a variety of jobs, on both sides of the law, that well acquainted him with the struggles of the impoverished. When his ability to deliver votes attracted the attention of prominent Republicans, Cox rose through the political ranks. Emerging as the boss of the city's Republican machine, Cox oversaw an expansion of municipal government that depended on expertise, centralized planning, and freedom from state interference (i.e., home rule).[7]

Cox's success in improving public services and utilities won him at least temporary support of silk-stocking Republicans in the city, despite his unsavory methods of bribery, graft, and election fraud. By the 1910s, however, the belief that the ever-present danger of disorder demanded a more vigilant citizenry turned a bipartisan set of reformers against Cox. Rather than blindly follow the machine, reformers argued, citizens had to be prepared to recognize competent experts, vote on complex issues, and join in civic-spirited organizations for the betterment of the city. To cultivate such citizens, reformers constructed a dense network of educational and civic institutions, including kindergartens, high schools, settlement houses, and other community organizations.[8]

Following World War I, the reformers created the Charter Party, a strictly local organization that advocated nonpartisanship. The "Charterites," as they became known, codified the metropolitan mode of thought in a new city charter, adopted in 1925. The new charter created a small city council, elected at large, that—at least theoretically—served the metropolitan interest rather than the narrow concerns of neighborhoods. The charter provided for nonpartisan elections conducted under the system of proportional representation to encourage the election of underrepresented minorities to council while also encouraging all candidates to appeal to all voters across the city. In the same year, Cincinnati became the first major city to adopt a comprehensive city plan to anticipate and guide future metropolitan growth.[9]

The unraveling of the metropolitan mode of thought over the following decades left central cities with a social and budgetary crisis that worsened even as *Boss Cox's Cincinnati* went to press. One of the last expressions of the metropolitan mode, the Cincinnati Metropolitan Plan of 1948 warned that the outward flow of population and the deterioration of the older parts of the city had "resulted in the decline of municipal revenues and a rise in the cost of municipal services." The plan pointed out that "Cincinnati has itself subsidized this outward development in that the residents of these surrounding communities enjoy many services daily at the expense of the central city." Cincinnati provided and maintained the streets and traffic controls, water and sewer systems, parks and airports, libraries, and museums that suburbanites depended on. But the 1948 plan also signaled the decline of the metropolitan mode of thought in observing that the metropolis had grown "to the point of diminishing returns in terms of the advantages which a city, as a social community, should provide for its inhabitants." Instead of pushing for metropolitan governance based on a collection of diverse and interdependent neighborhoods and suburbs, the 1948 plan called for a set of "self-contained" communities of twenty to forty thousand people, designed for the convenient delivery of services.[10]

By the late 1960s, the metropolis operated more like a fragmented collection of warring groups than an efficient vehicle for the delivery of services. Suburban jurisdictions with little allegiance to the larger metropolis proliferated, fragmenting metropolitan governance and leaving suburban resources unavailable to the central city. Resisting annexation to Cincinnati, suburban jurisdictions instead used zoning and restrictive covenants to keep out "alien" urbanites. Within Cincinnati, the great migrations of white Appalachians and African Americans taxed public services and tested a hard-won commitment to cultural pluralism. As Cincinnati's second ghetto expanded and deteriorated, violent civil disturbances in 1967 and 1968 punctuated the collapse of the metropolitan mode of thought.[11]

The metropolitan mode of thought nevertheless remained a lodestar for the rest of Miller's career. Miller had hoped that *Boss Cox's Cincinnati* would "help overcome the appalling neglect and widespread misunderstanding of our urban past." At a time "when many Americans are troubled by our cities," he wrote, "we badly need liberation from ancient myths and clichés." When Miller and his colleague the historian Henry D. Shapiro established the Laboratory in American Civilization at the University of Cincinnati in 1975, they continued the work of liberation. Convinced that "historians knew precious little about the relationship of urban and suburban neighborhoods to each other and to the life of the city as a whole," Miller and Shapiro used the laboratory to examine "the metropolis conceived as a set of communities, some inside and some outside the corporate limits of the big city." The rise of a neighborhood organization movement that erroneously treated the neighborhood "as a vital unit with a history of independence which only recently has been 'violated'" made their inquiry "a particularly timely topic." Partisans for the interdependence of the organic metropolis, Miller and Shapiro explored the shifting relationships between neighborhoods, suburbs, and the metropolis and the conceptions of community that produced and reflected those relationships.[12]

Taxonomies of Reality and Symptomatic History

Miller and Shapiro enjoyed an unusually long and productive collaboration. While Miller's metropolitan concerns provided the major focus of the partnership, Shapiro contributed the philosophy of history that guided their inquiries. What Miller called taxonomies of reality came from Shapiro's immersion in the European debate over structuralism. Emerging first in linguistic theory, structuralism held that an underlying conceptual system shaped everything that humans perceived, thought, and did. As the theory migrated to other fields from anthropology to literary criticism, structuralists held that culture—like language—depended on a set of hidden rules and relationships that people implicitly understood even if they could not articulate them. This underlying structure meant that everything must be understood in relationship to everything else. Hence the privileged place structuralists gave to cultural binaries (male-female, Black-white, civilized-savage).[13]

Critics assailed structuralism for minimizing the role of historical circumstances in shaping thought and action and obscuring the dynamics of change over time. In adhering too tightly to cultural binaries, critics added, structuralists obscured cultural diversity. Critics also found structuralism too deterministic in asserting that conceptual systems directed problem-solving along certain lines and foreclosed others. Poststructuralists, a loose grouping that included some structuralists, addressed these issues by incorporating a greater appreciation of historical change and cultural diversity. In doing so, the poststructuralists refined the theory and gave it wider currency. Shapiro developed his own distinctive version of structuralism in which taxonomies of reality, what Miller called an underlying conception of "what society is, is becoming, or ought to be," held center stage.[14]

Although structuralism made up a good part of Shapiro's teaching of both graduate and undergraduate students, he did not cite structuralists in his published work. The best evidence of his thinking on structuralism comes from his seminal work, *Appalachia on Our Mind: The Southern Mountains and Mountaineers in the American Consciousness, 1870–1920*. The book is not about Appalachia but about the vision of Appalachia in the minds of writers, missionaries, and social workers who defined it "as a discrete region, in but not of America." These people, Shapiro argued, saw not Appalachia but what they expected or needed to see in Appalachia. Those expectations and needs arose from a taxonomy of reality, "the process by which experience is defined, ordered, organized into coherent and actionable schemes."[15]

In the decades after the Civil War, for reasons Shapiro declined to speculate about, a belief in a unified and homogeneous American nationalism emerged as the reigning taxonomy. That belief generated a "cognitive dissonance" when faced with the white, native-born, Anglo-Saxon, Protestant people of Appalachia. Appalachia appeared to be "a strange land inhabited by peculiar people" that could not be explained away by geographic, chronological, or ethnic difference. Defining Appalachian otherness as a problem, writers, missionaries, and social workers tried to explain and reform that otherness. Gaining currency in the 1890s, the conception of Appalachian otherness shaped subsequent observations and interpretations of Appalachia and generated a host of philanthropic efforts.[16]

Although the footnotes and bibliography do not attest to it, *Appalachia on Our Mind* is filled with ruminations on the philosophy of history informed by structuralism. Shapiro carefully avoided determinism. He argued that historians must always keep in mind that what happened in the past did not have to happen in the way it did. But their task is not to argue with the past, only to understand it. It does us no good to protest that past actors worked from a faulty understanding of reality, for it was not reality that concerned those actors but "reality defined in a particular way." Ideas about reality "are not natural emanations from objective reality," Shapiro insisted, "but are the creation of men, and stand between consciousness and reality." People use ideas to define and to try to resolve the problems that cognitive dissonance presents. The task of the historian is to uncover these ideas and explore their consequences. "The present, however, is another matter," Shapiro insisted. He hoped his analysis of a past conception of Appalachia might free us to ask if that conception "proves useful in the present, and how, and to whom." Closing the distance between consciousness and reality, historical understanding might liberate us from the limitations of inherited ideas.[17]

The second distinctive element of Shapiro's (and Miller's) philosophy of history derived from the first. Reigning taxonomies of reality arose from collectivities—rather than from individual imagination or historical or immediate circumstances—making local histories symptomatic of larger, national trends. In 1970, Shapiro and Miller deployed this idea in their initial collaboration, a study of Daniel Drake, early Cincinnati's polymath builder of institutions. Rather than treat Drake as an exceptional man or the product of local circumstances, the authors assessed Drake's career "in the context of the problems which beset American science and American society during his lifetime." The ways in which Drake thought and acted revealed the characteristic ways of conceptualizing reality and defining problems in the early republic (in other words, the reigning taxonomy of reality).[18]

In May 1975, a phone call from a member of the city council of Forest Park, a northern suburb of Cincinnati, provided the occasion for the fullest elaboration of the philosophy of history that underlay the Laboratory in American Civilization. In the 1950s, a private developer built the planned community of Forest Park on land originally part of one of the New Deal's greenbelt towns (Greenhills, Ohio). Civic leaders in Forest Park wanted to commission a history of the community as part of the national bicentennial celebration. The project provided an opportunity to extend the laboratory's investigation of the relationships between cities, suburbs, and neighborhoods into a different geographic and chronological context. The laboratory tackled the job, and Miller later produced a book-length study, *Suburb: Neighborhood and Community in Forest Park, Ohio, 1935–1976* (1981). As Miller explained in his introduction, the study examined the symptomatic ways of defining and resolving metropolitan problems in the middle decades of the twentieth century.[19]

In the opening pages of *Suburb*, Miller lamented that the term *symptomatic history* mystified his colleagues, and he set out to explain it more carefully. Three things defined symptomatic history: a focus on structure, a radically historical approach to the past, and an analysis of the process of defining and addressing problems. Structure took the form of unspoken assumptions about the basic components of society, an unarticulated taxonomy of reality that shaped the definition and response to problems. Taxonomies of reality changed from time to time for reasons Miller professed no knowledge of and little interest in. By a radically historical approach, Miller meant that the past was truly past; previous taxonomies did not shape the present or influence the future in any linear or causal way. Rather than establish a genealogy of ideas, Miller identified "moments of redefinition" and sought to "understand and explain the consequences of the new modes of thought." He did this through an analysis of the process of problem definition and resolution. The consequences took the form of changes in existing institutions and the creation of new ones, as well as new relationships among institutions and in territorial arrangements.[20]

Despite symptomatic history's premise of radical historical discontinuity and its silence on cause and effect (at least at the level of changing taxonomies of reality), it did produce a narrative. Forest Park, in other words, had a story. The story focused on the process of problem definition and problem resolution *within a given taxonomy of social reality*. Once the taxonomy shifted, however, a new narrative had to begin. Miller found Forest Park a useful subject for symptomatic history because, while not appreciably different demographically from thousands of postwar suburbs, it had been "comprehensively"—and thus self-consciously—planned. Although that made Forest Park appear "special" to many people, it also meant that the reigning assumptions of the period would be particularly pronounced there. Moreover, a good part of the comprehensive and conscious planning centered on the creation of community, a central focus of Miller's work.[21]

As Miller explored what Forest Parkers meant by community, he found that the story of Forest Park involved three taxonomies of reality and thus three conceptions of community. And since Forest Park's development involved governments at the level of city, state, and nation, its history illuminated symptomatic assumptions about community as well as problem definition and institutional construction and arrangements characteristic of the entire nation. Everything from fragmented metropolitan authority and the obstacles to providing low-income housing to the excessive cost of urban utilities and racial tensions showed up in the story of Forest Park. So, too, did the assumptions that provided the structure in which such problems were defined and addressed.[22]

Changing Taxonomies from the Metropolitan Mode to the Community of Advocacy

To situate Forest Park in that national narrative, Miller first explored the conventional view of community in suburbanizing America. In the 1950s and 1960s, he argued, Americans saw suburbanization as an emerging phenomenon and tried to explain its meaning and consequences. The suburban way of life appeared homogenized, rootless, and shallow, culturally conformist and politically conservative. By the late 1960s and early 1970s, however, descriptions of suburbanization shifted dramatically. Despite his expressed lack of interest in explanations of cause and effect, Miller gave at least some suggestion as to why. Scholars and commentators discovered working-class and Black suburbs as well as antiwar, civil rights, and women's rights activists in the suburbs, overturning the view of suburbia's conformity and conservatism.[23]

By the early 1970s, the discourse about "suburbia" gave way to one about "the suburbs," the new term conjuring an image of a diversity of middle- and upper-income groups rather than a way of life. Similarly, "the city" no longer suggested a way of life but a set of "urban" problems associated with poverty and race. The city now appeared encircled by a ring of diverse suburbs that would either hollow out the core or, if historical preservationists and downtown revitalizers proved successful, would help to revitalize the core.[24]

Miller described these conventional views of community in suburban America only to subject them to critical historical examination. As artifacts and events from the past, these views themselves required interpretation. In interpreting discourse about suburbs and cities, commentators missed the "unarticulated assumption," the taxonomy of reality that underlay the division of the metropolitan world into "suburbs" and "cities" in the first place. Seeing the metropolis as the fundamental unit of the social order would have put a premium on seeing the organic interdependency between suburbs and cities. But mid-twentieth-century Americans had come to assume that the individual—rather than the metropolis—represented the fundamental unit of social order, and they acted on that assumption.[25]

The unarticulated assumption of the individual as the fundamental unit of society shaped problem definition and resolution in the period after 1950. Miller explicitly contrasted that assumption with the metropolitan mode of thought. As the dominant taxonomy of reality from the 1920s until around 1950, the metropolitan mode of thought encouraged an understanding of community as something akin to the public good, something beyond individual and group interests, indeed something worth sacrificing those interests for. This mode of thought shaped the earliest development of Forest Park. Designed by planners who understood the metropolis "as an organism in which all things are related," Miller argued, Forest Park would be part of a strategy for designing the social and spatial structure of the metropolis that would be conducive to a community of good citizens. Envisioned as a relatively self-contained residential community, Forest Park would still serve as part of a larger community. It would provide housing for those displaced by slum clearance and highway construction in Cincinnati, even as it depended on the big city for a host of services and attractions.[26]

But that future for Forest Park never materialized. The metropolitan mode of thought gave way in the 1950s to what Miller called the *community of limited liability*. As increasingly autonomous suburbs served a mobile population with a weaker allegiance to the metropolis, sharper distinctions between cities and suburbs made them seem less interdependent. The emphasis on the individual overturned the previous assumption that community arrangements should shape good citizens; now it seemed that individuals had an inherent right to shape their own local arrangements. What Miller called "the rediscovery of the local community" shifted the focus of civic participation from the metropolitan to the local level. Similarly, the search for community no longer seemed a metropolitan matter but a task for individuals who could make a variety of commitments to local places but also to translocal associations (unions, professional organizations, ethnic or fraternal groups). While Forest Parkers acknowledged a responsibility to sustain the civic community through voluntary associations, such as the Forest Park Civic Association, all understood that personal circumstances could legitimately excuse greater or lesser commitment to this community of limited liability.[27]

By the mid-1960s and early 1970s, yet another taxonomy of social reality gave rise to the era of the *community of advocacy*. Here the problem of community lost any civic focus whatsoever. In what Miller called the *inward-turning tendency*, individuals still appeared to be the basic unit of society, but now they had been "liberated," free to participate—or not—in civic life for the sake of individual well-being rather than community welfare. All conception of an organic metropolis gave way to multiple jurisdictions in competition with one another for scarce resources. What passed for civic life fragmented into a host of special-interest associations. Until the mid-1960s, Forest Parkers had still been capable of conceiving of social and economic problems as involving some greater whole and evaluating solutions in terms of the general welfare. But now, even when local actors invoked the civic interest, they shared no collective understanding of that interest. Indeed, Forest Parkers distrusted the term as a disguise for self-interest. Unable to formulate policies aimed at the public good, they lost faith in public solutions.[28]

At the end of *Suburb*, Miller drew the larger lessons from this symptomatic history. Pointing to the host of commentators (including President Jimmy Carter) who bemoaned "the narcissism" remaking American culture, Miller offered a new explanation for the current malaise. Dismissing such explanations as the energy crisis and stagflation, disillusionment following the traumas of Vietnam and Watergate, and the excessive bureaucratization of American life, he attributed the culture of narcissism to a new taxonomy of social reality. In the community of advocacy, individual concerns trumped everything else. It was not that Americans had turned away from social and economic issues. Individual concerns from careers to property values constantly raised larger social and economic issues, but no one bothered to address them in ways that promoted the public good. A political process once dominated by elections, bargains, and compromises now featured demonstrations, litigation, and referenda advancing particular rather than general interests. Political paralysis and stalemate ensued.[29]

A variety of issues illustrated the decline of any sense of an organic, metropolitan community. When the city of Cincinnati first introduced an earnings tax in the 1950s, for example, it reflected a belief in the central city as a distinctive place, the source of suburban growth, and the vital force that made the metropolis work. All who depended on the city should be expected to support it. But when Forest Park instituted its own earnings tax in 1974, the central city appeared to be just another jurisdiction in competition with other jurisdictions for resources and population. The same attitude animated the neighborhood movement within Cincinnati, underwriting the belief that each neighborhood should be as far as possible self-sufficient. Likewise, Forest Park's struggle with questions of racial justice illustrated the rise of the inward-turning individual. After the mid-1960s, as more African Americans fled the central city for Forest Park, residents agreed that all should have an equal right to move to the community. But no one debated whether and what kind of integration (racial or socioeconomic) best served the public interest and the well-being of the metropolis. Instead, debate centered on the individual interest in property values, the spread of blight, and the local municipality's need to attract affluent citizens and taxpayers.[30]

Although the metropolitan mode of thought provided a standard against which to measure the decline of the civic interest in Forest Park, and by extension the nation, in his final pages Miller pronounced it "irretrievably past." The radical discontinuity of history implied "the inappropriateness of past modes of thought and action for the present and the future." But Miller believed his symptomatic history raised two important questions: "Is the community of advocacy the only kind of community possible within the current mode of thought and action? If not, what kind of community do we want, and how, under current constraints, can we create it?" While deferring those questions to another and different sort of book, he thought his history might "free us of the past by suggesting that we can neither return to older modes of thought and action nor learn practical lessons from the past." Instead, he hoped his history would indicate that "we, as others before us have done, can think and act in new ways in the present and the future."[31]

The Response of the Profession: Taxonomies and Symptomatic History in the Dock

Recently reprinted, *Suburb* has earned praise as both an influential forerunner and, conversely, a neglected model for the new suburban history. One of the first serious studies of suburban history, *Suburb* avoided the simplistic notions of white flight to a homogenous suburbia that had caused historians to miss the complexity of suburban experience. Whatever else it might be, Forest Park is an example of Black (as well as white) flight from the city. Miller also avoided a condescending attitude to profit-seeking developers and middle-class homeowners, describing those who worked for a stable, racially integrated community as well as those who resisted this outcome.[32]

At the time of its first publication, however, *Suburb* received a rockier reception. Then as now, professional historians recognized and praised it as a pioneering effort to look objectively at the American suburb. Miller "steadfastly refused to trivialize the issues of suburban life," Terence McDonald wrote, "but instead emphasizes their human significance." Others welcomed Miller's close analysis of city planning and public policy in an American suburb and described it as an important and thoughtful work that would inspire further study and discussion. But the assertion of its symptomatic relevance, now at least more clearly understood, raised objections. McDonald thought Miller had made "very little attempt" to establish Forest Park's typicality in the Cincinnati region, much less nationwide. Jon C. Teaford concurred, writing that readers "might question whether the events in Forest Park are symptomatic of anything other than the local conditions of suburban Ohio."[33]

Nor did Miller's explication of his taxonomies of social reality win over his peers. Readers might well "dispute the validity of Miller's 'taxonomies,'" Teaford wrote. Miller's "rather narrow research focus and evidentiary base of the study," McDonald added, "do not fully support the much broader generalizations about community he wishes to make." Like McDonald, Thomas Bender bemoaned the lack of attention to the "social and cultural lives of people living in the community." Without considering what was happening in schools and professions, families and churches, Bender argued, an exclusive focus on city planning and politics could not reveal changing attitudes to community.[34]

In a generally positive review, McDonald nevertheless found something tendentious about Miller's argument. Without a social analysis of association membership or political participation, Miller could not convincingly establish either inward-turning or community fragmentation in the mid-1960s. Substituting institutions for individuals, Miller used the existence of the civic association as evidence of civic commitment despite his own evidence that the association "spent its time either bemoaning the lack of community participation or fending off charges that it was dominated by a political or neighborhood 'clique.'" The division between the white-collar and blue-collar residents of Forest Park that Miller brought out only in the section on the community of advocacy had likely been there ever since the developers' decision to erect "ticky-tacky" houses along with more upscale structures. The emergence of neighborhood and special interests in the 1960s, McDonald continued, "may have represented the recognition and political legitimation of divergent interests which had long existed." The community of advocacy thus "may have been a more authentic and democratic approach to politics," McDonald concluded, "than that of the assumed consensus in the era of civic association."[35]

Bender leveled the most direct challenge to Miller's philosophy of history. Bender found Miller's intellectual strategy provocative as it raised "some rather fundamental concerns in the writing of history." It "may be jarring to place the relaxed, informal, and essentially superficial historiographic speculations of Miller alongside the brilliant virtuosity of Michel Foucault," Bender wrote, but the "rather awkward explication of his methods" recalls "the fundamentally nonhistorical histories of Foucault." Bender also detected evidence of the anthropological work of Clifford Geertz on the "web of meaning sustained by culture that is open to inspection but not to causal analysis by historians." But Bender lamented that Miller seemed not to have followed the debates surrounding these theories, for "his position deserves a more rigorous and philosophically informed argument." It was no small matter, after all, for a historian to abandon causation or refuse to explain change over time.[36]

Taking the metropolitan mode of thought as an example of fuzziness about change over time, Bender questioned why Miller dated it to 1920. Daniel Burnham's *Plan of Chicago* (1909) would seem an obvious example of the metropolitan mode, but one might take it back even further to Frederick Law Olmsted's vision for a greater New York. "Dismissing questions of causation and change," Bender continued, "leaves categories and distinctions distressingly hard to fix." Without placing Forest Park in a longer history of community in the United States, we could not know whether Miller described "a distinctive mid-twentieth-century process rather than an endlessly repeated morphology of community-building in America." Indeed, Miller's description of a passage from "metropolitan linkage to civic unity to segmentation" resembled what other scholars documented as the "general morphology evident in nineteenth century American town development." Miller's methods raised "some fundamental problems troubling contemporary historiography," in a more concrete way than "Foucault's stratospheric flights." But they deserved much more discussion, Bender concluded, than Miller provided.[37]

In the two decades following the publication of *Suburb*, Miller wrote an array of essays, articles, book reviews, and review essays. Some of his writing addressed these philosophical questions; much did not. But he remained astonishingly productive and never stopped thinking about the bigger issues his work raised. In a project that went through many revisions, Miller returned to his central preoccupations in *Changing Plans for America's Inner Cities: Cincinnati's Over-the-Rhine and Twentieth-Century Urbanism* (1998, written with Bruce Tucker). A city neighborhood just north of Cincinnati's central business district, Over-the-Rhine was—and remains—a place of appalling contrasts, of trendy bars, restaurants, and condos astride homelessness, poverty, and despair. Over the course of the twentieth century, it had been the subject of a bewildering set of plans and transitions. By turns, native-born Americans, German immigrants, Appalachian whites, African Americans, the homeless, developers, and affluent "homesteaders" have tried to make it their own.[38]

As Miller and Tucker told it, the story hinged on a shift in taxonomies of reality, although one slightly altered from Miller's previous work. Planning between 1920 and 1950 still focused on the public interest, defined as the welfare of the metropolitan community. But now cultural groups took on greater importance as the basic units in society. Each cultural group possessed its own culture, acquired from its "history and experience in varying social and physical environments." But in the slum, a chaotic and deteriorating environment "eroded the coherence of cultural groups" and left only alienated and impoverished individuals. Slum clearance, aided by zoning and other planning tools, would produce stable and secure environments for cultural groups and encourage them to accept the obligation to interact with other groups. Segregation by race and class would continue, but improved environments, supplemented by civic education campaigns, would produce good citizenship and cultural pluralism. The city would enjoy a cosmopolitan character marked by "intergroup respect, understanding, and tolerance."[39]

After 1950, a new taxonomy of reality replaced cultural pluralism with cultural individualism as the city's mission. Slum clearance gave way to the preservation and rehabilitation of a diversity of city neighborhoods, maximizing individual choice. Some saw Over-the-Rhine's potential as a chic residential neighborhood, but others successfully defended it as a haven for the poor. Throughout the many debates, Miller and Tucker argued, one variety of cultural individualist faced off against another strain of cultural individualist, with neither side making a compelling case in terms of the public interest. In the 1960s, for example, developers seized on a historic preservation plan as a means of capitalizing on Over-the-Rhine's rich history and architectural distinction to attract affluent residents. But neighborhood activists used the federal mandate for "maximum feasible participation" in urban renewal planning to fight historic preservation. Recrimination and distrust led to political paralysis and left the residents of Over-the-Rhine mired ever deeper in poverty.[40]

Professional historians lauded *Changing Plans* as a detailed case study and found its indictment of cultural individualism convincing. "The new mode of thinking," Arnold Hirsch wrote, "championed individual and neighborhood autonomy while furnishing continued intellectual cover and comfort to a racially segmented city." In quoting the authors' assertion that race and poverty must be redefined as "multi-dimensional issue(s) with ramifications for every neighborhood in the city," Hirsch invoked Miller's organic ideal. Janet Bednarek agreed that none of the participants in the post-1950s debate "fully envisioned the neighborhood as a part of the city as a whole." I added in my own review of *Changing Plans* that "only when citizens articulated some larger vision for the city could competing claims be assessed and compromised in light of an unfolding public interest."[41]

As for the taxonomic method, it appeared in a somewhat altered form in this work, in a way that appeared to minimize radical historical discontinuity. Perhaps due to Tucker's participation or perhaps from Miller's own rethinking of the matter, *Changing Plans* offered some explanation for the shift in taxonomies at midcentury. The failure of slum clearance to advance cultural pluralism, Miller and Tucker wrote, "led to a rethinking of the nature of the metropolis problem that pushed the city in a new direction," toward mixed uses and diverse neighborhoods. The preference for cultural individualism, they added, stemmed from "our mid-twentieth-century fears of social determinism, totalitarianism, and conformity in the context of World War II." Influential Americans, they added, associated the program for promoting cultural pluralism with fascism, Nazism, and communism, for they all "projected cultural blueprints of the future and preached sacrifice for the welfare of the whole as necessary for realizing them."[42]

But these changes failed to win reviewers over to the taxonomic method. Skeptical readers, Hirsch wrote, might question the lack of "causal links between the various modes of thought and the urban policies associated with them." The "abhorrence of foreign totalitarianism and a sterile, domestic conformity," he added, is more asserted than demonstrated. Bednarek added that "the authors do not fully explain where the new ideas came from nor do they indicate to what degree they reflected mainstream planning thought." My review of *Changing Plans* extended these objections to the issue of historical continuity. Pointing to federal housing, mortgage insurance, and transportation policies that decimated inner-city neighborhoods (including the nearby West End from which many in Over-the-Rhine had come), I argued that the authors "minimize the historical burden the revitalizers carry." If "activists are skeptical of the public interest," I concluded, "it is because displacement, segregation, and neglect have too often been its product."[43]

Completing a Metropolitan Tour: From Suburb to Inner-City to Outer-City Neighborhood

Two years after the publication of *Changing Plans*, the prolific Miller published yet another study of our changing conceptions of community. *Visions of Place: The City, Neighborhoods, Suburbs, and Cincinnati's Clifton, 1850–2000*, a study of what Miller called an "outer-city neighborhood," appeared in 2000. Having explored the metropolis as a whole as it first emerged (*Boss Cox's Cincinnati*), an outlying postwar suburb (*Suburb*), and an impoverished inner-city neighborhood (*Changing Plans for America's Inner Cities*), Miller now rounded out his tour of metropolitan places and relations with a study of what local activists began to call an "in-city suburb." One of Cincinnati's first hilltop suburbs, annexed to the city in 1896, Clifton was also home to the University of Cincinnati and, for over thirty years, Miller himself.[44]

Visions of Place began as a longer, more professional version of the short book on Clifton that Miller, Shapiro, and the Laboratory in American Civilization published in 1976. Shapiro urged Miller to finish the book on his own, which he did. The work still bore the imprint of Shapiro, but it also returned to Miller's central concern with the metropolitan mode of thought and its eclipse. Miller described the emergence in the 1920s of a view that "defined the metropolis not as a collection of systems with mechanically interrelated parts but as an ecologically interdependent system of systems in which a defective part not only disrupted the functioning of the system but threatened the vitality of all the other systems, including the system of neighborhoods composed of specialized residential components." Clifton benefited from this strategy as the city used zoning regulations to protect it as a salubrious residential neighborhood that tied its affluent and educated population to the larger city.[45]

But after 1950, the metropolitan mode of thought gave way to one that emphasized the parts over the whole. The 1948 plan had already warned of Clifton's vulnerability to blight. As urban renewal and highway construction in Cincinnati's West End crowded the displaced into the Black ghettoes flanking Clifton, residents saw themselves as a besieged island inside the metropolis, not as an integral part of it. In December 1960, the announcement of an urban renewal plan for the neighboring Avondale-Corryville districts led residents to form the

Clifton Town Meeting (CTM) to halt the spread of blight. The CTM hoped to manage racial fears and forestall white flight and ghettoization. Some in Clifton supported integration, but others feared "the black cloud that is all set to move in from Vine Street." The CTM decided not to address race directly but to work quietly for integration while opposing ghettoization.[46]

In its first decade, the Clifton Town Meeting spoke of the public interest in its efforts to preserve Clifton's character. The CTM used zoning, building codes, traffic patterns, mixed-use development, and beauty "to preserve and develop the community of Clifton as a delightful in-town suburb, a fine residential area for all citizens." The CTM sought to minimize fear and panic, working block by block to encourage acceptance of Black integration but also establishing a quota that would prevent blockbusting and panic selling. It policed property maintenance, reprimanding those who littered or allowed junk to accumulate, and monitored new construction and troubled spots in the neighborhood. Fear of racial transition stood at the center of all these actions. But the CTM stressed that it wanted to exclude no one and valued a heterogeneous population. Meanwhile, the CTM also joined other organizations in a citywide campaign for school integration.[47]

Things changed in 1974, however, when the city initiated a neighborhood planning process that led to the development of a Clifton Community Plan. The plan, Miller wrote, "did not refer to other neighborhoods, the city of Cincinnati, or the metropolis of which Clifton might be seen a part." Unlike the 1925 and 1948 plans, Clifton's plan (and presumably that of other neighborhoods) "did not depict an ideal social and physical environment for realization in twenty of thirty years" but only guidelines for future piecemeal developments. In treating Clifton as an autonomous neighborhood, expressing opposition to the location of any more "citywide" institutions in Clifton, and in its solicitude for the "optimal personal and social development" of "individuals," the plan marked Clifton as a community of limited liability and reflected the inward turning of its residents. The plan sought to maintain the status quo in Clifton, which included the segregation of the Black quarter of Clifton's population to a narrow corridor along a busy street. Integration now appeared to be someone else's problem.[48]

Through the 1980s and 1990s, the Clifton Town Meeting opposed fast-food restaurants, saved an old theater, established a historical district, excluded big apartment complexes, and discouraged the placement of public housing in the neighborhood. In the 1960s, the CTM had allied with other civic and political organizations to attack citywide issues; it now turned inward. In 1992, the CTM erected a sign that read "Welcome to Clifton Village, Incorporated 1850." Reaching back to the period before annexation, Miller wrote, the sign "reinforced the idea of neighborhood autonomy and the dissociation of CTM with any concept of the public interest that embraced a local entity larger than Clifton." Even that entity sometimes seemed too large to hold loyalties, as some residents criticized the CTM as a tyrannical government running roughshod over the interests of individual streets or even households.[49]

In his concluding pages, Miller speculated that this isolationism might not hold. He cited the city's growing income gap and shameful conditions in Cincinnati's black ghetto as issues that might revive a concern for the public interest defined as the welfare of the whole. He described "residential apartheid" as "repulsive and dangerous" and called its persistence our "most pressing public interest problem." In yet another nod to the metropolitan mode of thought, he added that the ghetto "threatens the viability of the city as an agency for the nurturing of cultural pluralism." Citing the golden rule (from seven world religions), Miller warned of the dangers of neighborhood isolation and antigovernment animus. Racial segregation, he concluded, is a regional issue requiring a regional response. A regional strategy, organized by and around regional civic groups, might meet with representatives of suburbs, townships, and white city neighborhoods and persuade them to embrace and support integration.[50]

Professional historians embraced *Visions of Place* perhaps more than any of Miller's books since *Boss Cox's Cincinnati*. It earned praise as the culmination of a long and distinguished career that had broadened urban history beyond the central cores of a few major cities. It also won admiration as a complement to *Suburb* and *Changing Plans*. Reviewers understood and endorsed Miller's view of the dangers of the inward-turning, isolationist view. At least one reviewer commented favorably on the method as well, writing that Miller "permits the past to speak to the present without intervention of present assumptions."[51]

The most thoughtful review of *Visions of Place* came from David Stradling, Miller's colleague at the University of Cincinnati and fellow resident of Clifton. Stradling, too, saw the book as a "culmination of twenty-six years of research and contemplation," a "suitable capstone to a terribly important career in thinking and writing about the city." Stradling agreed that Miller's focus on the planning process—where participants articulated their conceptions of problems and potential solutions—best enabled him to capture the way people understood the world and how that understanding changed over time. But he also raised questions about "the intellectual problem that has occupied him for much of his career"—namely, "the ways in which conceptions of the city shape (and limit) perceptions" (i.e., taxonomies of social reality).[52]

Joining other reviewers, Stradling agreed that the isolationist attitude should trouble anyone who cared about cities. Comparing *Visions of Place* with *Changing Plans*, Stradling noted that even as urban decay generated calls for urban reform and revitalization, few people and few neighborhoods seemed willing to embrace change in the public interest. Activists in Over-the-Rhine and Clifton both called for stasis, the first fearing gentrification, the second fearing ghettoization. But Stradling also thought that Miller paid too little attention to the origins of the taxonomies that underlay these attitudes. The inattention to cause and effect left readers to question "whether or not urbanites more readily change their conceptions to fit their perceptions, rather than vice-versa as Miller would have us believe." Stradling also called for greater attention to the relative strength of these taxonomies and the question of who held—or did not hold—them. No doubt taxonomies of reality sometimes shaped perceptions, oversimplifying a more complicated reality (as when people ignore, for example, racial and income diversity in suburban America). But in focusing on taxonomies, Stradling concluded, Miller sometimes left too much unsaid about that complicated reality.[53]

Preserving the Metropolitan Mode of Thought: The Legacy of Zane L. Miller

Zane Miller left behind an impressive body of scholarship, four major monographs, an influential textbook, dozens of provocative articles, and an expansive new field, urban history, and a new organization, the Urban History Association—both of which he helped to create. He challenged historians to investigate neglected places and challenged us to think about the past in innovative ways. He mentored dozens of students and younger colleagues, the present author gratefully included. He edited three major series of monographs. A treasured friend, he conducted multiple simultaneous conversations over the years and, via email, over many an evening. And this does not even consider his record as an active and exemplary citizen. Aside from participating in a score of civic projects, he brought his—and our—scholarship to bear on public matters, not least in the successful and much-missed Cincinnati Seminar on the City.[54]

Others have and will have their say, but in my view, the metropolitan mode of thought stands at the center of Miller's work. He returned to it again and again in each of his monographs and many of his essays. Although at the end of *Suburb* Miller described the era of the metropolitan mode as "irretrievably past," he used the metropolitan mode of thought as a tool, to make sense not just of the past but of the present and future as well. This recognition of the enduring power of ideas is one of the things that long made me think (as I shall argue below) of Miller as more American pragmatist than European structuralist. "When communication occurs," the pragmatic philosopher John Dewey wrote in *Experience and Nature* (1925), "all natural events are subject to reconsideration and revision; they are readapted to meet the requirements of conversation, whether it be public discourse or that preliminary discourse called thinking. Events turn into objects, things with meaning. They may be referred to when they do not exist, and thus be operative among things distant in space and time, through vicarious presence in a new medium." Miller kept alive the idea of an organic metropolis governed by public policies attuned to the welfare of the whole, and it still operates among his many students, colleagues, and readers.[55]

Miller knew, of course, that the metropolitan mode of thought had sometimes unleashed a cocksure social engineering that paid little attention to people on the ground. But he saw the market fundamentalism that took its place as far worse. The "rise of cultural me-tooism, and its economic derivative, radically laissez-faire nostrums," Miller lamented, "have become grim and seemingly intractable problems for many who study and care about the vitality and fairness of life in metropolitan America." In an example of how taxonomies of reality shaped perceptions, he believed the focus on cultural individualism too often exalted "civil rights and liberties" not as a means to full public participation but only "as bulwarks against state-sanctioned cultural engineering." At the end of *Changing Plans*, Miller and Tucker urged us to "fortify our capacity for empathy and engage ourselves" in a democratic process aimed at the public interest. One reviewer may have identified Miller's precise purpose in praising *Changing Plans* for its "salutary argument for the recovery of a civic consciousness that takes account of the collective welfare without losing sight of the individual."[56]

As he tried to steer between the hubris of social engineering and the nihilism of market fundamentalism, Miller also addressed the matter of free will and determinism. He sometimes provided evidence for those who saw his embrace of taxonomies of social reality as a form of determinism that minimized human freedom. "Conceptions of reality *determine* what people look for when they examine reality," Miller wrote in the appendix to *Visions of Place* as he tried yet again to explain his philosophy, "and their conceptual 'bias' *determines* what they see and what they don't see in their examinations" (italics added). But he also believed that "people in the past managed, somehow, from time to time, to create new taxonomies of social realities that enabled them to handle current issues in new and more satisfying ways." Much is hidden in that "somehow," for example, the question of whether individuals as opposed to collectivities might change those taxonomies. But he saw a crucial role for historians. "It is through history," he wrote in that same appendix, "that the past influences the present and infringes on the future." This is what he meant by "liberation history," and although it seemed to qualify his assertion (on the same page) that "the past is past," it well describes what he tried to do.[57]

Miller did not hold consistently to the dictum of the radical discontinuity of history, as we have seen, supplying hints about how taxonomies change. Nor could he ignore the physical and institutional legacies of past taxonomies from schools and libraries to highways and slum clearance. And what are we to make of Miller's last, unfinished project? As a broad survey, and particularly one held together by the single theme of civic nationalism, it would seem to defy the idea of history's radical discontinuity. The word *taxonomy* or its variations appears in only one place in the pages he left behind, when he wrote that "mid-nineteenth city dwellers displayed a distinct tendency to segment and taxonomize their cities into a system of differentiated social spaces." But in that final work, the idea of liberation history remains, and a new conception—comity—seems to have taken the place once held by taxonomies.[58]

"A New Atom of Force": Miller as American Pragmatist

Comity means most simply courtesy and considerate behavior to others. But more broadly it points toward the goodwill and forbearance that enable people to act in concert for mutual benefit. In his final, unfinished work, Miller attributed the resilient, problem-solving capacity of cities to our "covenant with comity," a "willingness to make adjustments necessary for smoothing over the inevitable differences that would emerge in an extraordinarily pluralistic society." Comity exists in a society, the historian Richard Hofstadter (from whom Miller borrowed the concept) argued, when "its contending interests have a basic minimal regard for each other: one part or interest seeks the defeat of an opposing interest on matters of policy, but at the same time seeks to avoid crushing the opposition, denying the legitimacy of its existence or values.... The basic humanity of the opposition is not forgotten; civility is not abandoned; the sense that a community life must be carried on after the acerbic issues of the moment have been fought over and won is seldom very far out of mind." It is a hopeful idea for our partisan times.[59]

Hofstadter thought comity could best be understood from the evidence of its absence, pointing to anti-Catholic, anti-immigrant, and anti-Black episodes in our history. One can see why Miller felt drawn to comity at this historical moment. Comity also addresses some of the same issues that taxonomies of reality addressed, without the structural baggage. "A broad-based agreement on basics during a certain period is necessary for discussion and debate," Miller's student Alan I Marcus wrote of taxonomies of reality; "a shared vision of the nature of reality allows contemporaries to engage in conversations and arguments." A crucial difference, however, involves malleability. Taxonomies of reality, in Marcus's words, "bounded possibilities," or, in Miller's terms, determined what people looked for and could perceive. Comity, in contrast, seems to hinge on a sober second thought about the possibility of error, the possibility that one might be wrong and another right. Comity also shares something with philosophical pragmatism, a rejection of certitude (social engineering, market fundamentalism) but an embrace of the possibility of identifying a provisional definition of the public interest, always open to reconsideration and amendment.[60]

Comity is related to but should not be equated with civility. In his review of *Changing Plans*, Max Page complained that the book did not belong in the urban history section of the stacks but in the "civic virtue" section, "somewhere between Stephen Carter and Amitai Etzioni, and not far from the neo-con section, anchored by Allan Bloom, Nathan Glazer, and Irving Kristol." He argued that Miller and Tucker ignored the reality of slum clearance and racial segregation only to lay blame on "cultural individualists" and their intemperate, uncivil protests. The real cultural individualists, Page argued, might well be white, middle-class suburbanites fleeing cities on subsidized highways, not the minority activists defending neighborhoods. The authors wrote as if conflict and incivility posed the greatest threats to the city, Page concluded, and that only city planners could see the public interest.[61]

Page had a point. Miller's flirtation with radical historical discontinuity obscured the ways in which the injustices of urban renewal and highway construction burdened any new plan for urban revitalization. But Page's review might have benefited from a dose of comity. Written just after the impeachment of President Bill Clinton and as the Bush-Gore campaign got underway, the review exuded a righteous anger about how calls for civility policed what could be said and what could not. But Page got the argument in *Changing Plans* wrong. The idea of taxonomies meant that everyone embraced cultural individualism, suburban commuters as much as neighborhood activists (who were mostly white, by the way). And the injunctions against incivility and anger amounted to two brief passages in the entire book. But more to the point, Miller and Tucker went beyond civility. They addressed—rather than suppressed—the injustices of racial segregation and economic inequality. To invoke pragmatism again, they believed that reasoned debate depended on some sort of provisional assertion, open to revision, about the welfare of the whole. Self-righteous certainty precluded that as effectively as selfishness did.[62]

A more telling point might be that comity and civility are both endangered virtues. In his unfinished manuscript, Miller celebrated the "essential virtue embodied by the vast majority of city residents as they navigate their daily lives, obeying prevailing laws and cooperating with their fellow citizens." For all the emphasis on urban crises, Miller and other scholars point to the neglected fact that cities tend to work. City people, by and large, line up, take turns, negotiate transit, respect privacy, and properly dispose of wastes. Much of the effort to manage violence, confront external threats, and provide for health, safety, and welfare, all of which make civilization possible, originates not with the state but with city publics. City people also address bigger and more imposing problems. The U.S. Conference of Mayors' Climate Protection Agreement, for example, has enlisted more than one thousand cities to advance the goals of the international 2006 Kyoto Protocol (which the United States did not sign) to reduce carbon emissions.[63]

Miller believed that the future of the republic depended upon the "neglected civic temperament" found most abundantly in cities. He also knew that neither civility nor comity nor consensus could be taken for granted. The idea of consensus, Hofstadter argued in his discussion of comity, does not provide us with a theory of how society works but poses instead historical and political questions. To what extent does a consensus prevail, who takes part in it, and how is it arrived at? These are questions Miller never directly addressed in his scholarship because he turned taxonomies of reality into a theory of society. He went against his native pragmatism and failed to treat the idea of taxonomies as a problem-solving tool that arose out of cognitive dissonance, good for resolving some problems but not others. But Zane Miller lived these questions; as a scholar, teacher, citizen, and friend, he tried to craft and advance a better, more inclusive foundation for debate. Like the pragmatists, he abandoned the quest for certainty and guarded against the inevitable human tendency to classify and cling to categories. He avoided both the stance of mastery and the attitude of despair in favor of the role of hopeful reformer (the import, I take it, of his oft-used self-description as a "decadent liberal"). Notwithstanding his rich and productive friendship with Henry Shapiro, there are many reasons to consider Zane Miller—and perhaps Shapiro too—as more an American pragmatist than a European structuralist. If nothing else, their Laboratory in American Civilization recalls John Dewey's famous laboratory school at the University of Chicago, dedicated to learning by doing.[64]

Perhaps the best reason for considering Miller a pragmatist comes from what Justice Oliver Wendell Holmes Jr. called "bettabilitarianism." Engaged in the debate about determinism and free will, Holmes learned from his friend Chauncey Wright to never say "necessary" in reference to the universe because "we don't know whether anything is necessary or not." For the rest of his life, Holmes described himself as a bettabilitarian. "I believe," Holmes explained, "that we can bet on the behavior of the universe in its contract with us. We bet we can know what it will be. That leaves a loophole for free will—in the miraculous sense—the creation of a new atom of force." Holmes added, "I don't in the least believe in it." But some of us do believe that what we do and say and write can make a difference, and Miller was one of us. Zane added many new atoms of force to the world as he placed a lifelong bet on the value of the metropolitan mode of thought.[65]

NOTES

1. Sam Bass Warner, *The Private City: Philadelphia in Three Periods of Its Growth* (Philadelphia: University of Pennsylvania Press, 1968), ix–xii, 202; John D. Fairfield, "Private City, Public City: Power and Vision in American Cities," *Journal of Urban History* 29 (May 2003): 437–462.

2. Zane L. Miller, *Boss Cox's Cincinnati: Urban Politics in the Progressive Era* (Columbus: Ohio University Press, 2000; repr. of 1968 ed.). Although usually classed with those works that rehabilitated the boss and his machine, *Boss Cox's Cincinnati* anticipated the shift from that narrative to a focus on the expansion of urban services and infrastructure. See Timothy Gilfoyle, "White Cities, Linguistic Turns, and Disneylands: The New Paradigms of Urban History," *Reviews in American History* 26 (March 1998): 185–191. Miller's last project, with Patricia Mooney-Melvin and Larry Bennett, began as a revision of his well-known survey of urban history, Zane L. Miller and Patricia Mooney-Melvin, *The Urbanization of Modern America: A Brief History* (San Diego: Harcourt Brace Jovanovich, 1987), but had begun to blossom into an entirely new work. For Miller's critique of the private orientation of urban history, see Zane L. Miller, "Cheers! (but Is That All There Is, My Friend?)" [review of Richard B. Stott, *Workers in*

the Metropolis: Class, Ethnicity, and Youth in Antebellum (New York City], *Reviews in American History* 18 (December 1990): 485-492.

3. Zane L. Miller, *Suburb: Neighborhood and Community in Forest, Park, Ohio, 1935-1976* (St. Martin, Ohio: Commonwealth, 2016; repr. of 1981 ed.), "public interest" on xxvii, "the *metropolitan* mode of thought" on xxxiv (italics in original).

4. Miller, *Suburb*; Zane L. Miller, "Scarcity, Abundance, and American Urban History," *Journal of Urban History* 4 (February 1978): 131-155, "individuals constituted" on 147; Zane L. Miller, "The Role and Concept of Neighborhood in American Cities," in *Community Organization for Urban Social Change*, ed. Robert Fisher and Peter Romanofsky (Westport, CT: Greenwood, 1981), 3-32, "communities of limited liability" on 18-24, other quoted passages on 18 ("individuals constituted" appears here as well). Miller borrowed the phrase "communities of limited liability" from Morris Janowitz, *The Community Press in an Urban Setting* (Chicago: University of Chicago Press, 1952).

5. Progressive Era Americans, Miller wrote, "launched a desperate yet confident quest for a new urban discipline." Miller, *Boss Cox's Cincinnati*, xxi; Zane L. Miller, *Visions of Place: The City, Neighborhoods, Suburbs, and Cincinnati's Clifton, 1850-2000* (Columbus: Ohio State University Press, 2000), "taxonomy" on 167.

6. Miller, *Boss Cox's Cincinnati*, passim, "touchstone" on 241; the new conception of the city that underlay the machine-reform contests at the turn of the century is implicit in *Boss Cox's Cincinnati* and more fully articulated in Miller, "Scarcity, Abundance," and Miller, "Role and Concept."

7. Miller, *Boss Cox's Cincinnati*, 77-79, quoted passage on 77.

8. Miller, passim; see also William A. Baughin, "Murray Seasongood: Twentieth-Century Urban Reformer" (Ph.D. diss., University of Cincinnati, 1972).

9. Robert A. Burnham, "The Cincinnati Charter Revolt of 1924: Creating City Government for a Pluralistic Society," in *Ethnic Diversity and Civic Identity: Patterns of Conflict and Cohesion in Cincinnati since 1920*, ed. Henry D. Shapiro and Jonathan D. Sarna (Chicago: University of Illinois Press, 1992). I am indebted to Charles Casey-Leininger for pointing to the importance of proportional representation.

10. Miller, "Scarcity, Abundance"; Miller, "Role and Concept"; Cincinnati City Planning Commission, *Metropolitan Master Plan 1948* (Cincinnati: Cincinnati City Planning Commission, 1948), quoted passages on 8-11; Miller, *Suburb*, 9-17.

11. Miller, "Scarcity, Abundance"; Miller, "Role and Concept"; Charles Casey-Leininger, "Making the Second Ghetto in Cincinnati: Avondale, 1925-1970," in *Race and the City: Work, Community, Housing, and Protest in Cincinnati, 1820-1970*, ed. Henry Louis Taylor Jr. (Urbana: University of Illinois Press, 1993)

12. Miller, *Boss Cox's Cincinnati*, xxi; Zane L. Miller and Henry D. Shapiro, "Learning History by Doing: The Laboratory in American Civilization," *History Teacher* 11 (August 1978): 483-495.

13. Alan I Marcus, "In Memoriam: Henry D. Shapiro," Historians.org, April 2004, https://www.historians.org/publications-and-directories/perspectives-on-history/april-2004/in-memoriam-henry-d-shapiro; Alan I Marcus, "Re: Henry D. Shapiro and French Structuralism," personal email message, May 8, 2017. See also Marcus's short biography at the end of Henry D. Shapiro and Zane L. Miller, *Clifton: Neighborhood and Community in an Urban Setting; A Brief History* (St. Martin, Ohio: Commonwealth Book Company, 2014; repr. of 1976 ed.), 77–79. Shapiro found the work of Claude Levi-Strauss and Michel Foucault particularly useful.

14. The literature on structuralism and poststructuralism is vast, but one might start with Simon Blackburn, *Oxford Dictionary of Philosophy* (Oxford: Oxford University Press, 2008), and Craig Calhoun, ed., *Oxford Dictionary of the Social Sciences* (Oxford: Oxford University Press, 2002). My own encounter with structuralism came mainly from the works of Michel Foucault, who is sometimes described as a structuralist, other times as a poststructuralist.

15. Henry D. Shapiro, *Appalachia on Our Mind: The Southern Mountains and Mountaineers in the American Consciousness, 1870–1920* (Chapel Hill: University of North Carolina Press, 1978), ix–xix, passim, "discrete" on 4, "process" on ix; see also John Alexander Williams, "Henry Shapiro and the Idea of Appalachia: A Review/Essay," *Appalachian Journal* 5 (Spring 1978): 350–357.

16. Shapiro, *Appalachia on Our Mind*, vi–viii, 18, 267, 280, passim; Shapiro borrowed the theory of cognitive dissonance and its consequences from Leon Festinger, *A Theory of Cognitive Dissonance* (Evanston, IL: Row-Peterson, 1957).

17. It is an essential quality of humans that they divide reality into cognitive units, Shapiro explained (113), in a process that made language, culture, and society possible. These cognitive units turned perception into conception and made communication possible. But the process is invisible, and no one comments on it; it is simply what is assumed. The conservation of language further disguises these cognitive units from observers, including historians, because new ideas get hidden in old words, making what are actually new conceptions seem like new perceptions. But if historians could painstakingly reconstruct those new conceptions, we might bring them to consciousness and thus make them "subjects of discourse and the objects of action" (xvii). Shapiro, xvii–xix, 113–115. This is what Miller later called "liberation history" (see below). For a similar view of the task of historians, see the brief discussion of "the spiritual defense against resentment" as a historical discipline in "History as Social Criticism: Conversations with Christopher Lasch," interview by Casey Blake and Christopher Phelps, *Journal of American History* 80 (March 1994): 1331–1332; for a similar view of the role of ideas, see the discussion of "problematic, noncognitive situations" and the pragmatic theory of truth in Robert Westbrook, *John Dewey and American Democracy* (Ithaca, NY: Cornell University Press, 1991), 125–137.

18. On "symptomatic," see, for example, Shapiro, 30, 119–120; Henry D. Shapiro and Zane L. Miller, *Physician to the West: Selected Writings of Daniel Drake*

on *Science and Society* (Lexington: University of Kentucky Press, 1970); see also Miller's discussion of the Drake project in Miller, *Suburb*, xxiv–xxv.
19. Miller, xxiii–xxvi.
20. Miller, xxv–xxvi. Neither Miller nor Shapiro cited the European sources of their historical philosophies. But the references to "moments of redefinition" suggests critical engagement with the debates surrounding Thomas Kuhn, *The Structure of Scientific Revolutions* (Chicago: University of Chicago Press, 1970). Miller's discussion of radical historical discontinuity also suggests critical engagement with the debates surrounding Foucault's genealogy of ideas. Michel Foucault, *The Essential Foucault: Selections from the Essential Works of Foucault, 1954–1984* (New York: New Press, 2003).
21. Miller, xxvi–xxvii; community and the relationship between suburb, neighborhood, city, and metropolis had been the central focus of Miller and Shapiro's Laboratory in American Civilization at the University of Cincinnati. See also Zane L. Miller and Henry D. Shapiro, "Learning History by Doing: The Laboratory in American Civilization," *History Teacher* 11 (August 1978): 483–495; David Stradling, review of Miller, *Visions of Place: The City, Neighborhoods, Suburbs, and Cincinnati's Clifton, 1850–2000*, HUrban, H-Net Reviews, November 2001, http://www.h-net.org/reviews/showrev.php?id=5651.
22. Miller, xxvi–xxx.
23. Miller, xxix–xxxi.
24. Miller, xxix–xxxi.
25. Miller, xxxi–xxxvii. Miller raised several other objections, including that suburbanization—and consciousness of suburbs as distinctive places—stretched back into the nineteenth century. It is not clear why Miller thought "any urban or suburban history" must acknowledge the longer, nineteenth-century history of suburbanization. As Miller himself wrote, if history is radically discontinuous, then a "knowledge of those histories is not a prerequisite for understanding the Forest Park story." His explanation was that he raised the older stories only to "establish their historical distance and distinctiveness from this story."
26. To capture the shift at midcentury, Miller quoted the sociologist C. Wright Mills, who in 1951 wrote with anxiety about how the passivity of white-collar suburbanites had "transformed the tang and feel" of metropolitan life, threatening the civic process of finding common ground (reproduced as one of the three epigraphs to Miller's introduction). Miller, xxiii, xxvii, xxxi–xxxv, 3–27; "organism" is Cincinnati planner Ladislas Segoe, quoted on 25.
27. Thus the urbanist William H. Whyte could write in 1956 (in the second of Miller's epigraphs) of the "new suburbs" and the "organization man who has found in the suburbs an ideal way station." Miller borrowed the term "community of limited liability" from the Chicago sociologist Morris Janowitz. Miller, xxiii, xxiv–xxvi, 28–175.
28. Thus the columnist Ellen Goodman could write in 1978 (in the third of Miller's epigraphs) of a "lost faith in public solutions" in favor of a private salva-

tion of, among other things, vegetable gardens. Even the word *metropolis*—whose inclusion of *polis* implied some larger public good—fell out of favor, Miller explained. The neologism *metroplex* reflected the demotion of the metropolis to little more than a set of agencies delivering services. Miller, xxiii, xxv–xxxvi, 176–241. Cf. the discussion of the turning away from public solutions in Jeffrey C. Sanders, *Seattle and the Roots of Urban Sustainability: Inventing Ecotopia* (Pittsburgh, PA, 2010), 6–9 passim.

29. Miller, 227–240; Miller specifically referenced Christopher Lasch, *The Culture of Narcissism* (New York: Norton, 1979).

30. Miller, 227–240.

31. Miller, 240–241.

32. See Timothy J. Lombardo, "Foreword to the Second Edition," and Jon C. Teaford, "Afterword to the Second Edition," in Miller, ix–xix, 266–268.

33. Terence McDonald, review of *Suburb*, in *Public Historian* 3 (Autumn 1981): 87–90; Jon C. Teaford, review of *Suburb*, in *American Historical Review* 87 (June 1982): 879–880.

34. Teaford, review of *Suburb*; McDonald, review of *Suburb*; Thomas Bender, "Community and Culture," review of *Suburb*, in *Reviews in American History* 10 (June 1982): 255–258.

35. Without intending to, McDonald wrote, *Suburb* suggests that the "reality of diversity may be more important than the search for 'community.'" McDonald, review of *Suburb*. Miller's combination of a political history of Forest Park with an intellectual history of social taxonomies, Dwight Hoover added, "makes a volume that can, at times, be tedious, complex, and difficult to read." Dwight W. Hoover, review of *Suburb*, in *Indiana Magazine of History* 78 (March 1982): 67–69.

36. Bender, "Community and Culture." In his review, Bender broached some of his concerns about what he later called "narrative and its structural alternative" in his influential "Wholes and Parts: The Need for Synthesis in American History," *Journal of American History* 73 (June 1986): 120–136, "structural alternative" on 123. In his reference to the "structural alternative," Bender had the consensus historians in mind. Miller was certainly no consensus historian, but Miller's emphasis on shared assumptions about the nature of society as the foundation of problem-solving and his later idea (and ideal) of "comity" recall something of the consensus historians. Miller took the concept of comity from Richard Hofstadter's *The Progressive Historians: Turner, Beard, Parrington* (New York: Knopf, 1968), 440–454. I return to comity at the end of this essay.

37. Bender, "Community and Culture."

38. Zane L. Miller and Bruce Tucker, *Changing Plans for America's Inner Cities: Cincinnati's Over-the-Rhine and Twentieth-Century Urbanism* (Columbus: Ohio State University Press, 1998).

39. Miller and Tucker, *Changing Plans*, 9–12, passim.

40. Miller and Tucker, 9–12, passim. In the 1980s Over-the-Rhine made it onto the National Register of Historic Places, but Cincinnati's city council also designated it a low-income housing retention district. In 1985, the city council ap-

proved an urban renewal plan for Over-the-Rhine that favored revitalization but also made a commitment to a minimum of 5,520 low-income housing units in Over-the-Rhine. Three years after the publication of *Changing Plans*, Over-the-Rhine erupted in riots.

41. Arnold Hirsch, review of *Changing Plans*, in *American Historical Review* 105 (December 2000): 1759; Janet Bednarek, review of *Changing Plans*, in *Journal of the American Planning Association* 65 (1999): 125–126; John D. Fairfield, review of *Changing Plans*, in *Northwest Ohio Quarterly* 70 (Autumn 1998): 185–189.

42. Miller and Tucker, *Changing Plans*, "rethinking" on 12 (see also 43), "fears" on 166 (see also xvii–xix), "blueprints" on 44.

43. Hirsh, review of *Changing Plans*; Bednarek, review of *Changing Plans*; Fairfield, review of *Changing Plans*.

44. Miller, *Visions of Place*; John Bauman, review of *Visions of Place*, in *Indiana Magazine of History* 98 (June 2002): 154–155.

45. Miller, *Visions of Place*, ix–x, 1–6, 35–40, passim; quoted passage on 38. Thomas M. Spencer, review of *Visions of Place*, in *Journal of American History* 89 (December 2002): 1062–1063. The tendency to conflate Clifton's parklike northern reaches of large estates with its much more urban southern half of smaller lots, Miller wrote, suggested "the power of the new metropolitan vision of the city as a system of functionally differentiated groups and parts," the power of that conception to skew and limit perceptions (3).

46. Miller, 68–92, "cloud" on 77.

47. Miller, "preserve" on 79.

48. Miller, 113–131, "refer" on 116, "depict" on 130, "optimal" on 118. Miller did not use the term "community of limited liability" in this work. But he did refer to Clifton's "struggle to become a liberated entity" (157). On the "inward turning tendency," see 158.

49. Miller, 132–159, quoted passages on 158.

50. Miller, 161–165, "apartheid" on 161, "pressing" and "threatens" on 163.

51. Dwight Hoover, review of *Visions of Place*, in *Journal of the West* 43 (Spring 2004): "permits" on 100; Thomas J. Jablonsky, review essay on *Changing Plans* and *Visions of Place*, in *Ohio Valley History* 2 (Fall 2002): 34–36; Bauman, review of *Visions of Place*; Ann Durkin Keating, "Planning in Two Ohio Cities: Cincinnati and Columbus," *Journal of Urban History* 4 (May 2005): 182–187; Spencer, review of *Visions of Place*; Stephen J. McGovern, "Neighborhoods, Race, and the State," *Journal of Urban History* 29 (September 2003): 820–832.

52. Stradling, review of Miller, *Visions of Place*.

53. Stradling. Stradling's important question about who held and who did not hold a given taxonomy was reinforced in McGovern's review where he asked how representative the CTM was. McGovern, "Neighborhoods, Race," 827.

54. I met Zane Miller in 1984 when I took a job in Cincinnati at Xavier University. I estimate I have spent some forty hours—certainly not much more—in face-to-face contact, mainly at the Cincinnati Seminar on the City. But we

carried on a thirty-three-year correspondence, first via letters and later via email with the rare phone call thrown in, and I believe that I knew him well. We talked about almost every topic you could imagine, life and labor, friendship and love, basketball and movies, books and music, and, of course, cities and history. He shaped me and made me better in countless ways and brightened many an evening with his witty, thoughtful, and provocative messages. I have been privileged to have known him and feel his absence keenly, even as his voice remains in my head and his presence in my heart.

55. Miller, *Suburb*, "irretrievably" on 240; John Dewey, *Experience and Nature* (New York: Dover, 1958), 166.

56. Lombardo, "Foreword to the Second Edition" of *Suburb*, "me-too-ism" (from an email exchange between Lombardo and Miller) on xvii; Zane L. Miller, "The Death of the City: Cultural Individualism, Hyperdiversity, and the Devolution of National Urban Policy," in *The Social Sciences Go to Washington: The Politics of Knowledge in the Postmodern Age*, ed. Hamilton Cravens (New Brunswick, NJ: Rutgers University Press, 2004), 181–213; Miller and Tucker, *Changing Plans*, 188; "salutary" is from Jack Glazier (anthropology, Oberlin College), review of *Changing Plans*, in *Indiana Magazine of History*, June 1, 2000, 200–201. See Mary Ann Glendon, *Rights Talk: The Impoverishment of Political Discourse* (New York: Free Press, 1991); and Michael Sandel, *Democracy's Discontent: America in Search of Public Philosophy* (Cambridge, MA: Harvard University Press, 1996), on civil rights and liberties as an expression of cultural individualism (or what Sandel calls "the freely-choosing individual").

57. Miller, *Visions of Place*, 167.

58. Zane L. Miller, "The Mid-Nineteenth-Century Urban Crisis: Reconstructing Cities," unpub. ms., in possession of author, 12.

59. See Chapter 1, "From Istanbul to Philadelphia"; Richard Hofstadter, *The Progressive Historians: Turner, Beard, Parrington* (New York: Knopf, 1968), 440–454, quoted passage on 454. Miller shared an interest in comity with—and learned from—Daniel J. Monti Jr. See his *Engaging Strangers: Civic Rites, Civic Capitalism, and Public Order in Boston* (Madison, NJ: Fairleigh Dickinson University Press, 2012). Miller corresponded with and cited Monti on these matters.

60. Hofstadter, *Progressive Historians*; Alan I Marcus, "Back to the Present: Historians' Treatment of the City as a Social System during the Reign of the Idea of Community," in *American Urbanism*, ed. Zane L. Miller and Howard Gillette, Jr. (New York: Greenwood, 1987), 7–10. Christopher Lasch wrote that pragmatism "holds that the impossibility of certainty does not preclude the possibility of reasoned discourse—of assertions that command provisional assent even though they lack unimpeachable foundations and are therefore subject to revision." Christopher Lasch, *The Revolt of the Elites* (New York: Norton, 1995), 176–193, quoted passage on 188–189.

61. Max Page, review of *Changing Plans*, in *Journal of American History* 85 (March 1999): 1670–1671.

62. On the role of demands for civility in closing down debate, see Timothy J. Lombardo, "Making Urban Citizens: Civility and Civic Virtue in the Modern Metropolis," *Journal of Urban History* 41 (2015): 143–151; on "the lost art of argument," see Lasch, *Revolt of the Elites*, 161–175, esp. 170–171. Cincinnati is blessed with a forum called Beyond Civility that also addresses rather than suppresses issues. Its logic is that opposing sides must make each other's case effectively enough that each admits they could not express it better. This, of course, maximizes the possibility that one will be swayed by the argument of another. Miller would have loved it. See http://beyondcivility.org/.

63. See Chapter 1, "From Istanbul to Philadelphia"; Monti, *Engaging Strangers*; Lombardo, "Making Urban Citizens"; Elijah Anderson, *The Cosmopolitan Canopy: Race and Civility in Everyday Life* (New York: Norton, 2011); Jonathan S. Davies and David L. Imbroscio, ed., *Critical Urban Studies: New Directions* (Albany: State University of New York Press, 2010); Benjamin Barber, *If Mayors Ruled the World: Dysfunctional Nations, Rising Cities* (New Haven, CT: Yale University Press, 2013).

64. See Chapter 1, "From Istanbul to Philadelphia." Bender writes: "The notion of consensus, [Hofstadter] realized, was not a theory of society; rather it was a historical circumstance to be explained. The question, he wrote in 1968, 'is the extent to which agreement prevails in a society, who in fact takes part in it, and how it is arrived at." Bender, "Wholes and Parts," 124–125; Hofstadter, *Progressive Historians*, 454; on pragmatism, see Westbrook, *John Dewey*; and Louis Menand, *The Metaphysical Club: A Story of Ideas in America* (New York: Farrar, Straus, and Giroux, 2001).

65. Menand, *Metaphysical Club*, 214–230, quoted passage on 217.

5

Creating Cities in the Post–World War II Southwest

The Arlington, Texas and Mesa, Arizona Experiences

ROBERT B. FAIRBANKS

Zane L. Miller often reminded his students that there was more to urban history than studies of large, well-known cities such as New York or Chicago. His own scholarship clearly showed that by his books on Forest Park, a suburb of Cincinnati; Clifton, an outer-city neighborhood; and Over-the-Rhine, an inner-city neighborhood of the Queen City.[1] Miller approached these places not as traditional case studies but as what he called symptomatic histories and explained his interest in them because their histories reflected "changing taxonomies of social reality."[2] According to Miller, "from each taxonomy people create a dominant conception of what society is, is becoming, or ought to be." But since each taxonomy is peculiar to time rather than place, one can explore the consequences of that taxonomy by looking at various places, whether large cites, suburbs, or smaller towns, with an emphasis on how the taxonomy of reality influences how people define and respond to problems or opportunities.[3]

As a graduate student studying under Miller and his colleague Henry D. Shapiro, I found this approach to history both challenging and exciting—challenging because it questioned much of what I had learned in my earlier studies of history and exciting because it offered a new lens to view the past. It has had a profound impact on my own scholarship, starting with my first book, *Making Better Citizens*. This book used Cincinnati to explore the changing nature of housing reform for the needy between 1890 and 1960. Under Miller's guidance, I discovered that housing reform did not simply evolve but that different types of housing reform appeared during the first half of the twentieth century thanks to changing perceptions of the problem. Tenement reform at the turn of the century under one taxonomy responded to a problem defined differently than the community development strategy of the 1920s that spawned large-scale slum clearance and public housing, thanks to a different taxonomy. And by the late 1950s, still another type of housing "reform" took place[4] in response to new notions about what Miller has called "cultural individualism."[5]

My second book, *For the City as a Whole*, used Dallas to see if the same taxonomies there shaped political discourse, planning, and housing reform. My most recent book, *The War on Slums in the Southwest*, employed the similar approach I had used in the other books but this time as part of a comparative study of cities in the Southwest.[6]

Miller emphasized how important it was for scholars to closely read and analyze documents for not only what they said but what they did not say. For instance, he introduced me to the importance of a careful reading of housing reports and city planning documents when I was writing my book on Cincinnati to understand better the changing nature of housing reform in the Queen City. That careful reading led to my discovery of the changing taxonomies of social reality shaping housing reform.

How Miller approached urban history continues to influence my own scholarship in other ways too. For example, his belief in the importance of human agency rather than social forces in the development of modern metropolitan America has also affected my reading of the urban past and encouraged me to take seriously what policy makers and city builders said and did. Even more important, Miller's emphasis in his own research over the importance in defining and working for the public interest appears in all my books. Finally, his commitment to treat the actors as participants within a complex story in the context of their times rather than simply characterize them as heroes and villains underscores what he often characterized as the pastness of the past, an approach I take into my own research. His findings about the changing views of metropolitan America after World War II—from a type of organic community to a setting where individuals could pursue their own agendas and shape their own communities—helped me get a better understanding of the emergence of the new cities I write about in this chapter.

My curiosity regarding the growth of suburban cities in the Southwest led me to focus on two of the largest, Mesa, Arizona and Arlington, Texas. I soon discovered these really were a new type of city symptomatic of a new kind of urban growth that owed as much to cultural shifts about how we thought about the city and metropolitan America as it did to the automobile.[7] As a result, the southwestern metropolitan areas in places like Texas and Arizona became something very different than what had existed earlier.[8] They did not simply house suburbs dependent on the center city but included places that yearned to benefit from their location within the booming metropolis to develop as independent entities that might thrive because of the urban sprawl, instead of suffer from it, a fate of the traditional central city that emerged at a different time.

Indeed, my chapter starts by a reference to city building in the nineteenth century, but my exploration of southwestern city builders in the second half of the twentieth century suggests that their cities differed not only in appearance when compared to traditional late nineteenth-century cities, but they also reflected very different ideas about the metropolitan community and their place in it. City builders in the nineteenth century wanted to make their city the dominant center of their hinterland, while places like Mesa and Arlington in the late twentieth century aimed to be a significant urban component in what had become a multicentered metropolis in greater Phoenix and in the Dallas-Fort Worth Metroplex. The city makers of Mesa and Arlington desired to create communities that were independent and self-sustaining places of significant size even as they benefitted from their location within the metropolitan region. When it served their purposes, civic leaders were more than willing to cooperate with other metropolitan agencies, whether rival city governments or regional planning bodies, but the focus was always on what was best for Arlington or Mesa rather than what was best for the larger metropolitan community. My contribution to this volume follows the Miller tradition of exploring little-studied cities to understand larger developments in recent metropolitan America.

Building Cities within Metropolises

Although historians have documented the rapid growth of such established cities as Dallas, Phoenix, Houston, and Albuquerque in the southwestern United States after World War II,[9] they have given much less attention to the appearance of a new set of cities evolving from small towns in those Southwest metropolitan regions. Because these places often did not look like traditional cities, their emergence as large cities is often misunderstood. Even those recognizing their urban status often dismiss them as "accidental cities."[10] This chapter takes a different approach and argues that these communities were indeed intentional, taking advantage of their place within the new metropolitan region to attract businesses, industry, and population. As a result, they became the new cities of the late twentieth and twenty-first centuries. Just as city boosters of the nineteenth century had played a critical role in urbanizing the Midwest and took risks to develop new cities, so did a fresh set of post–World War II cities emerge thanks to leaders who took advantage of their communities' location within a booming metropolitan region. These urban boosters ultimately offered a different type of city shaped around the automobile and airplane that catered to the new priorities of Americans emphasizing freedom of choice and prioritizing good weather and access to recreational amenities as much as well-paying jobs. These cities catered to individual needs and the desires of residents more than trying to promote a traditional sense of community focused on a downtown. Early on they catered to white middle-class families, but as their population exploded and became increasingly diverse, both cities expanded their physical size to accommodate various lifestyles and welcomed non-Anglo ethnic and racial groups. In addition, the physical appearance of these cities seemed quite different from that of the traditional industrial cities of the late nineteenth century centered on the downtown.

No two cities demonstrate this change in urban America better than Mesa, Arizona, the thirty-fifth largest city in the United States, and Arlington, Texas, the forty-ninth largest city in the country. Mesa, an agricultural community initially settled by Mormons, is now larger than Atlanta, while Arlington, once a small rural college town and collecting point for cotton, has a population greater than New Orleans. Of the one hundred largest cities in the United States, sixteen of those emerged as significant cities only after World War II. This group includes six from Arizona and four from Texas.[11]

This chapter explores how these small towns became big cities, and it emphasizes the important role of civic leaders in fashioning a new type of city.[12] These boosters continued an American tradition of city building, doing every bit as much as those nineteenth-century city builders had done. The chapter also underscores the role of planners and the tactic of annexation in the quest to transform these small towns into cities. Arlington turned to planning in the early 1950s and by 1971 had produced four city plans. Mesa, slower to embrace planning, adopted three plans by 1969.[13]

Boosters in both cities not only convinced business and industry to relocate to their work places but focused on growing a tourism industry. Arlington boosters developed and promoted the Six Flags Amusement Park, while Mesa's Chamber of Commerce launched its first national advertising campaign in 1948 to convince winter tourists to locate or at least visit their town to enjoy the ambiance of the Old West.[14]

Both also went after the tourist dollar by seeking major league sports teams. Arlington secured the Texas Rangers baseball team in 1972, its goal since 1958, and city officials later lured the Dallas Cowboys football team away from the nearby suburb of Irving in 2009. Mesa developed spring training facilities for several major league baseball teams, including the popular Chicago Cubs, who now have access to a massive new baseball facility funded by the city.[15] Although their recent effort failed, Mesa also pursued the Arizona football Cardinals.[16]

There is no doubt that both cities benefitted from being near growing central cities as well as their location within rapidly expanding metropolitan regions. And like the larger southwestern cities, they took advantage of the development of large airports nearby and the creation of a massive highway system. Arlington was only ten miles from Fort Worth's new Greater Southwest Airport and about the same distance from the Dallas/Fort Worth International Airport that opened in the 1970s. Mesa, located about twelve miles from Phoenix's Sky Harbor, benefited greatly from that airport's expansion that included additional terminals in the 1960s and 1970s.

This chapter, then, explains how these once small towns took advantage of their setting within growing metropolitan areas to move away from a suburban identity and embrace an urban vision as a new type of city. Although some would argue about the inevitability of suburban city growth thanks to the explosive expansion of metropolitan regions, this chapter suggests that the specific form of that growth was not predestined and that the emergence of both Arlington and Mesa resulted from energetic civic leadership not unlike that found in the nineteenth century. But their vision of what a city should be differed from the earlier city builders.

Urban sprawl may have been inevitable, but the rapid growth and development of these new cities were not. Both Arlington and Mesa started out as agricultural communities in the second half of the nineteenth century, one established by the Texas and Pacific Railroad and the other founded by Mormons. Although both would have geographic advantages and benefitted from nearby cotton lands, their eventual growth stemmed from the rapid urban development of their regions and particularly the appearance of nearby big cities. Their specific location within the region would be a critical reason for their emergence as large cities. Arlington, located midway between Dallas and Fort Worth, was easily accessible by state and federal highways. Mesa, situated twenty miles east of Phoenix, established itself as the largest town in east Maricopa County and emerged as the business hub for that part of the county since farmers chose to use Mesa banks and shop in its stores rather than travel all the way to Phoenix.

From the late 1940s civic leaders in both Arlington and Mesa took advantage of the postwar migration to the Southwest and became more intentional about expanding their communities by developing new strategies to make them more appealing to not only those already living in the proximate area but as well to those drawn to the metropolitan region from outside the area. Whether it was attracting housing developers, luring new businesses and industries, promoting tourism, or encouraging the development and expansion of institutions of higher education, these strategies along with other efforts played important roles in promoting the rise of Arlington and Mesa from rural towns to major cities. The foundation for that growth appeared to be firmly in place by the end of the 1970s when the process of change was well underway.

World War II had a significant impact on both Mesa and Arlington, as well as the larger nearby cities of Phoenix, Dallas, and Fort Worth. Defense industries and military training facilities not only brought new people into Arizona's Salt River valley and north Texas but also would entice people and jobs from the central cities. Although some war industries and military camps located within the city limits of Phoenix, Fort Worth, and Dallas, many did not. For instance, military airfields and defense industries near Arlington and Mesa drew people away from the larger cities and provided opportunities for the two towns to grow. Following World War II, economic prosperity continued thanks in part to the Cold War–era defense buildup resulting from U.S.–Soviet Union tensions as well as the growing popularity of the automobile, the latter (along with commercial trucking) encouraged by accelerated street and highway construction. The commercial airline business also boomed thanks to increased federal aid for airports. Such developments made once out-of-the-way places easily accessible and provided new opportunities for small towns located within the Southwest's metropolitan regions. Air-conditioning also made life in the Southwest more livable.

Before World War II, Arlington, Texas, located between Dallas and Fort Worth, served as a market town for cotton farmers but also sported a thoroughbred racetrack (Arlington Downs) and parimutuel betting.[17] The town's junior college provided its other notable economic driver. Although there had been earlier efforts to create an educational institution, the state established Grubbs Vocational College in Arlington in 1917 as a branch of the Agricultural and Mechanical College of Texas (today's Texas A&M University). As a satellite of one of the state's land grant universities funded by the Morrill Act of 1862, the school's curriculum focused on agriculture, mechanical and industrial trades, and household arts for its female students. All male students were required to join the ROTC. By the 1922–1923 academic year enrollment had risen to a little over eight hundred students.[18]

World War II altered the town as defense industries populated north Texas, especially two giant airplane factories, one just west of Fort Worth and the other bordering the small town of Grand Prairie, located just east of Arlington and west of Dallas. As early as April 1942, the *Arlington Journal* reported, "Workers in war industries provide a steady increase in the population of Arlington." During the 1940s Arlington's population grew from 4,200 to 7,700. The town's location on the major highway between Dallas and Fort Worth (U.S. 80, also known as the Bankhead Highway) explains why defense workers ended up there.[19] During World War II, local civic leaders also established a chamber of commerce and charged its new president, B. C. Barnes, to create an organization that would make Arlington "a greater city."[20]

The town's development did not end after the war but would accelerate significantly in the late 1940s and 1950s as the metropolitan region grew rapidly, spurred in part by a growing Cold War defense sector. Aircraft manufacturer Chance Vought was located in nearby Grand Prairie, and there was a Bell Helicopter facility just northwest of Arlington in Hurst. Close by were also such emerging high-tech firms as Texas Instruments, as well as the traditional Texas staple, companies connected to the oil business. The Arlington Chamber of Commerce invited workers at Chance Vought to move to Arlington, promising that it was a much better alternative than living in Grand Prairie, an industrial suburb, or Dallas, a city beset by racial tensions at this time.[21] The chamber's efforts apparently worked since five hundred families of workers employed at the plant had moved to Arlington by 1949.[22] Chamber officials also urged Bell Helicopter employees to move to Arlington, promising they would pressure city and county officials to improve the road between Arlington and Bell's plant in Hurst.[23] To better manage that growth, in 1949 voters approved charter amendments that replaced the commission form of government with manager-council government. Shortly afterward, the city hired Arlington's first city manager, Albert Jones, after council members agreed that the ambitious community now needed a full-time administrator to make their community more attractive to outsiders.[24]

Arlington also benefitted from a generous refunding program that would reimburse developers their cost to provide sewer and water lines necessary for the development of subdivisions. This policy, employed throughout the 1940s and 1950s, attracted developers to Arlington and lowered the costs of homes for those wishing to buy there. This strategy demonstrated the aggressive posture of city government in promoting additional housing and provided an edge against nearby competing communities that did not follow a refunding policy.[25]

An inclination to grow Arlington was already present after the war, but it greatly accelerated on the return of native son Tom Vandergriff, who had recently graduated from the University of Southern California. Because both Fort Worth and Dallas experienced tremendous growth after the war, some Arlington civic leaders recognized the community's unique position to benefit from the region's expansion due to its location midway between the two cities. No one saw the potential for growth better than Vandergriff, son of a respected car dealer, who had witnessed the transforming power of the automobile in Orange County and understood that Arlington could likewise benefit from the coming sprawl.[26] When he came home from the university to help run his father's General Motors (GM) automobile dealership, Vandergriff, at age twenty-three, agreed to lead the town's chamber of commerce (in 1949) and became a vocal advocate for making Arlington more than merely a bedroom suburb.[27] He and fellow chamber members wanted to guide the community, so it would become a self-sufficient city within the growing metropolitan area. Alerted by his father that GM planned to erect a new factory in north Texas, Vandergriff initiated negotiations with GM to build the automobile plant in Arlington, using its location, between Dallas and Fort Worth, as a key selling point.[28]

A desire to have more say in the negotiations between the city and GM helps explain why at the age of twenty-five Vandergriff ran for mayor in the spring of 1951, defeating the incumbent, B.C. Barnes. A week after assuming office, Vandergriff called a meeting of business leaders to discuss how to promote Arlington's future. According to the *Arlington Journal*, all "agreed that the time is ripe for an intensive drive to make Arlington grow."[29] With their support, Vandergriff convinced GM to locate its new plant on a 250-acre site of newly annexed land just east of the former city limits.[30] That plant opened in 1954 and employed more than 3,400 assembly workers by 1955. Even before the factory was operational, civic leader George Hawkes, editor of the *Arlington Citizen Journal*, wrote that Arlington was "no longer merely a satellite suburb" but rather was "an industrial factor in its own right."[31]

Probably no one personified a modern-day city booster more than Tom Vandergriff. He served as mayor of the city for twenty-six years and managed to avoid serious challenges by city council or the general population. During his tenure, aided by his city manager, Bill Pitstick (hired in 1954), Vandergriff professionalized city government and, despite his strong pro-growth agenda that would significantly alter the quiet college town, managed to retain his popularity. From 1967 to 1975, he ran unopposed for each of his two-year terms. Vandergriff not only served as mayor during Arlington's boom times, but he, along with other family members, donated a nine-acre tract of land for the future hospital and played a major role in its construction. His family also donated numerous automobiles to the school system.[32]

Thanks to the efforts of Vandergriff and other civic leaders, the American Can Company opened a million-dollar factory on a twelve-acre tract east of the GM plant two years after completion of the automobile factory. It would employ two hundred and seemed to confirm what Hawkes had earlier boasted. After officials announced the plant's location, an editorial in the *Dallas Morning News* characterized Arlington as a "growing industrial city."[33] And in September 1955, the *Fort Worth Star Telegram* ran the following headline: "Industries Credited in Arlington' Growth."[34]

Mayor Vandergriff wanted more, however, and encouraged the development of a five-thousand-acre industrial park in a location that bordered Arlington and Grand Prairie. Unable to raise all the necessary financing locally to buy the Waggoner 3-D Stock Farm and develop it into a massive industrial park, Vandergriff contacted the famed developer William Zeckendorf of New York City, who had helped the Rockefellers manage their real estate empire. The mayor also convinced him to invest in the proposed industrial park. Zeckendorf teamed up with Angus Wynne Jr., a successful Dallas real estate developer, to purchase the land and develop it into the industrial park. The newspapers often referred to this undertaking as the Zeckendorf-Wynne industrial project.[35]

Zeckendorf and Wynne created the Great Southwest Corporation to establish and oversee the industrial park, with Wynne assuming the role of chair of the corporation. According to Zeckendorf, the massive industrial park would attract "desirable industries with steady employment and wholesome work conditions" that would attract population and bring prosperity to the area. The *Dallas Morning News* agreed, pointing out that the industrial park, located near the almost completed Dallas–Fort Worth Turnpike and situated just south of the proposed (but never completed) Trinity River Canal connecting north Texas with the Gulf of Mexico, would "be an economic boon to the entire region."[36] Arlington did everything it could to support the industrial park venture, including a promise to supply more water, thanks to a new lake the city created that freed it from its complete reliance on well water.[37]

Even as Great Southwest Corporation leaders focused on strategies to attract industry, its quest to secure an immediate return to fund the industrial park's infrastructure resulted in the creation of the Six Flags Over Texas amusement park.[38] For the first six years of its existence, the Great Southwest Corporation ran a budget deficit, but thanks to Six Flags, that changed.[39] Aware of the need for income, Angus Wynne suggested the development of an amusement park within the boundaries of the industrial park, a proposal that Vandergriff strongly supported. After a visit to Disneyland and a failed effort to get Disney to agree to build a themed amusement park in Arlington, Wynne decided to create a Texas version of a family amusement park and named it Six Flags Over Texas.[40] Opening in 1961, Six Flags turned out to be an enormous success, attracting over one million visitors during its second season.[41] Thus began the ascent of Arlington as a major Texas tourist destination.

The growth of Six Flags benefitted from the completion of the 29.6-mile Dallas–Fort Worth (DFW) Turnpike in 1957. Proposed in 1951 with the strong support of not only Fort Worth and Dallas but Arlington officials as well, the limited-access state toll road not only made the industrial district and Six Flags possible, but it also eased the commute between Arlington and both major cities and opened up the areas between the two cities for further development.[42]

Moreover, the turnpike also allowed Arlington boosters to make a strong case that Major League Baseball should come to their city. Baseball fans in north Texas had been lobbying for a team since at least 1958, when John Reaves, owner of the minor league Fort Worth Cats, applied to Major League Baseball for the first available franchise.[43] Toward that end, baseball enthusiasts created a bi-county commission that included Dallas, Fort Worth, and Arlington to secure a major league team for the Dallas/Fort Worth area. Led by Tom Vandergriff, the commission determined that Arlington's location between Dallas and Fort Worth would be the best site for the baseball stadium because each city's residents would have easy access via the DFW Turnpike. But the initial plan to have the three cities cooperate through the bi-county commission to erect the $9.5 million stadium, after winning voter approval, was rejected by a state court that ruled the two counties could not jointly fund the stadium.[44] Undeterred, Vandergriff developed a new plan and convinced Tarrant County voters in 1964 to approve a $1.5 million bond issue to secure land and build a baseball stadium in Arlington with the idea that it could eventually be converted into a major-league-level ballpark.[45] Vandergriff, at a Fort Worth Press Club meeting, claimed the passage of the bond for the stadium would increase the chance of the region securing a major league ball club. Its location near Six Flags just off of the DFW Turnpike would be a tremendous benefit for Arlington too. After the bond passed and workers completed Turnpike Stadium in 1965, the Dallas-Fort Worth Spurs of the Texas League became its initial tenant, but the minor league team was, in effect, a placeholder until civic leaders could secure a major league club.[46] The only problem was that Major League Baseball failed to grant Arlington a baseball franchise during its next expansion round. Frustrated by one failed attempt after another to secure a baseball franchise, in 1971 the ever-energetic Vandergriff finally convinced the struggling Washington Senators to relocate to Arlington.[47] To accomplish the franchise relocation, the city of Arlington used about $4 million to expand the ballpark to 35,000 seats, provide additional parking, and erect a scoreboard. This was done without an immediate tax increase using revenue bonds and some leftover bond money previously approved by local voters.[48]

Bob Short, owner of the Senators and deeply in debt, also secured loans from Arlington civic leaders, while the city helped out the owner by paying $7.5 million for the TV and radio broadcasting rights to the rebranded Texas Ranger ballgames and leasing the ballpark to the club for $1 a season.[49] Vandergriff's leadership and the city's willingness to spend extravagantly played a significant role in bringing Major League Baseball to Arlington and north Texas in 1972.[50]

Although Mesa did not have a Tom Vandergriff, it did have a chamber of commerce, an energetic junior chamber of commerce (Jaycees), and a city government that embraced a pro-growth philosophy and the ambition to promote Mesa as an independent community rather than a bedroom suburb tied to Phoenix. Mesa's first industrial trophy, secured in 1955, was a lingerie manufacturer, but soon the city would attract aerospace industries and massive shopping malls.[51] At the beginning of World War II, Mesa had purchased designated sites for airfields and then leased them to the federal government for $1 dollar a year to train pilots during the war. After the war, federal officials returned Falcon Field, located six miles northeast of downtown, and retained Williams Field, eleven miles away, to provide pilot training. Mesa converted Falcon Field into the Municipal Industrial Airport.[52] Soon the airfield not only accommodated airplanes but also offered sites for such industries as Rocket Power, Inc., established in 1958, and Talley Defense Systems in 1960. This was only the beginning as other aerospace companies located on sites bordering the airport. Around the same time, the Industrial Committee of the city's chamber of commerce created the Mesa Industrial Corporation "to assist industry locating in the Mesa Area." It offered land with utilities to prospective factories and made plans to construct an "all-purpose industrial building of 10,000 square feet available for lease or purchase."[53] The Industrial Corporation also established the Mesa Industrial Park to provide space for smaller businesses.[54] As a result of these activities, and because of Mesa's location in the booming Phoenix metropolitan region, the number of non-farmworkers in the Mesa area in 1959 now exceeded the area's agricultural workers.[55] A year later the city received an added boost as Motorola located its integrated circuit factory at the corner of Dobson and Main streets.[56]

Despite these successes in securing industry after the war, Mesa boosters continued to market their community as a tourist town. Ever since 1948, when the Mesa Chamber of Commerce initiated its first advertising campaign to attract tourists and winter visitors to their community, it had publicized the town as a tourist home for those of middle income rather than the wealthiest.[57] By the early 1960s, more than 130 hotels, motels, or motor home parks for winter visitors had located in Mesa. Positioned east of Phoenix, Mesa had easier access to major scenic and recreational areas, such as Superstition Mountain, the Tonto National Ruins, and both Apache and Roosevelt Lakes.[58]

Some of the city's growth advocates thought there were other ways to lure tourists and worked hard to secure a Major League Baseball club for spring training. With the full support of the chamber of commerce, the city paid $10,000 for improvements at the WPA-built Rendezvous Stadium located in the city's downtown. The boosters installed locker rooms for the players, seeded the infield, and moved the right and left field walls to achieve major league dimensions. As the result of an "aggressive campaign," the Jaycees convinced the Oakland Acorns, champions of the Pacific Coast League, to move its spring training site from Glendale, California to Mesa in 1950.[59] After the Acorns ball club announced that it would not return to Mesa the following year, the Jaycees, under the leadership of the rancher and land speculator Dwight Patterson, formed a new thirty-five-member organization called the HoHoKams and initiated a quest to host a Major League Baseball team for the following spring training.

Phil Wrigley, owner for the Chicago Cubs and winter resident in the Phoenix area, had been thinking about moving the spring training site of his ballclub to the Phoenix area. At the time, his team trained on Catalina Island off the California coast and had few opportunities to play other major league teams. Patterson convinced Wrigley to relocate the Cubs to Mesa for spring training after promising significant upgrades would be made to the Rendezvous Stadium with its three-thousand seat wooden bleachers. To secure the Chicago club, the city of Mesa agreed to put up $30,000 for improvements, and the HoHoKams provided an additional $50,000 to modernize the park. Once Wrigley realized how committed Mesa was to securing the Cubs, he agreed to move the team and provided an additional $40,000 to make sure the stadium's facilities were first-rate. The Cubs would train in Mesa until 1965.[60]

When the Cubs left for Long Beach the following year, Mesa was without Major League Baseball for three years. That changed in 1969 when Bob and Dwight Patterson secured the Oakland A's after convincing Charles Finley to move his team from Scottsdale to Mesa. That relationship lasted ten years. In 1975 the city purchased land that eventually became the site of HoHoKam Park, and city officials demolished the aging Rendezvous ballfield. Despite the new ballpark, opened for spring training in 1977, Finley decided to return his club to Scottsdale after 1978.[61] But persistent action taken by the HoHoKams persuaded the Cubs to resettle in Mesa. To this end, the city demolished the original HoHoKam ballpark in 1996 and replaced it with an updated facility the following year. The new ballpark not only had additional seating, better locker rooms, and more batting cages; it also sported a picnic pavilion and a new name, Dwight W. Patterson Field, HoHokam Park. The HoHoKams organization poured more than $1.5 million into the new stadium and was rewarded by record-setting attendance figures, including the single-game attendance record during spring training in 2007, as well the all-time attendance record for a spring training season that same year.[62] By the 1980s, economists estimated the Cubs economic impact on Mesa to be $37 million annually.[63]

When the Cubs threatened to bolt to Naples, Florida, in 2009, Mesa officials responded by developing a 140-acre site in West Mesa that included not only a new stadium seating 15,000 but an adjacent facility for training and rehab available year-round. The combined sports complex was funded by a $99 million bond issue passed by the residents of Mesa on November 2, 2010. Eight-four million dollars was budgeted for the sport facilities and $15 million for associated infrastructure. The city completed the complex in 2014. Mayor Scott Smith, a strong advocate for hosting spring training teams, predicted that the new Cubs training facilities would bring in $130 million a year to Mesa, making spring training baseball an important business proposition for the city.[64] In addition, the Oakland A's would return to Mesa and occupy the abandoned HoHoKam stadium, so Mesa would have two major league teams training each spring.[65] To secure the A's, the city signed an agreement that called for $20 million in stadium improvements. Fifteen million dollars was provided by the state and $2.5 million by the city, with the A's picking up the remainder.[66]

In addition to a strong tradition of civic boosterism shared by both cities, and a commitment to recruit industry as well as baseball, efforts to physically expand both cities through annexation proved another distinctive pro-growth strategy shared by these new cities. The annexation strategy suggests the intentionality of civic leaders in both communities to develop stand-alone cities. At the time of World War II, each city's physical scale was limited, but that would change as Mesa and Arlington undertook aggressive annexation campaigns that allowed them to become big cities. When World War II started, Mesa's city limits encompassed less than 3 square miles. By 1950 it had increased to 5.72 square miles, and during the rest of the decade, it added an additional 7.8 square miles of land.[67] During the 1970s, Mesa grew to cover 65.38 square miles as developers replaced farmland, citrus groves, and ranches with housing plats and industry.[68] Today Mesa covers 138 square miles.[69] Exploring why and how this happened helps explain Mesa's journey from small agricultural town to bedroom suburb to discrete city.

First, annexation guidelines in Arizona were not complicated. Outlying areas were allowed to vote over whether they would accept annexation, and if owners possessing 51 percent of the value of the property slated for annexation approved it, then the area would be annexed. Often ranchers or farmers who owned large acreage near Mesa realized that selling their land for subdivision development might produce more income than what they currently secured, and as a consequence, they frequently initiated annexation proceedings. This would allow those wanting to build on land beyond Mesa's city limits to secure city services, such as water and sewers, something the county did not offer. In addition to the water and sewer utilities the city provided, annexed areas could access other urban services, such as policing and fire protection, something that the county failed to do well.[70] The city's tax structure also made annexation less onerous. Unlike most cities that secured funding through property taxes, Mesa had not required citizens to pay a property tax since 1945. This was because the city owned, managed, and sold its own utilities that brought in significant revenue to its coffers. In addition to that income, the city levied a 1 percent sales tax implemented during the Egbert Brown administration in the 1960s and also relied on "intergovernmental revenue" from state and federal sources. Indeed, during and after the Nixon administration, Mesa benefitted significantly from the federal government's Revenue Sharing Program, and this became a considerable incentive to keep growing the city's population base through further annexation. One of the keys to the distributive formula under the State and Local Fiscal Act of 1972 was population size.[71]

The 1960s also witnessed the development of the first city plan for Mesa, prepared by the Maricopa County Planning and Zoning Commission. Until that time, Mesa had demonstrated little interest in planning, but its continued growth and the willingness of the county to help resulted in a ninety-page plan that provided an economic analysis and projection for the Mesa urban area, an examination of population trends and current land use, and a general land-use plan for the future.[72] At the time of the plan in 1961, Mesa occupied a bit less than fourteen square miles with a population of nearly 34,000, but the document identified Mesa's urban area as covering forty-two square miles of unincorporated land, mostly agricultural or vacant land. Implicit in the plan was that land outside of Mesa would be eventually part of the city.[73]

Although the plan acknowledged that "Mesa has had a significant role as a residential area for persons employed elsewhere in the Salt River Valley" and that it was a desirable residential community, the plan also predicted a significant expansion of employment in manufacturing over the next fifteen to twenty years.[74] Manufacturing had already risen by over 200 percent in the Mesa area, and the plan reminded readers that industry was now dispersing throughout the county as opposed to concentrating in Phoenix. The Mesa area seemed particularly attractive to light industry, including electronics and "other science related fields," because of its location near Arizona State University.[75] Still, there was little to suggest that at this time the county planners saw Mesa as a future independent city. Indeed, passages in the plan suggested that Mesa would continue to be a bedroom community, although it also warned that this would only work if better and faster roadways were constructed. At this time no limited-access highway connected Mesa to Phoenix. The plan also explored Mesa's attractiveness as a center for retirement and tourism.[76]

Just because county planners at this time embraced the notion that Mesa was a bedroom community for the Salt River valley does not mean that they had little to say about its future growth. The plan pointed out that 58 percent of the total gross land area within the city of Mesa was vacant and that "very little land within Mesa could be considered unsuitable for urban development by reasons of topography or other natural factors." In addition, much of the unincorporated land in the Mesa urban area already had city utilities that would make it more attractive to industry and developers.[77] After discussing factors that might promote as well as deter growth, the plan concluded that none of the potential barriers to growth of the area are insurmountable, and assuming that the desires of the community are effectively translated into action, the conclusion follows that *the rate at which Mesa develops will to a considerable extent, be dependent upon the rate at which it wants to develop.*[78] (italics added)

The plan urged Mesa officials to incorporate the best characteristics associated with suburban life but with the economic benefits associated with the city. Such a scheme would provide open space and recreational opportunities, planned subdivisions, and enough jobs so residents enjoyed a balanced community "in respect to travel time, between home and work, and to recreational areas and shopping centers." It would also maintain "high standards for schools, housing and other community facilities" and avoid the "defects of the city."[79]

The focus on annexation increased after Mesa became a home rule city in 1967. In addition, such civic leaders as Bob Evans, Wayne Pomeroy, Howard Godfrey, J. E. Petrie, and Charles Luster emerged as a new breed of city builders. They embraced the potential for Mesa's rapid growth and thought they could develop not just a large suburb but a new type of city that would dominate the East Valley. They anticipated future metropolitan growth and realized most of it would be to the south and east of Mesa since the Salt River blocked Mesa's growth to the north. As a result, in the 1970s the city undertook an ambitious annexation campaign that secured almost all the land between it and the municipality of Apache. City officials also annexed significant parcels of land to the south. Mesa met minimal resistance to this urban imperialism because it extended sewage lines, so the unincorporated areas no longer needed to depend on septic sewers.[80]

Despite the focus on the south and east, one of the earliest annexation efforts occurred on July 6, 1970, when the city council approved by a vote of 5–2 an ordinance to annex the community of Lehi, located north of Mesa, after receiving a petition for annexation from persons owning 68 percent of the property value of the area to be annexed.[81] To make the transition easier for Lehi residents, the city created a suburban ranch classification to avoid "urban and agricultural land conflicts." This allowed ranch owners and horse-riding enthusiasts in the newly annexed land to retain their lifestyle while benefitting from urban services.[82]

City officials, however, prioritized securing land beyond the municipality's southern border since the state had started construction of the Superstition Freeway (U.S. 60) in 1969, the first limited-access highway to reach Mesa from Phoenix. The city annexed land on both sides of the proposed highway. The rancher Cliff Dobson owned a significant amount of land and had requested annexation when he realized that developers wanted to erect housing there. The city intended to provide utilities critical for the development of a residential community. Soon after annexation, he sold two thousand acres of his property to Continental Homes of Phoenix, which in 1973 started building the master-planned community of Dobson Ranch just south of the proposed freeway. Within eight years, the development would house 32,000 residents. Other developers followed. About the same time, the city of Mesa bought the original Dobson family homestead and developed an eighteen-hole municipal golf course.[83] Dobson also sold land for the Fiesta Regional Shopping Mall, the Desert Samaritan Hospital, and the Mesa Community College, all very accessible after the highway was completed.[84]

This development took place shortly after Mesa had employed Victor Gruen and Associates to fashion the city's first truly comprehensive plan in anticipation of the rapid growth brought by the construction of Superstition Freeway. The new city charter approved in 1967 also required that Mesa create a planning department and a plan. Gruen, most famous for his early development of shopping malls and his failed plan to pedestrianize downtown Fort Worth, was hired with the help of a federal planning grant from the Department of Housing and Urban Development under the Housing Act of 1954.[85] Gruen and Associates produced an interim plan entitled "The Elements of the Comprehensive Plan" in June 1969 and published the final plan, in February 1971, titled *Mesa—1990 General Plan*. It became the city's guide for the next twenty years.[86]

The plan covered not only Mesa but also the "Mesa Planning Area" of now about seventy-eight square miles that included the two townships comprising eastern Maricopa County. The document, developed after consultation with the 144-member Mesa Citizen's Advisory Committee, provided a "long-range guide... for the development of the entire city of Mesa and its role in the Maricopa county region."[87] This plan emphasized the city's role in determining its own future in the rapidly expanding metropolitan region. If followed, according to Gruen and Associates, the plan would "make the community of Mesa a better place in which to live, to work, to shop, and to pursue leisure time activities" and "create the highest quality of social, economic, functional and physical environment in the Mesa Planning Area." The plan would allow Mesa to take the "fullest advantage of its opportunities."[88] Although growth was important, the plan warned that "Mesa should not attempt to sacrifice quality for quantity development," a warning that was not always heeded. Most importantly, the plan emphasized that Mesa should not be content to become "mainly a commuter-oriented 'bedroom' community with limited financial resources and employment opportunities." Rather it should focus on becoming a "balanced" community with "high quality commercial, tourist and industrial facilities as well as residential development."[89]

Providing options within Mesa also seemed a major theme of the planners. They called for a variety of residential environments, "which offer meaningful choices to the needs of present and future residents." For some areas, the plan called for flexible mixtures of cluster and multiunit dwellings with single-family dwellings. But other neighborhoods would be made up of people sharing "common social, economic and physical determinants." The plan also called for neighborhoods of both medium density and low density.[90] It clearly challenged the city's almost sole dependence on single-family detached housing and not only recommended more multifamily dwellings but also proposed more flexible zoning ordinances that would "help control mixtures of cluster and multi-unit dwellings with single family dwellings." Finally, the plan also proposed additional mobile home sites for snowbirds. These would be better designed than their predecessors, allowing improved circulation and more open space.[91]

When it came to shopping, the planners wanted "a strong and comprehensive base of good quality commercial facilities" in the Mesa planning area. This would give residents "a variety of choice facilities through encouraging the development of both local, sub regional and regional shopping areas." Aware that downtown Mesa would never again be the commercial center of the city, the plan concluded that an effort should be made to make the downtown a major office complex mixed with government facilities and attractions, such as a main library, community center, or auditorium and maybe even a baseball park.[92] Playing off the industrial base already established by Motorola and Talley and other aerospace industries, the plan called for the addition of both light and heavy industrial districts. Even though the plan conceded that "Mesa exists within the social, economic, political and functional constraints of the total metropolitan community," it insisted that there were "a number of activities to choose from in determining the future land use, including expanding residential build up, encouraging a strong industrial base, and providing retirement and tourist facilities."[93] As we have seen, the plan suggested that Gruen was not envisioning a bedroom suburb; rather, he promoted Mesa's growth as an independent city within the larger metropolitan community.

Thanks to the construction of the Superstition Highway, the 1970s would be a time of extreme growth. By 1975 workers completed the highway from Phoenix to Mesa, so the city now had easier access to the capital city and other areas of greater Phoenix. But even more important, it acted as a magnet and drew significant development into an area that had once been nothing but ranch land.[94] Not only did the construction of the highway draw significant residential development, but it attracted major commercial entities and other nonresidential usage, such as the Mesa Community College campus. Between 1975 and 1980, developers built the Fiesta Mall while significant development of office and retail buildings appeared nearby, leading one former official to conclude that Mesa's Main Street had moved south.[95] There is no doubt that the highway spurred this growth, but Mesa's plans and the civic boosters' energy made it possible. By the 1970s, boosters had committed to making Mesa a new type of city, and their effort to do that resulted in growth beyond their imagination. They established a framework for future expansion and benefitted from a completed state and federal highway system that made Mesa more accessible than ever before. And it offered various types of housing, recreational opportunities, numerous job opportunities, professional baseball, good schools, and low taxes that appealed to the diverse population moving into the Salt Valley and fleeing from Phoenix.

As we have seen, Arlington embraced planning earlier than Mesa, but both cities wanted growth and realized they also needed the appearance of orderly development so as not to impinge on the local quality of life.[96] A week after he was elected, Arlington mayor Tom Vandergriff held a public meeting to discuss how to encourage Arlington's growth and development. He called for a more active chamber of commerce with a full-time executive secretary and various committees to promote industrial development, commercial expansion, civic beautification, and city planning. Several weeks after the meeting, the *Arlington Journal* published an editorial entitled "Arlington's New Spirit." It identified Vandergriff as the main force behind it and endorsed his vision.[97] About the same time the editorial appeared, city council created a five-member planning commission and mandated that it "draw up a city plan that provides a basis for developments in general over an extended period of time."[98] Shortly after the creation of the commission, Arlington employed the Fort Worth engineering firm of Freese and Nichols to develop the plan. Robert W. Caldwell, formerly a planner for the Tennessee Valley Authority and subsequently a planner of other midsize Texas towns, oversaw the preparation of the 125-page document.[99]

According to the plan's introduction, its goal was "*an urban community* that would have as many of the basic improvements and advantages as would be necessary to produce an environment of convenience and desirability for good living" (italics added).[100] Indeed, the plan called for Arlington to take advantage of the growing decentralization of Dallas and Fort Worth and develop a balanced community including not only attractive homes but also expanded commercial and manufacturing assets.[101] The plan focused on land-use policies, including zoning objectives, subdivision control, and major street and highway planning, as well as the placement of public utilities. It also discussed how to accommodate automobile parking, airport development, and the location of public schools, parks, playgrounds, and public buildings.[102] The final section discussed how the plan would be implemented.[103]

If one is to judge from the local newspaper coverage, this was a central event in the history of Arlington. Numerous editorials and front-page stories highlighted the planning effort. Reports stressed how planning would allow the city to take advantage of the decentralization trend in urban America, observing that with careful planning Arlington might well avoid some of the mess that other north Texas suburbs had faced. The newspapers also viewed the plan as a booster tool, emphasizing how it marked the community as "progressive" and promised future businesses an orderly and efficient environment. The discussion of planning focused on how it would promote both residential and economic growth while also improving citizens' quality of life.[104]

By the 1950s Arlington civic leaders and government officials were clearly committed to growing Arlington into something more than a bedroom suburb; they wanted a balance of residents, commerce, and industry. Although city planners acknowledged the decentralizing tendencies of growth thanks to the automobile, they still emphasized the need to preserve and protect the Central Business District, claiming it was "vital to the continuing economic stability of the city."[105]

The rapid growth of Arlington resulted in a newly revised plan in 1959 that emphasized the importance of the neighborhood unit plan, a tool that later would be embraced by Gruen's plan for Mesa. It underscored the importance of developing local areas based around an elementary school and a park that provided a suburban-like setting in which families could raise their children and know their neighbors. Primary or secondary streets that provided boundaries would surround each unit, while commercial service areas would be located on the perimeter of major street intersections. Arlington had grown from a population of 5,000 in 1952 in an eight-square-mile city to a community of 46,000 in a twenty-square-mile footprint.[106] Despite this rapid growth, the plan observed that Arlington had "not lost its character as a peaceful, quiet, residential community, despite its growth as an industrial, commercial and cultural center." Acknowledging that Arlington's growth between Dallas and Fort Worth would be influenced by that location, it concluded that the city would "continue to grow and expand as an individual urban entity and as the axis and vital center of the ever-growing Dallas-Fort Worth metropolitan region," suggesting that this really was a new type of city.[107]

Caldwell and Associates updated the plan in 1964 and again emphasized the importance of the neighborhood concept for Arlington's continued residential growth. Under the plan, the neighborhood unit would be inwardly focused allowing for "a quiet, safe and healthy place in which people can live."[108] Despite the emphasis on single-family housing by Caldwell, the plan called for more apartments for singles moving into Arlington as well as young married couples arriving from outside of Texas to the city.[109]

To ensure that growth, Arlington took advantage of Texas's generous annexation laws to reserve an additional forty-eight square miles of land outside its city boundaries for future use. In Texas, all home rule cities had the power to annex unincorporated lands around them without the permission of residents living there, so long as the land was contiguous to the municipal boundaries. In addition, case law allowed Texas cities to freeze the status of unincorporated land by a first reading of intent to annex, thus preventing other communities from claiming those areas and keeping residents in the unincorporated land from incorporating those lands.[110] When added to the land already under first reading, if Arlington completed all its planned annexations, it would encompass ninety-six square miles.[111]

Such action clearly suggests Arlington civic leaders were committed to building a large municipality not only characterized by a variety of residential subdivisions but also aimed to attract commerce, industry, and recreation facilities. It would become a new type of city that would benefit from its location between two major cities and access to unlimited opportunities. Although it is a truism to assert that the area between Dallas and Fort Worth was destined to attract residents, commerce, and industry, it was in no way inevitable that a community like Arlington would seek to attract growth in the way that it did. The city builders of Arlington saw the possibilities and in the 1950s and 1960s were very intentional about their goal.

Another Arlington plan, written by former Dallas city planner Marvin Springer and published in 1971, acknowledged Arlington's success under the heading "Evolution of a Major City." The plan explored "the population, employment and related economic changes which were taking place in the Arlington Area" and those which would likely occur in the future. Such information, according to Springer, would guide the city's establishment of community development goals "directed toward the evolution of Arlington as the center of a vast urban complex and one of the significant urban communities of the Dallas-Fort Worth Region."[112]

By the end of the 1970s, the framework was in place for the development of Mesa and Arlington into large cities. Despite the economic downturn in the late 1970s, enough land had been annexed or reserved to provide the necessary housing for larger scale communities, and both cities had developed economies benefitting from such footloose industries as aviation and electronics. Other industries as well as a thriving service sector took advantage of an impressive network of highways and the accessibility of large airports. Both cities also benefitted significantly from tourism and their institutions of higher education.[113] Although suburban sprawl appeared inevitable in the southwestern metropolitan areas, Arlington and Mesa positioned themselves to benefit from the sprawl thanks to advice from city planners and their planning documents that from the beginning treated the communities as potential cities rather than merely one-dimensional suburbs. By the 1970s civic leaders in both Arlington and Mesa focused on strategies to grow these places into full-blown cities. And people came. Over the next forty years, Arlington grew from a 1970 population of 90,229 to 366,248. Mesa experienced an even greater growth rate, climbing from 63,049 in 1970 to 439,041 in 2010.[114] Just as a combination of location and leadership determined the fate of nineteenth-century cities (as well as conditions beyond their control), these new cities depended on the same. And they drew diverse and ambitious populations just as earlier nineteenth-century cities had done. Indeed, one index recently ranked Arlington, Texas, the tenth most diverse city in America.[115] Mesa is not as diverse, but more than 25 percent of its population is Hispanic, and like Arlington, its residents range from the very poor to the wealthy.[116]

Ambitious civic and governmental leaders in the 1950s clearly understood the opportunities that decentralization offered to their communities and sought to create a new type of city that benefited from its location within a sprawling metropolitan region. Today that is a reality. Indeed, by the 1990s Arlington's Mayor Richard Greene could assert, "We're nobody's damn suburb."[117] And had Mesa's mayor wanted to, he could have claimed the same thing.

Cities in a Postcivic Era

Greene's statement not only marked an acknowledgment that Arlington had truly gained city status, but it also reflected the modern mindset that Zane Miller has identified in his writings about contemporary urban America. Arlington, in the eyes of Greene, was dependent on neither Fort Worth nor Dallas and would base decisions on what was best for Arlington rather than a disposition emphasizing what was best for the larger metropolitan region. This might explain why Arlington, the third-largest city in the metropolitan region, refused to participate in the regional public transportation system seen by cost-conscious local officials as too expensive for the city. Gone was the idea of an organically constructed metropolitan region that encouraged a civic interest in the fate of the larger unit. Instead, a more mechanistic view replaced it that reflected a new assumption that inward-turning individuals composed the basic units of society and, in the words of Miller, "ascribed to those individuals not even a partial obligation for civic commitment to territorial community."[118]

Mesa's financial problems in the early twenty-first century, thanks to its residents' reluctance to support the establishment of a property tax, resulted in significant cuts in city services, which severely affected senior citizens and other disadvantaged residents. Again, one can discern a lack of empathy for the needs of the community as a whole.[119]

And there were other consequences for these new postwar cities. Both Arlington and Mesa exhibited an alarming lack of civic-mindedness despite the earlier efforts to promote neighborhood communities through planning. Neither city benefitted from a spatial center. Their original downtowns were practically nonexistent. Low voter turnout and the lack of thriving local newspapers also underscored civic indifference to the public interest.[120] These places had become what Miller called "communities of advocacy" made up of "liberated" persons who felt no "obligation for even partial commitment to civic participation for the sake of the community welfare (as opposed to individual well-being)."[121]

Although on the surface there are some parallels between the city-building efforts of civic leaders in Arlington and Mesa and those of the nineteenth century, the types of cities constructed after World War II were shaped by not only changing technologies and economies but, just as forcefully, by cultural changes in the way people thought about the city and the metropolitan community. This is one of Miller's most important contributions to the literature of urban history, encouraging us to take seriously how conceptions of the city and metropolitan region have had real consequences for the way people identified and responded to urban problems during separate eras in our history. Miller constructed a distinctive form of urban history chronology based on what he called taxonomies of reality, each reflecting a type of consensus of what cities were or could become. Those notions changed over time, but each shared basic assumptions permitting communication even among those who disagreed on specifics and helping to frame the parameters of debate among those with various agendas.

This framing of urban history has yet to be utilized by those outside the so-called Cincinnati School, a term Miller used to refer to a group of his Ph.D. students. The scholars who have adopted his approach to urban history have written narratives modeling his emphasis on changing taxonomies. This work has underscored the importance of changing discourses of what a city was or should be, which have in turn influenced how particular problems were identified and addressed over time. One of Miller's great achievements was his insight in taking what some might view as inconsequential events in urban history—the development of a postwar suburb such as Forest Park, Ohio; debate over the future of a declining area in Cincinnati, Over-the-Rhine; or the growth of the outer Cincinnati neighborhood of Clifton—and using these local histories to explore the changing ways in which people thought about their urban world over time and the consequences of those shifts in thinking. Indeed, his emphasis on the discontinuity of history as well as his redirecting the historian's traditional fascination with causation clearly affected my approach to history. For myself and many others among his cohorts of students, this approach allowed us to form unique insights on such historical subjects as housing reform, public health initiatives, community activism, race relations, and even the priorities of city and state governments. By examining changing discourses from one era to another, one could specify how solutions in one period became problems for later generations. For instance, the Progressive Era "problem" of inefficient government gave way in the 1970s to the "problem" of unrepresentative government as that decade's "problem," as a new public discourse replaced the need for government efficiency with the rights of individuals. The changing definition of problems (and solutions), according to Miller, reflected changing perceptions of reality over time. For many of his students, this approach provided an intriguing gateway to how urban history could be studied and allowed us to develop insights that other approaches to history have missed.

NOTES

1. Zane L. Miller, *Suburb: Neighborhood and Community in Forest Park, Ohio, 1935–1976* (Knoxville: University of Tennessee Press, 1981); Zane L. Miller, *Visions of Place: The City, Neighborhoods, Suburbs, and Cincinnati's Clifton, 1850–2000* (Columbus: Ohio State University Press, 2001); Zane L. Miller and Bruce Tucker, *Changing Plans for America's Inner Cities: Cincinnati's Over-the-Rhine and Twentieth-Century Urbanism* (Columbus: Ohio State University Press, 1998).

2. Miller, *Suburb*, xxxvi.

3. Miller, *Visions of Place*, 167.

4. Robert B. Fairbanks, *Making Better Citizens: Housing Reform and the Community Development Strategy in Cincinnati, 1890–1960* (Urbana: University of Illinois Press, 1988).

5. Miller has argued that cultural individualism emphasized "the ultimate integrity of the individual" and encouraged people "to define their own lifestyles and cultures" rather than have them defined by where they lived. Miller, *Changing Plans*, 44.

6. Robert B. Fairbanks, *For the City as a Whole: Planning, Politics and the Public Interest in Dallas, 1900–1965* (Columbus: Ohio State University Press, 1998); Robert B. Fairbanks, *The War on Slums in the Southwest: Public Housing and Slum Clearance in Texas, Arizona, and New Mexico, 1935–1965* (Philadelphia: Temple University Press, 2014).

7. Miller's best discussion of the emergence of consequences of this new taxonomy can be found in his book *Suburb*, xx–xxxvi.

8. Probably the best example of the transition not only in the Southwest but in the nation can be found in John C. Teaford, *The Metropolitan Revolution: The Rise of Post-Urban America* (New York City: Columbia University Press, 2006), esp. chaps. 1 and 5.

9. See, for example, Bradford Luckingham, *The Urban Southwest: A Profile History of Albuquerque, El Paso, Phoenix, and Tucson* (El Paso: Texas Western Press, 1982); Philip VanderMeer, *Desert Visions and the Making of Phoenix, 1860–2009* (Albuquerque: University of New Mexico Press, 2010); Elizabeth Tandy Shermer, *Sunbelt Capitalism: Phoenix and the Transformation of American Politics* (Philadelphia: University of Pennsylvania Press); Marc Simmons, *Albuquerque: A Narrative History* (Albuquerque: University of New Mexico Press, 1982); Michael F. Logan, *Fighting Sprawl and City Hall: Resistance to Urban Growth in the Southwest* (Tucson: University of Arizona Press, 1995); Patricia Evridge Hill, *Dallas: The Making of a Modern City* (Austin: University of Texas Press, 1996); Fairbanks, *For the City*; Roger Hanson, *Civic Culture and Urban Change: Governing Dallas* (Detroit: Wayne State University Press, 2003); Harvey Graff,

The Dallas Myth: The Making and Unmaking of an American City (Minneapolis: University of Minnesota Press, 2008); David G. McComb, *Houston: A History* (Austin: University of Texas Press, 1981); Robert D. Thomas and Richard W. Murray, *Progrowth Politics: Change and Governance in Houston* (Berkeley: IGS, 1991); Joe R. Feagin, *Free Enterprise City: Houston in Political and Economic Perspective* (New Brunswick, NJ: Rutgers University Press, 1988); Martin V. Melosi and Joseph A. Platt, eds., *Energy Metropolis: An Environmental History of Houston and the Gulf Coast* (Pittsburgh: University of Pittsburgh Press, 2007).

10. Jennifer B. LeFurgy, *Boomburbs: The Rise of America's Accidental Cities* (Washington, DC: Brookings Institution, 2007). There has been much written on the new suburban cities, from Robert Fishman's account of technoburbs to Joel Garreau's edge cities as well as Jon Teaford's insightful books about post suburbia and what he calls the municipal revolution. Joel Garreau, *Edge City: Life on the New Urban Frontier* (New York: Anchor Books, 1992); Robert Fishman, *The Rise and Fall of Suburbia* (New York: Basic Books, 1987); Jon C. Teaford, *Post-Suburbia: Government and Politics in the Edge Cities* (Baltimore: Johns Hopkins Press 1997); Teaford, *Metropolitan Revolution*.

11. Biggest US Cities (website), "Top 100 Biggest US Cities by Population," last updated February 3, 2022, https://www.biggestuscities.com/.

12. This took place during a period that Miller called the era of cultural individualism. According to Miller, it emphasized "'the ultimate integrity of the individual' by encouraging people to define their own lifestyles, and cultures" and "took individuals rather than groups as the basic units of concern." This would help shape Mesa and Arlington as much as the automobile would. Miller and Tucker, *Changing Plans*, 44.

13. City Planning and Zoning Commission, "The City Plan for Arlington, Texas" (Fort Worth: Freese and Nichols, Consulting Engineers, Robert W. Caldwell, Associate Planner, 1952); City and Zoning Commission, "Arlington City Plan: Studies and Revisions, 1959" (Fort Worth: Caldwell and Caldwell planners, 1959); Arlington Planning and Zoning Commission, "Comprehensive Master Plan 1964: A Guide for Future Development, Studies and Revisions," (Fort Worth: Robert W. Caldwell and Associates, Freese Nichols and Endress, 1964); Arlington Planning and Zoning Commission, "Arlington, Texas: Urban Development Framework" (Dallas: Marvin Springer and Associates, 1971); Maricopa County Planning and Zoning Department and City of Mesa Planning and Zoning Department, "Comprehensive Plan for Mesa, Arizona" (Phoenix: Western Business, Consultants Associates, 1961); City of Mesa Planning and Zoning Department, "The Elements of the Comprehensive Plan" (Los Angeles: Gruen Associates, 1978); City of Mesa Planning and Zoning Department, "Mesa—1990 General Plan" (Los Angeles: Gruen and Associates, 1978).

14. Mark C. Simpson, *Parks and Recreation: City Planning and Urban Development in a Southwest Suburb; Mesa, Arizona 1980–2000* (Lincoln, NE: iUniverse, 2007), 12.

15. Gary Nelson, "Part One: Mesa's Cactus League Roots Go Back to '40s," *Arizona Republic*, January 21, 2014, http://archive.azcentral.com/community/mesa/articles/20140121mesa-cactus-league-roots-go-back-spring-training-prog.html; Gary Nelson, "Part Two: Mesa Wages Bitter Fight to Keep the Cubs," *Arizona Republic*, January 23, 2014, http://archive.azcentral.com/community/mesa/articles/20140123part-two-mesa-wages-bitter-fight-keep-chicago-cubs-prog.html.

16. Gar Nelson, "Mesa Voters Sacked Cardinals Stadium," *East Valley Tribune*, August 28, 2016.

17. Donald Frazier, "Arlington Downs Racetrack," *Handbook of Texas Online*, accessed May 31, 2021, https://www.tshaonline.org/handbook/entries/arlington-downs-racetrack.

18. University of Texas at Arlington (website), "History of the University," accessed September 2, 2020, https://www.uta.edu/uta/about/traditions/history.php. The school changed its name to the North Texas Agricultural College in 1923 and kept that name until 1949 when it became Arlington State College. Also see Robert B. Fairbanks, "The Morrill Land-Grant Act and American Cities," in *Science as Service: Establishing and Reformulating Land-Grant Universities*, ed. Alan I Marcus (Tuscaloosa: University of Alabama Press, 2015), 180–182.

19. Freese and Nichols, Consulting Engineers, Robert W. Caldwell, Associate Planner, *City Plan for Arlington*, 5.

20. "Announces Formation of Arlington Chamber of Commerce," *Arlington Journal*, May 1, 1952.

21. Fairbanks, *For the City*, 159–161, 192–194; Michael Phillips, *White Metropolis: Race, Ethnicity, and Religion in Dallas, 1841–2001* (Austin: University of Texas Press, 2006), 120–126.

22. *Fort Worth Star-Telegram*, May 12, 1949, untitled from *Star-Telegram* clipping file, Special Collections, University of Arlington (UTA).

23. *Fort Worth Star Telegram*, April 3, 1951, untitled from *Star-Telegram* clipping file, Special Collections, UTA.

24. "First City Manager Assumes Duties as Arlington Goes on Business Basis," *Fort Worth Star Telegram*, January 8, 1950, *Fort Worth Star Telegram* clipping files, Special Collections, UTA. A year earlier, Arlington residents had overwhelmingly voted for a charter amendment allowing the commission to employ a city manager. "News in Review," *National Municipal Review* 38 (September 1949): 401.

25. Victor Di Sciullo, "A New Line of Thinking: Changes in Spatial Development Stimuli of America's Modern and Post-Modern Cities," unpub. paper for History 3351, UTA, Fall 1996, 8–9. According to the political scientist Allan Saxe, Arlington was the only city in the state that employed such a generous policy. Allan Saxe, *Politics in Arlington Texas: An Era of Continuity and Growth* (Austin, TX: Eakin, 2001), 28–29.

26. Guest lecture by Tom Vandergriff, History 3351, UTA, April 27, 2000.

27. Saxe, *Politics in Arlington Texas*, 24–25. Also see David Lynn Cannon, "Arlington's Path to Post Suburbia" (Ph.D. diss., UTA, 2000).

28. Guest lecture by Tom Vandergriff.
29. "Build Arlington Meeting Called," *Arlington Journal*, April 13, 1951.
30. "General Motors Buys East Arlington Site," *Arlington Journal*, August 5, 1951. Arlington annexed six square miles of land between Arlington and Grand Prairie. Cannon, "Arlington's Path," 37.
31. "GM to Drop 600 at Arlington," *Dallas Morning News*, May 16, 1956, 1; Irvin Farman, "Arlington 'No Longer Suburb,' Flexes Industrial Biceps at Man of the Year Fete," *Fort Worth Star Telegram*, June 10, 1953.
32. Cannon, "Arlington's Path," 34, 53–54, 80–81. Also see Saxe, *Politics in Arlington Texas*.
33. Ken Hand, "American Can Plans Factory at Arlington," *Dallas Morning News*, April 27, 1955, 1; William K. Stuckley, "Million-Dollar American Can Plan Dedicated," *Dallas Morning News*, September 9, 1956, 5; Editorial, "Arlington Plant," *Dallas Morning News*, April 30, 1955, 2.
34. Tony Slaughter, "Industries Credited in Arlington's Growth," *Fort Worth Star Telegram*, September 6, 1955.
35. Cannon, "Arlington's Path," 44; James J. Cockrell, "Rockefeller Brothers Join 3-D Development," *Dallas Morning News*, July 11, 1956, 1. Other investors included Angus Wynne Jr.'s uncle and a Fort Worth group including Amon Carter Jr., Marvin Leonard, Ken Davis, and Sol Brachman. "Great Southwest Corp. Adds Banker to Board," *New York Times*, July 16, 1956, 33; "$10,000.00 Investment Reported for Project," *Dallas Morning News*, July 19, 1956.
36. James A. Cockrell, "Realtor Bares Industry Plan," *Dallas Morning News*, January 7, 1956, 1; Francis P. Raffetto, "Zeckendorf Envisions Multi-Million Project," *Dallas Morning News*, January 10, 1956, 1.
37. 3,200 acres of what would become the Great Southwest Industrial District would be in Arlington. "Rapid Growth of Arlington Expected," *Fort Worth Star Telegram*, January 11, 1959. Amon Carter Jr. and several other prominent Fort Worth leaders joined Angus Wynne Jr. as investors in the industrial park too. "James A. Cockrell, GSC Work Underway on New Building Idea," *Dallas Morning News*, April 14, 1957, 2; Panel Study by the Urban Land Institute; *An Evaluation of Land Use and Development for Great Southwest Corporation, Arlington, Texas* Washington, DC: 1968), https://openlibrary.org/books/OL5689655M/An_evaluation_of_land_use_and_development_for_Great_Southwest_Corporation_Arlington_Texas#editions-list, accessed on March 5, 2020.
38. O. K. Carter, "Six Flags Waved in Boom that Exceeded Leader's Hopes," *Fort Worth Star Telegram*, May 8, 1994, 17.
39. Rudy Rochelle, "GSC, Now in the Black, to Open New Area," *Dallas Morning News*, October 23, 1962, 6.
40. "Heritage of State's Past Coming Alive near Dallas," *Dallas Morning News*, May 8, 1961, 12; O. K. Carter, "Six Flags Waved," 17.
41. "Six Flags Fly High," *Dallas Morning News*, November 13, 1962, 4.
42. Ken Hand, "Turnpike Links Twin Cities," *Dallas Morning News*, August 25, 1957, 1.

43. "Stadium Plans," *Fort Worth Star Telegram*, March 21, 1958.
44. Frank Jackson, "Arlington Stadium," *Handbook of Texas Online*, accessed May 31, 2021, https://www.tshaonline.org/handbook/entries/arlington-stadium.
45. To get the necessary county votes for the stadium bond, Vandergriff agreed to include a $15 million Tarrant County Convention Center bond issue on the ballot that would be built in downtown Fort Worth. Eddie S. Hughes, "Tarrant Approves Center, Stadium," *Dallas Morning News*, April 26, 1964, 1.
46. Eddie S. Hughes, "Think 'Big League,' City Leaders Told," *Dallas Morning News*, February 7, 1964, 7; Fun while It Lasted (website), "1965–1971 Dallas-Fort Worth Spurs," accessed on May 15, 2020, https://funwhileitlasted.net/2013/10/20/1965-1971-dallas-fort-worth-spurs/#.
47. "Six Flags Baseball Luncheon Tuesday Makes It Official," *Dallas Morning News*, November 21, 1971, 3.
48. "Arlington Confident on Park," *Dallas Morning News*, September 24, 1971, 6; "Arlington Ponders Stadium," *Dallas Morning News*, November 9, 1971, 10.
49. "Arlington's Growth Shaped by Vandergriff's Successes, Setbacks," *Arlington Star Telegram*, June 15, 1997, 16; Mark S. Rosentraub, "Financial Incentives, Locational Decision-Making and Professional Sports: The Case of the Texas Rangers Baseball Network and the City of Arlington," in *Financing Local Government: New Approaches to Old Problems*, ed. Mark S. Rosentraub (Fort Collins, CO: Western Social Science Association,1977), 56–57. Arlington created its own network and lost $868,796 in its first two years of operation.
50. Cannon, "Arlington's Path," 73–74. Not all of Vandergriff's efforts to make Arlington a beacon for tourists worked. With the success of Six Flags and the forthcoming Texas Rangers, the mayor decided to secure one more major tourist attraction. After being turned down by Walter Knotts to build a Knotts Berry Farm–like park in Arlington, Vandergriff decided to imitate the success of Sea World in San Diego and develop a sea park in Arlington. Once again working with Angus Wynne Jr., Vandergriff convinced Arlington voters to pass a $7.5 million bond issue that would allow Arlington to finance the building of the park on land near Six Flags while Wynne and the Six Flags developers would design, construct, and operate it. When Wynne was unable to fulfill his commitment and resigned, the city decided to construct and operate the park through its own Arlington Park Corporation. A delay in construction created serious problems for the park, and when it opened in 1972, the project was already $2.5 million over budget. Attendance also failed to reach projections. Even when George Millay, San Diego Sea World's founder, took over the management in a joint venture with the American Broadcasting Company yet failed to right the ship, the city lost more than $500,000 a year. Despite efforts to rebrand the park, the council voted to close the park in 1976. Although the venture was a financial disaster for the city, it again suggests how the city used its location to try to become a major tourist center. Al Hirting, "Remember Seven Seas," *D Magazine*, February 1980 https://www.dmagazine.com/publications/dmagazine/1980/february/remember-seven-seas/.

51. *Our Town: Mesa, Arizona, 1878–1978*, Centennial Edition (Mesa, AZ: Mesa Public Schools), 152.
52. *Mesa Tribune*, June 27, 1941, 6, newspaper clipping, Mesa Historical Society; *Our Town*, 154.
53. Western Business Consultants, *The Industrial Advantages of Mesa, Arizona*, prepared for Mesa Chamber of Commerce, pamphlet, 31, Mesa Chamber of Commerce papers, box 1 Mesa Room, Mesa Public Library; Maricopa County, Planning and Zoning Departments, *Part 1, Our Town*, 150.
54. "Get Acquainted with MIDC," *Mesa Journal*, October 26, 1966, clipping in Mesa Chamber of Commerce papers, box 1, folder 19, Mesa Room, Mesa Public Library.
55. *Our Town*, 152.
56. *Our Town*, 55.
57. Simpson, *Parks and Recreation*, 20.
58. Western Business Consultants, *Industrial Advantages of Mesa*, 9.
59. Thomas Rhodes, "A History of the HoHoKam's of Mesa," typescript, 1997, 3; "Top Notch PCL Nine to Be at Rendezvous," *Mesa Tribune*, July 26, 1949.
60. Rhodes, "History," 4–8.
61. Rhodes, "History," 4–8.
62. Rhodes, "History," 4–8.
63. Rick Thompson, "History of the Cactus League," *Spring Training Magazine*, accessed May 20, 2020, http://springtrainingmagazine.com/history4.html.
64. Carrie Muskat, "New Spring Training Ballpark, Complex Unveiled in Mesa," MLB.com, February 12, 2014, https://www.mlb.com/news/cubs-spring-training-ballpark-complex-unveiled-in-mesa/c-67698502.
65. Kevin Reichard, "Mesa Launches HoHoKam Park Renovations for A's," *Ballpark Digest*, March 14, 2014, https://ballparkdigest.com/201403147163/major-league-baseball/features/mesa-launches-hohokam-park-renovations-for-as; Kevin Reichard, "New Cubs Spring Facility Approved by Mesa Voters," *Ballpark Digest*, November 3, 2010, https://ballparkdigest.com/201011033232/major-league-baseball/news/new-cubs-spring-facility-approved-by-mesa-voters.
66. Kevin Reichard, "Oakland, Mesa Reach Final Agreement on HoHoKam Park Move," *Ballpark Digest*, March 1, 2013, https://ballparkdigest.com/201303016102/major-league-baseball/news/oakland-mesa-reach-final-agreement-on-hohokam-park-move.
67. *Our Town*, 9.
68. *Our Town*, 182; also see Carol E. Heim, "Border Wars: Tax Revenues, Annexation, and Urban Growth in Phoenix" (2006), Economics Department Working Paper Series 55, 56.
69. *Our Town*, 182.
70. *Our Town*, 182.
71. *Our Town*, 178; interview manuscript, Howard Godfrey interviewed by Sarah Zafra, September 4, 2001, tape 1 of 3, Mesa Room, Mesa Public Library; also see Heim, "Border Wars." According to Heim, "the primary argument for annexa-

tion, from the perspective of municipal authorities, often was to obtain tax revenues and fees." Also see Staff of the Joint Committee on Internal Revenue Taxation, *General Explanation of the State and Local Fiscal Act Assistance and the Federal-State Tax Collection Act of 1972*, February 12, 1973, http://www.jct.gov/s-1-73.pdf.

72. Maricopa County Planning and Zoning Department, *Part 1*.

73. Maricopa County Planning and Zoning Department, "Comprehensive Plan," 8, 11, 77.

74. Maricopa County Planning and Zoning Department, "Comprehensive Plan," 5.

75. Maricopa County Planning and Zoning Department, "Comprehensive Plan," 14, 25, 36.

76. Maricopa County Planning and Zoning Department, "Comprehensive Plan," 6–7, 22, 38.

77. Maricopa County Planning and Zoning Department, "Comprehensive Plan," 77.

78. Maricopa County Planning and Zoning Department, "Comprehensive Plan," 31.

79. Maricopa County Planning and Zoning Department, "Comprehensive Plan," 82.

80. Interview manuscript, Wayne Balmer interviewed by Sarah Zafra, September 4, 2001, tape 1 of 3, Mesa Room, Mesa Public Library.

81. Interview manuscript, Wayne Balmer interviewed by Sarah Zafra, March 29, 2000, tape 1 of 3, Mesa Room, Mesa Public Library; Ordinance no. 672, City of Mesa, Arizona Council Meeting Minutes, July 6, 1970, https://web.archive.org/web/20100527224035/http://www.mesaaz.gov/Planning/pdf/LongRangePlanning/Lehi/CC-Minutes07-06-1970.pdf.

82. Tanya Collins, "Council Hears Pro, Con On Lehi Area Zoning," *Mesa Tribune*, vertical newspaper clipping, file. Mesa Room, Mesa Public Library.

83. Howard Godfrey interviewed by Sarah Zafra, September 4, 2001, tape 1 of 3, Mesa Room, Mesa Public Library; Jason Carey, "Impact of Highways on Property Values: Case Study of the Superstition Freeway Corridor, Final Report 516, for Arizona Department of Transportation," Mesa Chamber of Commerce Collection, 1965–1982, Mesa Room, Mesa Public Library.

84. Dobson Ranch, homepage, accessed February 7, 2020, http://www.dobsonranchhoa.com/the-best-place-to-live/in-the-beginning/.

85. Gruen and Associates, "Mesa, Arizona: The Elements of the Comprehensive Plan." The money came from the Urban Planning Assistance Program authorized by section 701 of the Housing Act of 1954, as amended.

86. Gruen and Associates, "Elements," iii. Most of the following references are from the interim report, "The Elements of the Comprehensive Plan," which also appears in Gruen and Associates, *Mesa—1990 General Plan*.

87. Gruen and Associates, "Elements," iv; Gruen and Associates, *Mesa—1990 General Plan*, 1. The advisory committee made up of various Mesa residents ac-

cording to the plan "would serve as an essential link in the communication process between citizens of Mesa and the Planning Commission."

88. Gruen and Associates, "Elements," 22.

89. Gruen and Associates, "Elements," 23; Gruen Associates, *Mesa—1990 General Plan*, 14.

90. Gruen and Associates, "Elements," 31.

91. Gruen and Associates, "Elements," 23–25.

92. Gruen and Associates, "Elements," 30.

93. Gruen and Associates, *Mesa—1990 General Plan*, 22.

94. Jason Carey, "*Impact of Highways on Property Values: Case Study of the Superstition Freeway Corridor*," for the Arizona Department of Transportation, Final Report 516, October 2001, iv, 1. The Superstition Freeway was completed to Power Road in east Mesa in 1985.

95. Carey, *Impact of Highways*, 23.

96. Editorial, "Community Instead of Suburb," *Arlington Journal*, June 15, 1951.

97. *Arlington Journal*, April 20; Build Arlington Meeting," *Arlington Journal*, April 13, 1951; Editorial, "Arlington's New Spirit," *Arlington Journal*, April 27, 1951.

98. "City Planning Board Studied by Council," *Arlington Journal*, May 4, 1951; Editorial, "Toward Planning, What Next?," *Arlington Journal*, May 11, 1951; June 22, 1951 (quote). Arlington residents probably did not miss the fact that shortly after Vandergriff appointed the planning commission, GM finalized its deal to build an automobile plant in their community. "Business Men Enthusiastically Support 'Build Arlington Movement,'" *Arlington Journal*, July 20, 1951.

99. "City Planning Board Studied by Council," *Arlington Journal*, May 4, 1951; Editorial, "Toward Planning, What Next?" *Arlington Journal*, May 11, 1951; June 22, 1951 (quote). Freese and Nichols, Consulting Engineers, Robert W. Caldwell, Associate Planner, *City Plan*.

100. Freese and Nichols, Consulting Engineers, Robert W. Caldwell, Associate Planner, 16 (italics mine).

101. Freese and Nichols, Consulting Engineers, Robert W. Caldwell, Associate Planner, 23.

102. Freese and Nichols, Consulting Engineers, Robert W. Caldwell, Associate Planner, 41–75.

103. Freese and Nichols, Consulting Engineers, Robert W. Caldwell, Associate Planner, 118–121.

104. "New City Planning Commission Can Be a Big Thing for Arlington," *Arlington Journal*, June 29, 1951, 2; "A Master Plan Can Help Community Avoid Headaches," *Arlington Journal*, September 21, 1951; Tommy Vandergriff, "Zoning Is a Part of Effort to Keep Eyes on Arlington's Great Future," January 19, 1952. Even before Caldwell completed the plan, the city commission adopted its revised zoning proposal and its subdivision rules and regulations. Freese and Nichols, Consulting Engineers, Robert W. Caldwell, Associate Planner, *City Plan*, 9. Planning officials held a public meeting at the First National Bank Building

to present the master plan to the public on September 23. "City Plan to be Presented Tuesday," *Arlington Journal*, September 19, 1952, 1.

105. Freese and Nichols, Consulting Engineers, Robert W. Caldwell and Caldwell, 2. For a broader discussion of early planning efforts in Arlington, see Arlington Planning and Zoning Commission Department, "Comprehensive Plan: Arlington, Texas, 1986," 11–14.

106. Caldwell and Caldwell, *Arlington City Plan*; Arlington Planning Department, *Comprehensive Plan*, 12.

107. Caldwell and Caldwell, *Arlington City Plan*, 1.

108. Robert W. Caldwell and Associates, Freese Nichols and Endress, *Comprehensive Master Plan 1964*, 117.

109. Robert W. Caldwell and Associates, Freese Nichols and Endress, Planning Consultants, 133–134.

110. Constitution of the State of Texas, art. 11, sec. 5, repr. in John P. Keith, *City and County Home Rule in Texas* (Austin: Institute of Public Affairs, University of Texas, 1951), 29; "Cities and Towns—Authorizes Cities of More Than 5,000 Inhabitants to Adopt and Amend Their Charters," *General Laws of the State of Texas Passed by the Thirty-Third Legislature at Its Regular Session* (Austin, TX: Von Boeckmann-Jones, 1913), chap. 147, p. 310. Later legislation by the state in 1963 changed the rules but still allowed cities.

111. "Suburb Beats Cowtown in Annexation 'Grab,'" *Dallas Morning News*, May 18, 1958, 12. Also see Robert W. Caldwell and Associates, Freese Nichols and Endress, *Comprehensive Master Plan 1964*, 68. Although the state eventually voided a home rule provision that allowed cities to reserve unincorporated land by claiming its intention to eventually annex, under a 1963 state law, cities in Texas could still reserve land by extending city limits through strips or "protector boundaries."

112. *Arlington, Texas: Urban Development Framework* (Dallas: Marvin Springer and Associates. 1971), 2–3.

113. By 1982, Mesa Junior College had an enrollment of 14,674, and the University of Texas at Arlington student population was over 20,000 then. Mesa Community College (website), "About," accessed February 4, 2022, https://www.mesacc.edu/about/history/timeline/timeline-list.

114. U.S. Census Bureau, "Quick Facts, Mesa Arizona," accessed February 4, 2022, https://www.census.gov/quickfacts/fact/table/mesacityarizona/PST045216.

115. Adam McCain, "2018's Most Diverse Cities in the U.S.," WalletHub.com, April 19, 2021, https://wallethub.com/edu/most-diverse-cities/12690/#main-findings.

116. "Mesa Population (2018-06-12)," WorldPopulationReview.com, accessed June 16, 2018, http://worldpopulationreview.com/us-cities/mesa/.

117. Richard Greene, "Nobody's Damn Suburb Keeps Getting Stronger," *Fort Worth Star Telegram* (November 3, 2013), 79.

118. Miller, *Suburb*, 229.
119. Jeffrey I. Chapman, "What Happens When a Large City Doesn't Have a Property Tax but Attempts to Enact One: A Case Study of Mesa Arizona," working paper for the Lincoln Institute of Land Policy, 2007, accessed June 9, 2020, https://www.lincolninst.edu/publications/working-papers/what-happens-when-large-city-doesnt-have-property-tax-attempts-enact-one.
120. For instance, in August 2010, only 29 percent of registered voters in Mesa participated in a municipal primary election. Arlington had similar low turnouts. Subscriptions to local newspapers declined as subscriptions to the big-city dailies of Fort Worth, Dallas, and Phoenix increased.
121. Miller, *Suburb*, xxv-xxvi. This new trend may also help explain why a report from the Pew Research Center in 2014 identified Mesa (#1) and Arlington (#6) as two of the most conservative cities in America. Indeed, many of the new postwar suburban cities listed in this report found their way to the list. Drew Desilver, "Chart of the Week: The Most Liberal and Conservative Big Cities," Pew Research Center, August 8, 2014, https://www.pewresearch.org/fact-tank/2014/08/08/chart-; Zane L. Miller, *Suburb: Neighborhood and Community in Forest Park, Ohio, 1935-1976* (Knoxville: University of Tennessee Press, 1981); Zane L. Miller, *Visions of Place: The City, Neighborhoods, Suburbs, and Cincinnati's Clifton, 1850-2000* (Columbus: Ohio State University Press, 2001); Zane L. Miller and Bruce Tucker, *Changing Plans for America's Inner Cities: Cincinnati's Over-the-Rhine and Twentieth-Century Urbanism* (Columbus: Ohio State University Press, 1998).

6

Claiming Space

Petrified Ethnics, Identity, and Civic Space

PATRICIA MOONEY-MELVIN

Lorado Taft, a Chicago sculptor known for his championship of public sculpture, lamented the creation of a "petrified congress of nations" that dotted the open spaces of his city's parks. These statues, wrote Taft, ruined the "sylvan beauty" of the parks. Natural settings, he believed, should be reserved for statuary more at one with nature, such as nymphs, animals, or Indians. The "sculptural card-index of the peoples represented in Chicago's mighty melting pot," strewn across parkscapes, benefitted no one.[1] As far as Taft was concerned, parks were to be showcases of natural beauty, green oases in an increasingly developed urban landscape. They were not to be the resting place for the likes of Schiller, von Humboldt, Reuter, Ericson, Linnés, or Garibaldi.

Although Taft failed to appreciate the importance of this use of space by urban ethnic groups, Zane L. Miller would have interpreted the situation quite differently. Miller understood the city as a crucible for forging good citizenship and identity. Good citizens, Miller argued, possessed a "civic responsibility to tolerate, understand, empathize with, and treat as equals the many different cultural groups" that inhabited the nation's urban centers. In this way, Miller suggested, it was possible to translate the one and the many into a large civic whole.[2]

While there existed many avenues to address the interaction of identity and participation in burgeoning urban communities as the nineteenth century drew to a close, Miller's appreciation of the nature of space and its ability to define and shape understanding and action in the "emerging modern city"[3] suggests that his musings on urban ethnic group identity[4] could easily accommodate the notion that ethnic communities wished to utilize space as a way to inscribe ethnic identity on the urban landscape. In the process of inscription, they marked out arenas in which to bolster simultaneously identity in both the group and the larger urban community.

It is this combination of ideas and space that signifies one of the most important ways Miller influenced my understanding of urban history. Miller emphasized ideas as modes of thought distinctive in particular periods. While some of these modes appear to transcend periods, each period retains a distinctive approach and articulation that defines it as separate, even if linked, from other chronological periods.[5] My formative experience as Miller's mentee occurred between *Boss Cox's Cincinnati: Urban Politics in the Progressive Era* (1968) and *Suburb: Neighborhood and Community in Forest Park, Ohio, 1935–1976* (1981).[6] Particularly compelling in our discussions was the idea of the city as an organism, which shaped my MA thesis and dissertation work, as my understanding of this notion emerged from the ways in which turn-of-the-century urban activists utilized the organic metaphor to visualize and then act upon this visualization in their approach to defining the city and its constituent parts—that is, the metropolis and its neighborhoods. This mode of thinking was symbiotic. It described the historical actors' beliefs about how things should be while at the same time it shaped their actions, creating programs and influencing policy in ways that put their ideas into action while simultaneously promoting their vision of the city. Our conversations on the nature of the city and why the subjects of my study operated in the way that they did owed much to the process of discussing, writing, and revising my dissertation chapters and, as I finished up, Miller's engagement with the Forest Park study.

The men and women in my dissertation—and later book[7]—wrestled with the challenge of the large urban space and the disruption they saw as a result of the rapid social and economic changes in the urban communities in which they lived as the nineteenth century drew to a close. These urban reformers crafted a vision of the city that allowed them to impose order on an exploding city that appeared no longer to be a whole but rather composed of parts with little binding them together. Even as they engaged in action to confront the problems they found in the urban environment, they searched to understand how their actions contributed to an understanding of the nature of the city. As men and women of their time, they borrowed an analogy popular in discussions about society and envisioned the urban community as an organism composed of interdependent parts. For the larger whole to work well, the problems facing the various parts needed fixing so that the city in its entirety would function well for the benefit of all of its inhabitants.[8] The University of Chicago sociologists dismissed these men and women as sentimental reformers who only saw the city as a "'happy hunting ground' of movements" without possessing an understanding of the new urban world they faced.[9] However, these men and women emerged from my research and analysis as something much different. They were, in fact, men and women who directly confronted the dynamics of the late nineteenth- and early twentieth-century city and developed theories and strategies for addressing it.

As Miller pushed me to disentangle the actions of the reformers from their ideas and then reengage with them by comparing and contrasting what they did and said, it became clear that through a dynamic interaction between theory and praxis they articulated a conception of the city that provided the base upon which to confront the problems they found facing urban dwellers as the twentieth century dawned. What Ernest W. Burgess and the other Chicago sociologists dismissed as action without theory was, in fact, a failure on their part to understand that people organized reality differently during different periods and that no theory of the city transcended time and place. In his announcement that he and his colleagues had "the" theory of the city in the 1920s, Burgess demonstrated that a new mode of thought had replaced one that no longer seemed useful in understanding American urban communities. Even if the words used by Burgess and his colleagues appeared the same as those they called sentimental reformers, the meanings Burgess ascribed to the words meant something different—no more right or wrong than what came before.[10]

Our engagement with the relationship between the large and the small community and civic health during the conversations about my work and Miller's reviews of my dissertation drafts revealed the multitude of ways that turn-of-the-century citizens adjusted to the cityscape of late nineteenth- / early twentieth-century America. The clear takeaway from the process was that discussing urban form contextually offered the opportunity to understand the "particular notions of reality popular during different historical periods and the attempts of contemporaries to address the various issues or problems confronting them based on prevailing beliefs."[11] At the same time, these conversations underscored the visualization of ideas on the urban landscape and the ways that contemporaries utilized this approach to signify points of view.

Long before the publication of current discussions of the landscape, Miller brought space and place into his analytical framework. His approach to the understanding of the spatial elements of the modern city reflects that category of landscape study that rests upon a historical sensitivity toward the nature of change, suggesting that landscapes are not static but change over time and can reflect a variety of historical experiences.[12] Dell Upton characterizes such understanding as the "seen and the unseen." The analysis of multiple texts, in addition to the visual, and contextualizing the landscape in time and place,[13] allow us to appreciate what Miller would see as the interaction between modes of thought and the cityscape over time. Miller's geographic sensibility in *Boss Cox's Cincinnati* and the way in which he utilized space as an interpretive tool in combination with ideas represent a central component of his mentorship. In the world of mid-1970s urban history with its emphasis on quantification, ideas and space provided me with the tools to make sense of the late nineteenth- / early twentieth-century city.

Urban Statuary and Civic Space

It is the intersection of ideas, place, and action or, one could say, the visualization of ideas on the cityscape, that brings us back to Chicago's petrified ethnics. Any understanding of a landscape's meaning rests on an appreciation of the intersection of people and place. Landscapes, as Paul Groth has suggested, represent "crucibles of cultural meaning."[14] For Chicago's ethnic communities during the late nineteenth century, the placement of granite and bronze ethnics in public parks represented important statements about who they were. Situating a monument in a public space represented a "ritual occasion" at which members of a group created an interruption in local life and utilized this intrusion in time to highlight issues deemed important to the ethnic community.[15]

Ethnic statuary served both a commemorative and didactic purpose. As a touchstone for ethnic memory, these statues offered immigrant communities the opportunity to honor someone important in their past. At the same time, however, these statues represented a physical way to assert that ethnic groups were a part of a larger American—in this case, Chicago—community. Their existence in Chicago's parks reflects the often tenuous balance between the retention of cultural identity and the pressure to assimilate into American society, the reality of the one and the many played out in physical form. The monuments and the activities surrounding their placement and celebration allowed ethnic communities to combine issues of descent and consent in a dynamic way that enabled them to assert agency in the urban community.[16] Despite Taft's condemnation of such statuary in Chicago's parks, ethnic communities saw parks as recognized civic arenas, appropriate places to reinforce community identity and be seen as a part of the fabric of urban life.

The statues were civic art with a purpose and, as such, conformed to the larger impulses that shaped an explosion of civic art in urban areas between the 1880s and the 1920s. In the years following the Civil War, sculptural biography emerged as an important form of urban public art as communities sought to come to terms with a divisive war, transforming private mourning into public emotion through monumental form and elaborate commemorative public rituals. The sculptural program of the 1893 World's Columbian Exposition generated interest in civic monuments as well. Biographical statuary, in particular, was believed to serve as a way to translate the relatively nebulous notion of civic loyalty into tangible form. The granite and bronze portraits commemorated individuals designated as significant and imbued with some larger meaning for the general public.[17] Across the nation between the end of the Civil War and the New Deal, both small and large communities erected statues that compose, in essence, a secular pantheon of role models for the public.[18]

The placement of this sculpture in parks reflected a belief on the part of many turn-of-the-century park planners and developers that park landscapes could affect individual character, social relations, and civic identification.[19] This interpretation of the role of parks had not always been the dominant one. Mid-nineteenth-century park advocates reacted against what they perceived as an artificial urban environment completely lacking the serenity and rejuvenating qualities they associated with the natural world. Even though they too were constructed spaces, rural parks characterized by woods, grassy open spaces, meandering paths, and ponds would stand in sharp contrast to the mind-numbing grid of the city. The rustic park environs proponents envisioned would promote the larger public health—physical as well as mental—of urban dwellers. As a synthesis of nature and city, mid-nineteenth-century planned parks offered a "middle landscape" nestled between the world of man and nature.[20] Like Taft, these individuals saw parks primarily as calming green spaces designed to provide a restorative tonic to urbanites or as a refuge from a man-made environment, not places for civic engagement.[21]

While late nineteenth-century advocates of urban parks did not reject beliefs about the importance of communing with nature for city residents, this element of urban park ideology grew less compelling by the 1880s. According to David Schuyler, "nostalgic pastoralism or the silent influence of natural scenery"[22] seemed increasingly inadequate in cities with burgeoning foreign populations. As part of the civic landscape, parks should demonstrate, instead, social responsibility beyond the provision of health and natural interaction. In this context, perceived as places that promoted notions of respectability and character development, parks possessed the ability to provide a unifying aspect in what seemed to be an increasingly "fractious city society."[23]

One source of that friction, immigration, doubled between 1870 and 1890, and to many Americans, park planners included, it appeared that American society resembled a collection of ethnic enclaves that existed without "cultural endorsement or mutual understanding." The belief that the nation possessed an unlimited ability to absorb diverse groups and fuse them into one entity no longer held much currency.[24] American culture appeared not to be unified but particularistic, and distance rather than absorption seemed to characterize society. Urban conditions demanded, as Schuyler has argued, "a new civic order"[25] that utilized park space in a different way. The situation represented "a moment of redefinition," in Miller's parlance, during which urbanities reenvisioned the world around them and then acted in new ways to solve perceived problems.[26]

In this context, late nineteenth-century park planners emphasized the relationship between public arenas and civic education. As constructed civic spaces, parks combined opportunities for reflection, recreation, education, individual displays of cultivation, and social mingling. According to Daniel Bluestone, "park planners and designers ascribed to particular design elements the capacity to affect the character of individuals who experienced the landscape," and "the idea that landscape might shape thinking, sensibility, and social experience was central to park rationale."[27] As manipulated spaces, parks provided an excellent slate upon which to sketch the basic tenets of civic identity believed critical in urban areas experiencing the twin traumas of dramatic economic growth and massive in-migration of newcomers.

Monumental art provided an avenue to transform ideals about the importance of civic life into physical form. Public monuments, of which statues are a part, contain three essential attributes. First, their public designation anticipates a wide audience. These structures are not intended solely for private use but provide the opportunity to engage with a diverse audience. Indeed, the success of public monuments rests on their ability to communicate with the public, eliciting a range of responses from those who encounter them intentionally or through happenstance. Second, the site and scale of public monuments suggest something about the level of relevance to a community and the available resources.[28] Third, these monuments were imbued with didactic or commemorative purposes. Statuary, in particular, was identified as a three-dimensional vehicle for nurturing civic consciousness. Situated in public areas, statues emphasize the fact of existence, celebrate identity, and foster a sense of community through a shared experience and as well reflect prevailing values and cultural norms. They represent a way to make aspects of the past more tangible. As public art, they not only reflect but also contribute to a culture. In so doing, statues possess the potential to influence thought and experience.[29]

Monuments have embodied different meanings at different times, and this is no less true of their settings. In the antebellum rural cemetery, monuments promoted the "contemplation of moral subjects." Mid-nineteenth-century park advocates believed that monuments detracted from the "contemplation of natural beauty."[30] By the end of the century, as Paul Boyer has pointed out, reformers worried about the paucity of "landmarks, traditions, and civic symbolism."[31] What was needed, they believed, were tangible symbols whose very presence could help stimulate the "surge of civic loyalty"[32] necessary to integrate a city's disparate elements into a larger whole. Statues, monuments, and other types of civic edifices that pictorially represented history and American traditions could stimulate patriotism and civic loyalty. Slowly but surely in the years after the Civil War, park landscapes became less "natural" and more "educational and associational,"[33] representing canvases upon which the social life of urban communities grappled with the economic and political positioning of various groups.

In the turmoil of the late nineteenth-century city, central elements of the process of situating ethnic monuments in urban parks, which included the use of the street and large gatherings in public parks, ran up against larger political concerns about order and perceptions of violence. These events simultaneously generated a fear of the "foreign" on the part of some members of the urban community and represented the opportunity to stress inclusion for others. The tension inherent between fear and opportunity during this period reveals another way in which particular groups attempted to establish both imaginative and physical control of the cityscape.[34] Susan G. Davis has suggested that nineteenth-century urbanites utilized "collective gatherings and vernacular dramatic techniques—reading aloud, oratory, festivals, work stoppages, mass meetings, and parades—to propose ideas about social relations."[35] Such activities utilized space to define identity in urban settings.[36] If rhetoric and street theater offered opportunities to show power and make a point, the physicality of monuments suggested a way to ensure the transcendence of memory beyond the contemporary world. The planting of monuments and such associated activities as parades and oratory represented a "desire of all parties involved to dramatize and thereby validate their view of current social reality."[37] At the same time, they provided official sanction through securing of the rights to use the street and the necessary governmental approval through the process of site selection.

Although the emphasis of civic leaders stressed the development of an ethic of civic loyalty that, not surprisingly, was grounded in the identification with American culture and government, specific ethnic commemoration and recognition had a role to play. This was particularly true in communities with sizeable ethnic populations like Chicago. Although its ethnic composition has varied over time, ethnicity represents a central component of Chicago's demographic experience. Prior to the 1840s, the Irish, Germans, and Norwegians diversified Chicago's population. During the 1840s and 1850s, an additional surge of Germans and Irish further swelled the area's population. After the Civil War, the ethnic makeup of Chicago's residents grew increasing diverse. Bohemians, English, Swedish, Canadian, Polish, and Norwegian migrants joined the Germans and Irish as identifiable ethnic communities in the rapidly growing metropolis. By 1920, over two million foreign newcomers had arrived, and the Poles, Russians, Bohemians, Italians, Dutch, Hungarians, Austrians, and Czechs represented the significant immigrant sources.[38] Each group carved out spaces for itself—work, religious, recreational, and political—and navigated the boundaries between ethnic identification and the larger "American" (U.S. national) community.[39] Within Chicago, ethnic groups altered the dynamics of the workplace, diversified the city's religious architectural infrastructure and denominational practices, and shaped the routine of local life and neighborhood identification. These internal tribal markers of ethnic identity and community-building efforts notwithstanding, ethnic groups desired a more public citywide recognition that moved beyond their localistic worlds to a place within the greater civic landscape.

Reflecting an approach to the study of ethnicity that has focused on immigrant gifts rather than a dynamic interrelationship between assimilation and empowerment,[40] Daniel Bluestone has argued that the energetic efforts of Chicago's ethnic groups to establish monuments to their national heroes reflected the desire of immigrant communities to emphasize the contributions they had made to America. In so doing, their campaigns for public sculpture helped "[knit] immigrant Americans into a cosmopolitan nation rather than [celebrate] diversity or separateness of immigrant life."[41] The "petrified congress of nations,"[42] in this context, "enriched American life" rather than posed "an alternative." The petrified ethnics served as a prop for a larger civic unity.[43]

While this approach to understanding the reasons for commemorative activity—enshrine ideals, bridge communities, and stress unity—represents an element of ethnic ritual activity, an interpretation grounded in immigrant gifts, such as Bluestone's, reflects in effect the perspective of those involved in the creation of an "official culture." There is an alternative perspective that appreciates the way in which members of ethnic communities pursue agendas of their own. Through such vehicles as festive rituals or statuary campaigns, for example, ethnic groups drew on elements of their own culture in ways that inserted their presence more visibly into the public sphere while at the same time not threatening civic disorder as the types of activities chosen were part of American civic culture.[44] While these agendas, as interpreted by the larger society through a particular lens, in this case that of a larger civic unity, reflected a desired image, the construction placed on this activity by the proponents of granite and bronze ethnics differed both in the meanings attached and the purposes to be served. As Miller suggested in his musings on German immigrants in Cincinnati, immigrant communities wanted both to promote the group and see the group as a part of a larger pluralistic urban community.[45] Groups campaigning for the placement of their particular petrified ethnic did not necessary eschew identification and participation in the larger American polity. What they wanted was an opportunity to celebrate, on their terms, heterogeneity that was not necessarily divisive but rather part of a larger collective whole.

Chicago's Germans and Spatial Politics

As Chicago's park system developed, associational monuments populated its vistas and highlighted the importance of park spaces as landscapes for group identity. The Chicago park system formally began with the passage of legislation in 1869 that established large, landscaped parks along the lakefront and at the edge of the city. Three commissions—the Lincoln, West, and South—were organized to guide the destinies of Chicago's parks. Park commissioners were empowered to accept "personal property" for the parks, such as works of art initiated and financed by private individuals and groups. Once in the parks, these items became park property.[46] By the 1870s, Lincoln Park, located along the lakefront north of the Loop, emerged as the city's "showcase" park. Heroic sculpture served as a popular expression of civic character, and the arrival of each piece of statuary in the park came amid a range of ceremonial events and public spectacles.[47] As the twentieth century opened, Lincoln Park possessed more commemorative portraiture statuary than any of the other Chicago parks,[48] and the park commissioners noted in their 1895 annual report that the park was "indebted to prominent citizens and societies for a number of pleasing statues."[49] The public nature of these monuments, whether publicly funded or not, utilized park space as a "special imprimatur" for the message of the monument and its supporters.[50] The desire to include memorials in Lincoln Park suggests the importance contemporaries placed on the park as an associational center.

Not surprisingly, then, Lincoln Park became the home of the city's first petrified ethnic since it was "the" park in which to be located. The Germans, one of the largest ethnic groups in Chicago during the late nineteenth century and one that possessed a belief in its own cultural equity—if not cultural superiority—with American culture, inaugurated the efforts of the city's immigrant communities to "people" the parks.[51] Melvin G. Holli has suggested that the scope of "public expression of German ethnicity"[52] falls far short of the size of the German migration to America and the subsequent expansion of the larger German American community. Miller and Guido Dobbert found Germans in Cincinnati during the late nineteenth century feeling the need to think about the nature of group identity despite the sizeable nature of German migration to the city. Of concern to Germans in Cincinnati was process and sustainability. How should groups work toward a particular identity and how, once in place, to ensure that it lasted? Their concerns, Miller and Dobbert noted, were not unique among German communities throughout the United States although the tactics of these identity crusaders varied.[53] Although each of the major ethnic communities in Chicago participated in the monument enterprise, given Miller's attention to Cincinnati's German community's engagement with identity, only the efforts to utilize park space to promote German identity in Chicago are highlighted in this chapter. The Germans, ultimately, set the pattern for late nineteenth- / early twentieth-century monument building in the city, and the protocol they established was followed by the Czechs, Italians, Scots, Swedes, Danes, and Norwegians.

During the late nineteenth century, Chicago's German community sought to inject physically the German presence into the larger civic consciousness in a manner that attempted to move beyond an association with labor radicalism toward a more nonpoliticized identification. In retrospect, this desire seems prescient as it is clear that the late nineteenth century represents both the high point and commencement of a steady decline of German labor activism in Chicago. Middle-class sentiments, a relatively high level of economic success, cultural predominance, and increasing political acceptance converged as the predominant theme as many of German descent constructed a group identity in the years after the conclusion of the Civil War until the outbreak of World War I.[54]

The German community possessed a rich associational life, with clubs and organizations established for cultural activities, recreational pursuits, and relief efforts. Among the most significant clubs was the Schwabenverein, organized in 1878. A compatriotic club whose membership transcended German regional identification for the pursuit of larger common goals, the Schwabenverein took the lead in the establishment of the German monumental presence in Chicago.[55] Drawing upon an established tradition of public commemoration among German Americans across the United States, Chicago's German American community combined parades and monumental presence to highlight its place within a specific community as well as to suggest sympathy with larger themes in American life. According to Kathleen Neils Conzen, German Americans possessed a festive ritual repertoire that combined assembly, parades, performance, and, on occasion, monumental specificity. This activity served a twofold purpose, providing information to an internal as well as an external audience. Despite the differences in religious affiliation, class, political persuasion, and region of descent, these festive occasions offered the opportunity to present a communal front to the outside world, stress a commonly held belief in the "superiority of homeland culture,"[56] promote a sense of group consciousness and ethnic identity,[57] and assert membership in the larger community in which they lived.

As one of its earliest projects, the Schwabenverein launched a drive to memorialize the Schwabian Johann Friedrich von Schiller on November 18, 1879.[58] A donation of five hundred dollars to what became the "Schiller fund" set things in motion.[59] The club called on all Germans to participate in the fundraising drive and earmarked some funds from its own treasury to help defray the cost of the monument.

The monument committee contacted the Lincoln Park commissioners, received approval for the project, and secured a site for the monument east of the Webster Avenue entrance of the park as well as a commitment from the Lincoln Park commissioners to pay for the statue's foundation.[60]

Schiller, one of Germany's renowned dramatists and poets who argued passionately for the cause of human freedom, served as the centerpiece of German festive and memorial culture in nearly every city with a German immigrant population. In keeping with other Schiller commemorations, Chicago's Germans found in Schiller an example of the best in German culture that reflected the essence of freedom found in the immigrants' new homeland, the United States. In many respects, Schiller represented the "ideal" German to commemorate. His contributions to culture and freedom rendered him uncontroversial both within the German community and without. He was an acceptable symbol to make a statement about the community's existence in the present.[61]

The idea of the statue moved toward reality by the mid-1880s. On November 11, 1885, the cornerstone of the monument was laid in the park before a crowd of about four thousand people. Julius Rosenthal, chair of the Schiller Monument Committee, addressed the gathering. He stressed that support came from across the German community, a situation made possible by Schiller's standing as a proponent of liberty and individual freedom. The date of May 8, 1886, the anniversary of Schiller's death, was set for the unveiling of the statue.[62] However, Schiller's formal arrival at Lincoln Park did not take place until May 15, 1886. In response to the Haymarket Riot of May 4, 1886,[63] Mayor Carter H. Harrison issued a proclamation that limited the use of streets and other public gathering places. The Schwabenverein's Monument Committee asked the mayor if the unveiling of the statue could continue since the festivities included not only a parade but also a large crowd of Schiller supporters. According to the *Chicago Daily Tribune*, the mayor indicated that in the context of the Haymarket violence, "if a large crowd assembled in Lincoln Park . . . it would be claimed that workingmen should be allowed to meet in public places to discuss labor topics." As a result, the club postponed the unveiling of the monument for a week in deference to the mayor's wishes, who then used the postponed ceremony to make a point about the limits of liberty and the need for order.[64]

Despite inclement weather, approximately eight thousand people watched as the Chicago Citizens of German Descent unveiled the statue of Johann Christoph Friedrich von Schiller and presented it to the park commissioners on May 15, 1886. A copy of the 1876 statue erected in his memory in his hometown of Marbach, Germany, the Schiller monument was the work of the German sculptor Ernst Rau. The bronze figure, cast in Stuttgart, portrays Schiller with a scroll in one hand and a pencil in the other. The granite base, designed by John Gall, is typical of Victorian stonework.[65] The address by Mayor Carter H. Harrison applauded the committee for its efforts. He noted to a round of applause that "Schiller loved liberty, but he loved liberty with law" and that "he died not to arouse the people to become rioters and anarchists but to be orderly lovers of liberty." In his address to the crowd, William Rapp of the *Staats-Zeitung* reiterated the distance between those involved in the Haymarket Riot and the larger German American community. According to Rapp, "all true German-Americans live as Schiller taught and they are in no way responsible for the crimes of ungrateful, half-crazy fools neither German nor American but internationalists, and without a fatherland." A banquet in the park boathouse rounded out the event.[66]

In the context of the riot, ethnic disorder seemed a manifestation of the explosive tendencies of urban culture, and the selection of Schiller served as an antidote to the larger controversy about immigrants and their place in urban society. While this was not necessarily the original intent of the selection of Schiller and the drive for the installation of the statue, the mayor and other speakers used him to present a less radical view of life in a city with a sizeable immigrant population. Over time, the statue served as a gathering place for other German American events and can be seen as a touchstone of German American cultural politics.[67] The construction campaign and the festive event reminded the larger public that the Germans possessed a seat at the table as equals and reminded members of their own community that elements of German culture and thought represented important points of individual identification and ties to the culture of descent.[68] Additionally, it offered the German American community an opportunity to frame how it wished to be viewed.

The Schiller monument served as the general model for the monument drives subsequently launched by the Germans as well as those organized by other immigrant groups. Once an ethnic group decided to support the construction of a monument, the group raised money, selected a sculptor who often was a member of the ethnic group in question, worked with the city to find a proper site, and highlighted the dedication day with parades, speeches, and other festivities. While the monument represented the permanent piece of the event, the parades and large gatherings in the parks were equally as important as they reflected a "right" to use the street and the park in ways beyond the ordinary. Like parades and festivities before the Civil War, these activities had a point to make; however, after the Civil War, the point included, among other things, a statement about a group's importance in the city and the ability to demonstrate order and respectability.[69] Commemoration committee organizers created activities that stressed ethnic affiliation as well as commitment to America. Event orators also reflected this duality. The contemporary narrative structure of public addresses[70] shaped their organization and included information already known to the community being honored as well as larger references to the relationship between the ethnic community in question and universal American ideals. The public ceremonial activity allowed citizens of a particular descent to "learn, invent, and practice a common language," showcased at the event but useful at other times and in other places, and statues represented a very physical insertion of the group into the city's civic space.[71]

Schiller's arrival in Lincoln Park marked the beginning of an ethnic presence throughout Chicago's park system. Ethnic statuary entered the West Park system in 1892, and, as was the case in Lincoln Park, the Germans led the way. On October 16 of that year ten thousand people attended the unveiling of the Alexander von Humboldt monument in Humboldt Park, a gift of Francis J. Dewes, president of the Francis J. Dewes Brewery, who, like von Humboldt, hailed from Prussia.[72] The German Press Club orchestrated the festivities to honor the German scientist who launched expeditions in the Americas as well as Europe. According to the *Chicago Times*, Mayor Hempstead Washburne extolled the German people's many gifts to the world as he accepted the statue on behalf of the city. Situated in a central spot along the park's main boulevard, von Humboldt (Felix Görling, sculptor) looks out over a grassy plain. At his side is a globe; his hands hold his book, *Cosmos*, and an iguana, all symbolizing his travels and the role his work played in the development of physical geography and geophysics.[73] Like Schiller, von Humboldt represented for the German American community a twin mirror. During the nineteenth century, von Humboldt emerged as both a proponent of republican values forged during the French Revolution and a renowned scientist whose studies in the Americas earned him the respect of the Western scientific community. In the United States, his ecological sensitivity that integrated the scientific, physical, and human elements of life influenced not only American scientists but also the artistic and literary community as well. His funeral in 1859 in Berlin far surpassed what was commonly seen for a private citizen, and American supporters and members of the German American community initiated a series of von Humboldt memorial activities across the nation.[74]

On May 14, 1893, another German notable, Fritz Reuter, joined von Humboldt in the park. Fritz Reuter, a German novelist, was known for his contribution to the creation of a distinctive German literature and his struggle against political oppression. Approximately sixty thousand members of the German community came out to celebrate Reuter's arrival. Most of the orators spoke in German and stressed that Reuter's statue (Franz Englesman, sculptor) would stand as a "reminder to German-Americans of the freedom of speech and of the press which they enjoyed in their adopted land, but which Germans, [such as Reuter], had not always enjoyed." William Vocke, speaking in English, described Reuter as a writer admired by readers across the world while at the same time being Germany's special pride.[75] As with Schiller and von Humboldt, the German American community used this occasion to highlight the ties between German and American culture while at the same time celebrating the strengths of their German heritage.

Balancing the Culture of Assent and Descent

What can this cursory review of Chicago's German petrified ethnics tell us? Many turn-of-the-century Americans, concerned about the transformation of foreigners into Americans, believed that if immigrants felt that the host society appreciated immigrant culture, the newcomers would more readily accept the way of life of their adopted country. It would be easier, according to this view, to gently but firmly guide immigrant groups into active participation in the host society.[76] If park commissioners let ethnic groups place commemorative statuary in the same parks with American patriotic memorials, then immigrant communities, so the logic ran, would see this as a sign that they were accepted as part of the larger American society. In addition, since the host society had to approve all proposed memorials, those possessing official cultural power shaped the representation available for the various ethnic groups to use.

Certainly, as Bluestone suggests,[77] the desire on the part of Chicago's ethnic communities to have their representative of choice in the parks reflects their interest in calling attention to what they have contributed to America. Virtually all selections during the late nineteenth and early twentieth century not only emphasized the compatibility of ethnic heritage with American ideals but also reminded the communities of descent of the importance of their ethnic origins. At least one of the speakers during each of these dedication ceremonies focused on identifying a contribution to celebrate and that was relatable to American life as well as voicing the group's attachment to its adopted homeland. What appears central, however, in their public statements and in the choice of subjects was the use of selected symbols that served to rejuvenate loyalty to ethnic as well as American heritage.

In doing so, they may not have, as Bluestone indicates, wanted to pose a divisive alternative. Nonetheless, while members of ethnic communities may have sought to become an integral part of American society, they did not necessarily wish to do so at the expense of their own sense of attachment to their culture of descent. They preferred to accommodate in ways that did not negate their own experience and values. John Bodnar has argued in his discussion of urban public memory that while individual ethnics or specific ethnic groups were interested in becoming part of the American political and economic world, they continued to hold ties to their ancestral cultures. They adopted strategies that allowed for an expression of "patriotism and consent but in clearly ethnic terms."[78] As Michele Bogart found in New York City, ethnic communities utilized ethnic "hero memorials" to insert both "literally and figuratively" themselves "in the metropolis."[79] Their decision to juxtapose simultaneously loyalty to communities of consent and descent suggests that they read into and drew out of the commemorative process what they—not necessarily the host country—wanted. Additionally, even if all members of each ethnic group did not fully support the selected symbol, these statues represented a cultural defense against the imposition of solely American notions of who was appropriate to honor and what type of lessons to be learned from national heroes. As both Bodnar and Michael Wallace have pointed out, symbols are manufactured.[80] Regardless of their origin, their proponents hope to use this form of monumentality to shape perceptions about what is important to their present. Certainly, cultural elites used statuary and historic sites as visible symbols of the lessons to be learned by a larger public. What is important to recognize, however, is the way in which others co-opted the medium for a different sort of message—humoring the elite prescriptions of appropriateness while at the same time sending a message that bolstered ethnic pride and identity. Such a situation suggests that "national" and "ethnic" (or elite and vernacular) visions can coexist but that the motives for construction and meanings inferred may resonate differently depending on the audience. Coexistence, however, is not necessarily a case of parallelism. Rather, it is a dynamic mixture that can satisfy two masters simultaneously. As Miller suggested, ethnic communities drew from their past to bolster contemporary ethnic group identity while at the same time set the stage "for the emergence and nurture of something different"[81]— that is, pluralism rather than homogeneity. Statuary situated in the public sphere represented a vehicle for Chicago's ethnic communities to balance uniqueness and integration and exert agency in the face of efforts to enforce conformity.

Claiming Space and Civic Engagement

Ethnic communities drew on their past to make a statement in their present about the fact of their existence and utilized spatial politics as a part of their representational strategy. As Mary Ryan has suggested, civic arenas such as parks provide opportunities for interaction during which "people can actually see each other in all their diversity and can mobilize, debate, form identities, and forge coalitions."[82] The creation of associational moments acknowledge life in a heterogeneous city while at the same time foster group identification. The nineteenth century's "instability of nationality" fractured into, among other things by the late nineteenth century, campaigns for American national conformity and drives for what become known as cultural pluralism. Into this debate over the nature of nationality, ethnic monuments inscribed the idea of the one and the many on the landscape in a highly scripted and public manner. These ritual moments, Ryan suggests, served dual roles as "staging grounds and exercises of public life."[83] Miller would see these moments as good citizenship and identity forged in the civic arena. The ethnic actors participating in these ritual events may have lived in parts of the city defined during their period as ethnic enclaves à la the Chicago sociologists' vision of ethnicity characterized by supposed homogeneity and distance and separation from the large body politic.[84] However, they defined their world as something larger. Their engagement in the public sphere was shaped by both tribal and inclusive motivations.

By selecting the medium of memorial civic statuary, ethnic communities desired remembrance, one that seemingly transcended time as statues present an image of permanence. Taft's concerns about the injection of petrified ethnics into urban parks represented a requiem for a changed view of parks as civic spaces. While park designers and managers allowed for spaces within parks that boasted "sylvan beauty" and a tonic from the bustle of city life, parks increasingly became home to a wide range of statuary, "educational and associational" elements that represented efforts to stimulate national loyalty and civic identification.[85] As Henri Lefebvre has suggested, "space is permeated with social relations; it is not only supported by social relations but it is also producing and produced by social relations."[86] The placement of petrified ethnics in Chicago's parks reflected the proposition that the urban landscape represented a "spatial form of social life and power relations" designed to encourage good citizenship.[87] Miller's emphasis on the civic responsibility of urban dwellers to "tolerate, understand, emphasize with, and treat as equals the many different cultural groups"[88] inhabiting the city and his appreciation for the dynamic combination of ideas, space, and action in the urban setting suggest that he understood the importance of space as both a lens of analysis and a physical reflection of ideas and action.

When one visits Lincoln Park or Humboldt Park, the statues of Schiller, von Humboldt, and Reuter tug the eye and, in so doing, proclaim their existence. As physical representations of the social production of public space, they transcend silence by the sheer fact of their existence. The historic landscape and the contemporary one intertwine in dynamic ways. While the moment of their production and celebration has passed, they provide evidence of decisions made in the past and raise questions about whom and what should be remembered. At a very basic level, they bear witness to another time[89]—despite their seemingly inactivity or silence—and, as tangible traces of the past, they ask for remembrance.

Additionally, the very fact of their existence serves as a reminder of a degree of ethnic complexity easily hidden in today's city of African, Asian, and Latin American immigrants. The "old immigrant" communities set the accepted parameters for expressing ethnic pride, and they provided a model for using public art to mark public space. Although the period, memory space, and ethnic group are different, the large-scale metal Puerto Rican flags that bookend Chicago's Paseo Boricua, the heart of the Puerto Rican community on Division Street, reflect the same duality of meaning as the statuary of the nineteenth-century petrified ethnics. Their ability to simultaneously express consent and descent in ethnic terms, whether as monuments or public art, allows these installations to transcend the official memory desired by those managing public space and create a memory environment that validates the experiences of both past and present ethnic communities.

Zane L. Miller's appreciation of the interaction between space and ideas highlights the ways in which urban dwellers inscribe decisions, predispositions, and meanings they deem important in the cityscape. Civic spaces represent arenas in which to grapple with the challenges and opportunities of urban life. In the spirit captured in Zane L. Miller's *Boss Cox's Cincinnati*, ethnic communities utilized statuary and public art to impose intellectual order on and find meaning in the urban environment. The manipulation of urban space over time and the uses to which it has been put suggest the important role cities play in the forging or dismantling of community and identity.

NOTES

1. Lorado Taft, "The Monuments of Chicago," *Art and Archaeology* 12 (September–October 1921): 124.

2. Zane L. Miller, "Thinking, Politics, City Government: Charter Reform in Cincinnati, 1880–1990s," *Queen City Heritage* 55 (Winter 1997): 28.

3. Zane L. Miller, *Boss Cox's Cincinnati: Urban Politics in the Progressive Era* (Chicago: University of Chicago Press, 1968), 55.

4. Zane L. Miller, "Cincinnati Germans and the Invention of an Ethnic Group," in *Ethnic Diversity and Civic Identity: Patterns of Conflict and Cohesion in Cincinnati since 1820*, ed. Henry D. Shapiro and Jonathan D. Sarna (Urbana: University of Illinois Press, 1992), 165–179.

5. Zane L. Miller to Patricia Mooney-Melvin, email, June 2, 2015; and Patricia Mooney Melvin, *The Organic City: Urban Definition and Neighborhood Organization 1880–1920* (Lexington: University Press of Kentucky, 1987), 9.

6. Miller, *Boss Cox's Cincinnati*; and Zane L. Miller, *Suburb: Neighborhood and Community in Forest Park, Ohio, 1935–1976* (Knoxville: University of Tennessee Press, 1981).

7. Mooney Melvin, *Organic City*.

8. Mooney Melvin, 11–26; and Patricia Mooney-Melvin, "The Neighborhood-City Relationship," in *American Urbanism: A Historiographical Review*, ed. Howard Gillette and Zane L. Miller (Westport, CT: Greenwood, 1987), 257–270.

9. Ernest W. Burgess, ed., *The Urban Community* (Chicago: University of Chicago Press, 1926), viii.

10. Mooney Melvin, *Organic City*, 1–2.

11. Mooney Melvin, 2; and Miller, *Suburb*. Other studies useful in thinking through these issues include John Brewer, *Party Politics and Popular Politics as the Accession of George III* (Cambridge: Cambridge University Press, 1976); Thomas Bender, *Community and Social Change in America* (New Brunswick, NJ: Rutgers University Press, 1978); and Philip Abrams, "History, Sociology, Historical Sociology," *Past and Present* 87 (May 1980): 3–16.

12. Michael P. Conzen, "Introduction," in *The Making of the American Landscape*, ed. Michael P. Conzen (New York: Routledge, 1990), 1–7.

13. Dell Upton, "Seen, Unseen, and Scene," in *Understanding Ordinary Landscapes*, ed. Paul Groth and Todd W. Bressi (New Haven, CT: Yale University Pres, 1997), 176.

14. Paul Groth, "Frameworks for Cultural Study," in *Understanding Ordinary Landscapes*, ed. Paul Groth and Todd W. Bressi (New Haven, CT: Yale University Press, 1997), 1,3.

15. Robert Bocock, *Ritual in Industrial Society: A Sociological Analysis of Ritualism in Modern England* (London: George Allen and Unwin, 1974), 39.

16. Werner Sollors, ed., *The Invention of Ethnicity* (New York: Oxford University Press, 1989), 6.

17. Paul Boyer, *Urban Masses and Moral Order in America 1820–1920* (Cambridge, MA: Harvard University Press, 1978), 261–262; Michele H. Bogart, *Public Sculpture and the Civic Ideal in New York City, 1890–1930* (Chicago: University of Chicago Press, 1989), 4; Timothy J. Garvey, *Public Sculptor: Lorado Taft and*

the Beautification of Chicago (Urbana: University of Illinois Press, 1988), 75–81; Theodore J. Karamanski, "Memory's Landscape," *Chicago History* 26 (Summer 1997): 54; Meredith Arms Bzdak, *Public Sculpture in New Jersey: Monuments to Collective Identity* (New Brunswick, NJ: Rutgers University Press, 1999), 4.

18. Bogart, *Public Sculpture*, 2; Bzdak, *Public Sculpture in New Jersey*, 6.

19. Daniel Bluestone, *Constructing Chicago* (New Haven, CT: Yale University Press, 1991), 2, 37–38.

20. David Schuyler, *The New Urban Landscape: The Redefinition of City Form in the Nineteenth-Century America* (Baltimore: Johns Hopkins University Press, 1986), 35, 59, 61; Stanley K. Shultz, *Constructing Urban Culture: American Cities and City Planning, 1800–1920* (Philadelphia: Temple University Press, 1989), 155–156.

21. Garvey, *Public Sculptor*, 86; Taft, "Public Monuments," 4; Galen Cranz, *The Politics of Park Design: A History of Urban Parks in America* (Cambridge, MA: MIT Press, 1982), 3, 5, 55–56; Bluestone, *Constructing Chicago*, 22. See also Thomas Bender, *Toward an Urban Vision: Ideas and Institutions in Nineteenth-Century America* (Lexington: University of Kentucky Press, 1975); Roderick Nash, *Wilderness and the American Mind* (New Haven, CT: Yale University Press, 1982); Roy Rosenzweig and Elizabeth Blackmar, *The Park and the People: A History of Central Park* (Ithaca, NY: Cornell University Press, 1992); and Morton White and Lucia White, *The Intellectual versus the City* (Cambridge, MA: Harvard University Press, 1961).

22. Schuyler, *New Urban Landscape*, 185.

23. Bluestone, *Constructing Chicago*, 37.

24. U.S. Bureau of the Census, *Historical Statistics of the United States, Colonial Times to 1970*, Bicentennial ed., vol. 1 (Washington, DC: Government Printing Office, 1975), 14; John Higham, *Strangers in the Land: Patterns of American Nativism, 1860–1925* (New York: Atheneum, 1971), 20–39, 234; William Gaymon and John R. Garrett, "A Blueprint for a Pluralistic Society," *Journal of Ethnic Studies* 3 (Fall 1975): 59; Patricia Mooney Melvin, "Building Muscles and Civics: Folk Dancing, Ethnic Diversity and the Playground Association of America," *American Studies* 24 (Spring 1983): 89–90.

25. Schuyler, *New Urban Landscape*, 185.

26. See Mooney Melvin, *Organic City*; and John D. Fairfield, "'The *Metropolitan* Mode of Thought': Zane L. Miller and the History of Ideas," Chapter 4 in this volume.

27. Bluestone, *Constructing Chicago*, 37.

28. Marianne Doezema, "The Public Monument in Tradition and Transition," in *The Public Monument and Its Audience*, ed. by Marianne Doezema and June Hargrove (Cleveland: Cleveland Museum of Art, 1977), 9, 63.

29. Doezema, "Public Monument," 9–21, 63; Garvey, *Lorado Taft*, 1–6; Bogart, *Public Sculpture*, 81–82.

30. Schuyler, *New Urban Landscape*, 61.

31. Boyer, *Urban Masses*, 262.

32. Boyer, 190–193, 261–264.
33. Schuyler, *New Urban Landscape*, 108.
34. Carl Smith has explored the creative tension between disorder and order and the varied narratives employed to exert control—actual as well as intellectual over the late nineteenth-century American city. See Carl Smith, *Urban Disorder and the Shape of Belief: The Great Chicago Fire, the Haymarket Bomb, and the Model Town of Pullman* (Chicago: University of Chicago, Press, 1995).
35. Susan G. Davis, *Parades and Power: Street Theatre in Nineteenth-Century Philadelphia* (Berkeley: University of California Press, 1988), 4. See also Mary P. Ryan, *Civic Wars: Democracy and Public Life in the American City during the Nineteenth Century* (Berkeley: University of California Press, 1997).
36. Dolores Hayden, "Urban Landscape History: The Sense of Space and the Politics of Space," in *Understanding Ordinary Landscapes*, ed. P. Groth and T. W. Bressi (New Haven, CT: Yale University Press, 1997), 130.
37. Smith, *Urban Disorder*, 102. See also Rosenzweig and Blackmar, *Park and the People*, 328–332.
38. Melvin G. Holli and Peter d'A. Jones, eds., *Ethnic Chicago: A Multicultural Portrait*, 4th ed. (Grand Rapids, MI: William B. Eerdmans, 1995), 5.
39. Holli and Jones, *Ethnic Chicago*, 1–14.
40. Kathleen Neils Conzen, "Phantom Landscapes of Colonization: Germans in the Making of a Pluralist America," in *The German-American Encounter: Conflict and Cooperation between Two Cultures, 1800–2000*, ed. Frank Trommler and Elliott Shore (New York: Berghahn Books, 2001), 10.
41. Bluestone, *Constructing Chicago*, 193.
42. Taft, "Monuments," 124.
43. Bluestone, *Constructing Chicago*, 193.
44. John Bodnar, *Remaking America: Public Memory, Commemoration, and Patriotism in the Twentieth Century* (Princeton, NJ: Princeton University Press, 1992), 42; and Geneviève Fabre and Jürgen Heideking, "Introduction," in *Celebrating Ethnicity and Nation: American Festive Culture from the Revolution to the Early Twentieth Century*, ed. Geneviève Fabre, Jürgen Heideking, and Kai Dreisbach (New York: Berghahn Books, 2001), 12.
45. Miller, "Cincinnati Germans," 170.
46. William H. Beckman, comp., *Laws and Ordinances concerning Lincoln Park Annotated* (July 1, 1928), 1, 3, 18–19, 132–133; Bluestone, *Constructing Chicago*, 27, 44–46. For information on similar practices in New York City, see Bogart, *Public Sculpture*, 81–87; and Rosenzweig and Blackmar, *Park and the People*, 330.
47. Bluestone, 191.
48. Bluestone, 12, 20.
49. *Annual Report of the Commissioners of Lincoln Park from April 1, 1894 to March 31, 1895* (Chicago, 1895), 8.
50. Sanford Levinson, *Written in Stone: Public Monuments in Changing Societies* (Durham, NC: Duke University Press, 1998), 89–90.

51. *Inter Ocean*, May 20, 1892, as cited in James L. Riedy, *Chicago Sculpture* (Urbana: University of Illinois Press, 1981), 193.

52. Melvin G. Holli, "German American Ethnic and Cultural Identity from 1890 Onward," in *Ethnic Chicago: A Multicultural Portrait*, 4th ed., ed. Melvin G. Holli and Peter d'A. Jones (Grand Rapids, MI: William B. Eerdmans, 1995), 93. Rudolph A. Hofmeister, *The Germans in Chicago* (Champaign, IL: Stipes, 1976), chap. 1.

53. Miller, "Cincinnati Germans," 165–168. See also Guido Dobbert, *The Disintegration of an Immigrant Community: The Cincinnati Germans, 1870–1920* (New York: Arno, 1980), chaps. 1–5.

54. Holli, "German American Ethnic," 93–109. For the importance of German American associationalism and its relationship to culture, see Conzen, "Phantom Landscapes of Colonization," 16.

55. Hofmeister, *Germans in Chicago*, 118.

56. Conzen, "Phantom Landscapes of Colonization," 12.

57. Kathleen Neils Conzen, "Ethnicity as Festive Culture: Nineteenth-Century German America on Parade," in *The Invention of Ethnicity*, ed. Werner Sollors (New York: Oxford University Press, 1989), 47–48.

58. Hofmeister, *Germans in Chicago*, 118.

59. Hofmeister, 118.

60. Once created, Lincoln Park was given the power to accept personal property within the limits of the park under terms negotiated between the donor and the park. Once accepted, the park commissioners possessed the power to manage such property and decide its location and longevity in the park. Beckman, *Laws and Ordinances*, 18–19, 132–133; "The Schiller Statue: German Americans Making Arrangements for It in Lincoln Park," *Chicago Daily Tribune*, November 12, 1884, 8; "A Schiller Monument," *Chicago Daily Tribune*, May 9, 1885, 8; and "Schiller's Monument," *Chicago Daily Tribune*, November 12, 1885, 3.

61. Riedy, *Chicago Sculpture*, 192; Conzen, "Ethnicity as Festive Culture," 44–76.

62. "A Schiller Monument."

63. During the 1880s, the Knights of Labor, an inclusive organization that included trade unionists, small producers, and unskilled workers, called for a variety of worker-related reforms. In 1886, trade union members of the Knights called for a national eight-hour-day strike. Workers from across the country went on strike. Although generally peaceful, the Chicago strike took a violent turn. Skirmishes at the McCormick Reaper Works between the striking workers and the scabs ended in a confrontation with police and the death of two workers. Local labor radicals and anarchists called a protest meeting at Haymarket Square that evening which was peaceful until a bomb was thrown, police shot into the crowd, and eight policemen were killed. For more information, see Paul Avrich, *The Haymarket Tragedy* (Princeton, NJ: Princeton University Press, 1984); James Green, *Death in the Haymarket: A Story of Chicago, the First Labor

Movement, and the Bombing that Divided Gilded Age America (New York: Pantheon, 2006); and Smith, *Urban Disorder*.

64. "The City," *Chicago Daily Tribune*, May 7, 1886, 8.

65. "Schiller's Statue," *Chicago Times*, May 16, 1886, 14; Riedy, *Chicago Sculpture*, 190–192; Ira J. Bach and Mary Lackritz Gray, *A Guide to Chicago's Sculpture* (Chicago: University of Chicago Press, 1983), 138.

66. "Schiller's Statue."

67. Until the outbreak of World War I, the German American community held periodic celebrations around either anniversaries of Schiller's birth or death. These events were orchestrated in part by the Schwabenverein and included ceremonies at the monument as well as talks and musical performances held elsewhere in Chicago. See, for example, "Begin the Schillerfest: Germans of Chicago Celebrate Centenary," *Chicago Daily Tribune*, May 7, 1905; "Poet Schiller Is Extolled," *Chicago Daily Tribune*, November 11, 1909, 3; "Honor Birthday of Poet Schiller," *Chicago Daily Tribune*, November 10, 1913, 3.

68. Conzen, "Festive Culture," 55–56.

69. William A. Blair, *Cities of the Dead: Contesting the Memory of the Civil War on the South, 1865–1914* (Chapel Hill: University Press of North Carolina, 2004), 13; and Michele H. Bogart, *The Politics of Urban Beauty: New York and Its Art Commission* (Chicago: University of Chicago Press, 2006), 12, 106.

70. David Glassberg, "History and the Public: Legacies of the Progressive Era," *Journal of American History* 73 (March 1987): 960–961.

71. Ryan, *Civic Wars*, 15; and Fabre and Heideking, "Introduction," 13.

72. Bach and Gray, *Guide*, 320; John William Leonard and Albert Nelson Marquis, *The Book of Chicagoans: A Biographical Dictionary of Leading Living Men of the City of Chicago* (Chicago: A. N. Marquis, 1905–1917), 163.

73. Bach and Gray, *Guide*, 320; "Von Humboldt," *The Graphic*, November 12, 1892, 351; "Dedicated to Humboldt," *Chicago Times*, October 17, 1892.

74. Laura Dassow Walls, *The Passage to Cosmos: Alexander von Humboldt and the Shaping of America* (Chicago: University of Chicago Press, 2009), 303.

75. Bach and Gray, *Guide*, 319; "In Reuter's Memory," *Chicago Tribune*, May 15, 1893; "The Fritz Reuter Monument," *The Graphic*, May 20, 1893, 330.

76. Mooney Melvin, "Building Muscles," 91.

77. Bluestone, *Constructing Chicago*, 193.

78. Bodnar, *Remaking America*, 41–61, 100–108.

79. Bogart, *Politics of Urban Beauty*, 106–107.

80. John Bodnar, "Symbols and Servants: Immigrant America and the Limits of Public History," *Journal of American History* 73 (June 1986): 147; and Michael Wallace, "Visiting the Past: History Museums in the United States," *Radical History Review* 25 (October 1981): 63–96.

81. Miller, "Cincinnati Germans," 171.

82. Ryan, *Civic Wars*, 8.

83. Ryan, 12, 15

84. Zane L. Miller, "Pluralizing America: Walter Prescott Webb, Chicago School Sociology, and Cultural Regionalism," in *Essays on Sunbelt Cities and Recent Urban America*, ed. Robert B. Fairbanks and Kathleen Underwood (College Station: Texas A&M University Press, 1990), 162–163. See also Robert E. Park, Ernest W. Burgess, and Roderick McKenzie, *The City* (Chicago: University of Chicago Press, 1925); Burgess, *Urban Community*; Harvey Zorbaugh, *The Gold Coast and the Slum: A Sociological Study of Chicago's Near North Side* (Chicago: University of Chicago Press, 1929).

85. Taft, "Monuments," 124; Boyer, *Urban Masses*, 262; and Schuyler, *New Urban Landscape*, 108.

86. Henri Lefebvre, *The Production of Space*, trans. Donald Nicholson-Smith (Oxford: Blackwell, 1991), 286.

87. Gyan Prakash, "Introduction," in *The Spaces of the Modern City: Imaginaries, Politics, and Everyday Life*, ed. Gyan Prakash and Kevin M. Kruse (Princeton, NJ: Princeton University 2008), 2.

88. Miller, "Thinking, Politics, City Government," 28.

89. W. James Booth, *Communities of Memory: On Witness, Identity, and Justice* (Ithaca, NY: Cornell University Press, 2006), 73–78.

PART III

Reflections on Zane Miller

7

"I See My Job as Helping You"

Zane L. Miller the Scholar, Mentor, and Friend

CHARLES LESTER

As far as I can tell, I am Zane L. Miller's youngest and last mentee. I first met Miller in a rather unorthodox way, and our relationship developed over the years along equally unorthodox terms. Nearing the end of my second year in the MA program studying history at the University of Cincinnati, I received an email from Miller one evening inquiring about my work. I was stunned. Though he was retired for several years at this point and no longer a physical presence in McMicken Hall, his body of work and reputation as an eminent scholar were held in high esteem among my graduate student cohort. Why was such an important and accomplished scholar interested in a fledgling graduate student project, I thought. I fired off a quick and stammering reply with elation and a bit of confusion. From the first, he was interested in my project, and his excitement and encouragement for my work buoyed my own confidence and set me on the path of a professional historian. Over the next eight years, until the end of his life, Miller and I shared a relationship that grew from a traditional mentor/mentee rapport to a genuine friendship. (I am far from alone in that regard.) But our relationship was anything but traditional; it was conducted entirely via email. We never met in person; we never shook hands, never broke bread or shared cocktails. Nonetheless, I grew to know the measure of the man and was fortunate to experience a mentorship every bit as rewarding and stimulating as any I have had with more traditional advisers.

Miller's entire approach was rooted in relationships. I thought of him as a "great man" as a graduate student—the dean of American urban history—but I came to find out his greatness lay as much in his cultivation of others as it did in his academic output. For him, history was truly a collaborative form. Miller insisted that the craft of the historian is rooted in certain agreed upon standards and rigor, but he was also democratic in his belief that anyone could potentially do it—including a second-year MA student with no record of publication. Miller remained a historian even in retirement. It was in his DNA—a historian to the core. He may have stopped teaching, but he did not stop his advocacy for urban history as a field. He continued to serve as a brilliant editor and engage in scholarly production. And he never stopped fostering relationships and mentoring others. For that, I am eternally grateful.

As many other former students, colleagues, and friends can attest, Miller had a habit of emailing well into the night. Often armed with a cocktail or two, these exchanges typically began in the early evening and continued in a free-wheeling manner as premises were challenged, points argued, jokes exchanged, encouragement extended, or new avenues explored. Eventually, a cease-fire would be called and the conversation carried forward to the next morning. Invariably, the terms of the cease-fire were renegotiated the following day and still new conclusions drawn. It was a twenty-first-century Enlightenment salon in digital form. Perhaps because he was such a brilliant editor, he refused to revise his prose in these conversations.

It turns out that Miller and I were kindred spirits. We were both musicians (I, a drummer, and he, a saxophone player) who had an unbridled love for jazz and a passion for urban life and history. My scholarship blends these mutual interests with the story of the Jazz Age in urban America. Consequently, our many discussions often revolved around scholarly details and urban historiography but also could be as simple as listening recommendations for two musicians in the know. He also introduced me to other scholars via email, including a former student of his, Robert Burnham. At the time, Burnham was working on a project about African American music forms centering on Macon, Georgia (including two native sons, Otis Redding and Little Richard). Here, Miller's enthusiasm and humor shine through (I have left a portion of our email exchange unedited for errors, as well as subsequent email excerpts cited in this essay, to give a sense of our dynamic):

> To my knowledge, or recollection, Bob was not a jazz fan until he met me, and then he rather took to it. At least he would listen to it, my records (lps), or go to clubs with me in Cincinnati (I hung out a lot at the Blue Wisp, in part becuase I once played on aband with Al Nori, the trumpet player (now deceased, alas) in the Bllue Wisp Big Band, and thereby got to know von Ohlen and Steve Scjhmidt pretty well—von Ohlen told some wonderful Stan Kenton June Christie stories, ihnvolving vodka, lots of it).[1]

Miller's gift for building relationships often meant introducing likeminded scholars to one another and encouraging the sort of collaboration that was a hallmark of his approach to the field.

We shared more than just a common interest in jazz and urban history. Though I did not fully realize it at the time, our work touched on similar themes. We both advocated theories of civic nationalism and held a mutual affinity for outsiders and urban boosters. I explore these topics at length in my book (currently under revision) on the dissemination of jazz as an emerging art form during the New Negro Renaissance. I return to these themes in a second project that examines Cincinnati's contribution to rock 'n' roll history and more recent attempts of local activists to memorialize those efforts.[2] Miller's influence on my career cannot be overstated. I first knew him while a graduate student through his work as a scholar, but after we met and as our relationship evolved over the years, I was privileged to know him as a mentor. I am honored, finally, that I got to know him as a friend.

Jazz Capitals

Given our shared interests—the significance of place, boosterism, music (specifically jazz in this instance), and the impact of culture on urban life—it became clear why Miller was attracted to my work from the start. My scholarship centers on the political activism associated with the formation of jazz in the first decades of the twentieth century in a variety of urban settings from New Orleans to Memphis, St. Louis, Kansas City, Chicago, and New York City. I situate the political and social connections of early jazz within the context of the broader social movements of the day, including the first Great Migration and the Harlem Renaissance. Jazz activists articulated a vision of civic nationalism that challenged inherited modes of thought from the dominant culture and created a new language of artistic expression and urban boosterism. As such, my book project employs an interdisciplinary approach to questions of cultural identity, political mobilization and organization, migration, economic cooperation, and cultural production. Thanks in no small part to the first Great Migration, when over one million African Americans left the South to stake their claim on the American Dream in the urban North, jazz transitioned from a regional musical form to *the* national music in the 1910s and 1920s.[3] A number of scholars of the Great Migration have shed light on the grassroots leadership that facilitated northern emigration.[4] In the first few decades of the twentieth century, African Americans in scores of cities across the country were busy forging a new collective identity, known as the New Negro, expressed in the visual and performing arts, political protest, and economic enterprise culminating in the Harlem Renaissance.[5]

Consequently, my work examines the Great Migration through the lens of jazz to explore why New Orleans musicians left the city at the turn of the twentieth century, why Chicago, New York, and other urban centers were such attractive places to ply their crafts, and what relationship these locales have to the Great Migration, the dissemination of jazz, and the Harlem Renaissance. As a result, the manuscript synthesizes the scholarly traditions of urban, African American, and jazz histories and challenges the traditional interpretations of the Harlem Renaissance. While jazz was a central cultural component of life in Harlem, it was also crucial to scores of cities across the country as African Americans journeyed north during the Great Migration. Jazz musicians were just as active politically as other migrants. In fact, Black artists in Chicago organized collectively to build the largest African American musicians' local in the American Federation of Musicians. Meanwhile, Black jazz activists in New York City pushed for increased political power in the nation's largest integrated musicians' local. Despite the common stereotype that characterizes musicians as apolitical, my work demonstrates that the musicians of the period were no different than their counterparts in the literary arts by shedding new light on the grassroots activism that emerged alongside the music. Thanks to historians like David Levering Lewis, the political activism of the literary arm of the Harlem Renaissance is well known.[6] Unfortunately, few have made the same connections regarding the musicians of the period. Indeed, jazz made its own Great Migration on the backs of a cadre of grassroots musician leaders whose political awareness has yet to be fully appreciated. As the clarinetist Sidney Bechet explained in 1960, "You know, there's this mood about the music, a kind of need to be moving. . . . You just can't keep the music unless you move with it."[7] This movement of the music and musicians mirrored the exodus of millions of African Americans out of the South, and it set the stage for the Jazz Age that followed. Consequently, by casting a wider net on the political and artistic achievements of the period, investigation of the New Negro of jazz broadens our understanding of Black activism of the day so closely associated with the visual and literary artists of the Harlem Renaissance. All too often, the accomplishments of the musicians of the period are relegated to a supporting role in the cultural and political engagement of the New Negro movement. These considerations lead to a deeper analysis of jazz, the Great Migration, the Harlem Renaissance, and the political activism of musicians beyond 135th Street and Lenox Avenue that will uncover the New Negro of Black music.

This work is an examination of the role jazz and jazz musicians played in forging cultural and civic institutions in New Orleans, Memphis, St. Louis, Kansas City, Chicago, New York City, and other locales in the first decades of the twentieth century. To be sure, jazz was not a phenomenon exclusive to these cities. Innovations in the music were made in dozens of urban centers across the country, including Detroit, Cleveland, Pittsburgh, and Los Angeles, to name but a few. But the work of musicians and activists in New Orleans's Storyville, Memphis's Beale Street, St. Louis's Levee District, Kansas City's 18th and Vine Neighborhood, Chicago's South Side, and in Harlem particularly illuminate New Negro activism in relation to jazz artists. It was the work of artists and activists in these communities that fundamentally transformed Black life and, with it, American culture at the turn of the twentieth century. As Miller well understood, the vitality of dynamic neighborhoods fosters the richness of urban life. The South Side and 18th and Vine communities not only made Chicago and Kansas City exciting places for African Americans to live in the first decades of the twentieth century; they also made the Great Migration and the Jazz Age watershed moments in the history of the United States.

As I discussed with Miller on several occasions, once our relationship evolved and deepened, we felt it important to detail the vibrant scene at the local, neighborhood level *and* widen the proverbial lens to compare and contrast with the broader implications for society at large. As Miller wrote (in Chapter 1 of this volume), the role dynamic cities play in national culture cannot be understated: "But it is the mix of the progressive and the conservative, the proper and the improper, that gives urban life its zest and its resilience, and the capacity of cities to function as centers for creating, sustaining, and sometimes for transforming whole societies, often by dismantling empires, ousting royal dynasties, or revolutionizing nation-states." By situating jazz musicians at both the local level *and* within the larger framework of the Great Migration, it becomes evident that elements of the jazz musicians' experiences were representative of the out-migration from New Orleans. The migrating musicians share certain characteristics, such as their motivations to journey north, which echo the stories of other migrants. However, a number of characteristics set them apart from the typical African American who left the South during the Great Migration. Jazz musicians had an additional incentive to migrate north; they were hard-pressed to find profitable public outlets to ply their craft that offered both material *and* artistic satisfaction. This dynamic pushed them from the region and on to places that were receptive to the new musical form and the culture it fostered. In addition, the existence of Black benevolent societies coupled with the long history of Creole and African American activism in New Orleans conditioned musicians to political activism, which they continued in the North. Once in Chicago, the African American musicians' union protected jazz artists and fostered greater political participation. Additionally, due to cultural innovations in language, styles of dress, and demeanor, New Orleans musicians developed a consciousness that separated them from other migrants. These developments created an environment of political activism that combatted the repressive mechanisms that dictated the status of African Americans as second-class citizens in American society.

The central argument of this study is that jazz musicians joined the political activism that preceded and followed migration. In his study of Black working-class culture and politics, *Race Rebels* (1994), Robin D. G. Kelley argues that, all too often, conventional scholarship only views as "legitimate" those forms of protest and resistance that take place within the parameters of civil rights organizations or trade unions. Kelley asserts that, by doing so, scholars diminish disparate viewpoints within these groups and downplay resistance that takes place outside of these institutions. Instead, he advocates redrawing the map of political discourse by questioning common notions of what constitutes "legitimate" protest and resistance. To do so, Kelley rejects "the tendency to dichotomize people's lives, to assume that clear-cut 'political' motivations exist separately from issues of economic well-being, safety, pleasure, cultural expression, sexuality, freedom of mobility, and other facets of daily life. Politics is not separate from lived experience or the imaginary world of what is possible; to the contrary, politics is about these things." He further explains, "Politics comprises the many battles to roll back constraints and exercise some power over, or create some space within, the institutions and social relationships that dominate our lives."[8] Miller touched on these same themes in a piece for *Reviews in American History* in 1990. He described an antideterministic sentiment in the latter half of the twentieth century, writing that "participants in this revolt against determinism have assumed and sometimes asserted that individuals are and should be free to determine their own lifestyles and group affiliations as a means of achieving self-fulfillment, that sense of contentment with one's lot in life deriving from the sense that one devised it and chose to occupy it."[9]

Viewed in this light, the story of the development of jazz in New Orleans, and the subsequent migration of Black musicians out of the city to northern locales, is one rife with political overtones. Jazz musicians bolstered political discourse in New Orleans, Memphis, St. Louis, Kansas City, Chicago, and New York. Both before they left New Orleans and once they arrived elsewhere, musicians attempted a number of mobilizing and organizing activities to better their conditions and adjust to living in a new environment.[10] Additionally, jazz music acted as a vehicle for social change both in New Orleans and elsewhere.

Finally, the distinct and recognizable brand of jazz that developed in New Orleans became *the* national music as a result of the cultural forces set loose by the Great Migration. Given the extent of repression African Americans faced across the South and the lack of respect and full equality they were accorded in the North, that jazz, as a byproduct of Black culture, claimed a central place in American popular culture was no small feat. We often take for granted the 1920s identity as the Jazz Age, without fully considering the implications of this association for American society. Though jazz did not tear down all racial barriers during the Jazz Age, the 1920s saw Black and white customers interacting on American dance floors, the first nationally recognized and positively portrayed Black celebrities, and white jazz artists clamoring to emulate the latest innovations from men like Joe Oliver, Louis Armstrong, and Duke Ellington. Black musicians developed a distinct brand of language that persists to this day—terms like "gigs," "chicks," and "squares." In music conservatories across the country, contemporary students study the work of classical composers like Beethoven and Bach *and* the work of Armstrong and Ellington. Black musicians shared their artistic achievements with the nation during the Great Migration, and their creativity forever altered American society. Few could have envisioned such a transformation at the turn of the twentieth century.

What is now a full-fledged book project began as an MA research paper on Chicago jazz and political activism. When Miller introduced himself via email, the research paper was not yet finished. Once the paper was completed, I sent him what I had. He was elated and offered to include a revised version of my upcoming dissertation in the Urban Life, Landscape, and Policy Series for Temple University Press, where he served as an editor:

> I'm an admirer of your MA paper. Well organized, well written, well researched, and just plain interesting. Look forward to workiing with you more later. . . . But I think I found, gasp, one error. At the bottom of p. 39 you refer to a jam session as a form of employment, like a gig. Not in my time, at any rate. Musicians jammed in private for their own amusement after the gigs, sometimes, but also sometimes on other occasions—a jobless night, or an afternoon. You may want to coonsider the construction

of a glossary for your dissertation and book, for the benefit of theuninitiated.[11]

I was jubilant, and I got a glimpse of his editing prowess. He read carefully; he could have easily given the paper a cursory glance, since I was a young scholar quite a way off from a formulated manuscript. Rather, he offered insightful comments, a critical eye, and encouragement to carry the project to fruition.

He was also very considerate. My dissertation adviser was one of Miller's protégés, David Stradling. Miller was concerned that if he became too involved with the project while it was in the dissertation stage, he could potentially overstep and interfere with the relationship Stradling and I were developing. Instead, he asked for updates only when I had completed portions or fleshed out ideas to show him. Once accepted to the Ph.D. program, I envisioned the dissertation beginning the story in New Orleans. I wanted the project to next examine the jazz scenes in Chicago and New York, thus telling a more national story that focused on urban culture and activism. I shared this vision with Miller, and he was, of course, intrigued and ebullient. As I finished my Ph.D. coursework, I completed a second research paper on New Orleans jazz activism, which I passed along to Miller. He was critical, once again offering probing and insightful comments. But he also made certain to remind me that he believed the overall project was not only a worthwhile endeavor but one that would make a scholarly contribution. "I do indeed (in general) like the way you write, its clear, straightforward and will appeal to academic and non-academic audiences," he wrote. "I think this dissertation revised as a book will make you rich and famous, or at least richer and more famous than you now are, by which I mean quite a bit more, a whole lot."[12] It was his reassurance that made me *believe* my work was significant to the field. Given the incredible stress of graduate school, the dissertation phase, and the academic job market that I was soon thrust into, it was invaluable to have that encouragement from such a prolific scholar.

With the dissertation in hand, the next step was to begin thinking about how to fashion the project into a coherent manuscript. Once again, Miller's comments and advice were challenging and rewarding. In a flurry of emails over the course of two weeks, Miller dissected my dissertation and offered new lines of analysis and paths of inquiry.

We agreed that there was yet more to the story. I would expand my study to include Memphis, St. Louis, and Kansas City. With additional research, the book could reach academic and nonacademic audiences alike and tell a story that was missing in the literature on urban history. He also made certain that I was the architect of the project; he was a facilitator: "And remember, I'm working as an editor, and as an editor make suggestions for consideration—no mandates—things to accept, reject, or amend, to fit your taste and your argument as you see it. I see my job as helping you to write the best book that YOU [Miller's emphasis] want to write."[13] This was Miller's skill as a mentor on full display. He was not *telling* me how to write history; he was *empowering* me to write history.

As is often the case for freshly minted Ph.D.'s, I was overwhelmed by the job hunt. I eventually landed a two-year visiting position after much effort. All the while, Miller and I remained in touch, but I had little time to devote to the manuscript. He continued to offer possible leads and advice, nonetheless. I was able to secure funding to complete the additional research in Kansas City, St. Louis, and Memphis, and I was very happy I finally had some progress to report on the book project. His response was, as always, helpful, encouraging, and filled with humor: "Glad you're research is going so well. Memphis should be fun. There's a tolerably good book on Boss Crump that may or may not prove useful to you for contextual purposes. All's well for us in northwest Florida except that it's cold (for here, at this date) today. Nevertheless my wife and I played golf this afternoon, and are now warming up with a little merlot. It works pretty well."[14] It was the last time we were in contact.

Since his passing, I realize more clearly how much my work speaks to the broader themes Miller explored throughout his career—namely, conceptions of civic nationalism and his affinity for both outsiders and boosters in urban society. The musicians I write about began their respective careers as proverbial outsiders—African Americans deprived of full citizenship in the South during the nadir of Jim Crow America. But these musicians envisioned a different world than the one they inherited. As Amiri Baraka noted, "What seems to me most important about these mass migrations was the fact that they must have represented a still further change within the Negro as far as his relationship with America is concerned. It can be called a psychological realignment, an attempt to reassess the worth of the black man within the society as a whole, an attempt to make the American dream work, if it were going to."[15] Due to the power of jazz as a dynamic art form embraced by wide sections of American society during the Jazz Age, these outsiders became, perhaps ironically, cultural harbingers. As Miller wrote (in Chapter 1 of this volume), Louis Armstrong, Duke Ellington, and other jazz icons represented "radical thinkers and opponents of the status quo eager and capable of rallying others to their cause." Boosters promoting their respective cities as jazz capitals soon embraced these jazz outsiders, but Miller was also dubious of such claims of civic individuality in the era of mass culture. He expressed as much in one email exchange:

> I bet that these city labels—New Orlean Jazz, Kansas City and whatever—have little to do with musicianship and alot to do with something else—the human urge to classify things by some more orl ess meaningful taxonomy to the folks alive at the time and thereafter.... It has to do with city ubris, and city boosters, directly or indirectly (I mean, it sounds better to say that Count Basie;sband is Kansas City stuff than it;s cairo, Illinois stuff). I dunno. From my limited expeience as a musician, and from talking to (jazz(musicians, a gig is gig, and it would be real nice to find a gig with a band that you lked, frm the point of view of jazz, but a studio job isOK and also playing for commercial ads helps to pay for booze, ne reeds, and other nececcessities of life.[16]

Few took jazz seriously in its infancy—aside from the musicians themselves—but by the 1920s, this new cultural form became a point of civic pride. This development marked a radical departure in American society—African Americans recognized by the dominant culture as artists, not just as musicians. Miller's approach was a reminder that my work must make clear that these jazz outsiders were also intellectuals with their own conceptions of civic nationalism.

King Records

I was working on a second project when Miller passed away, and like my jazz capitals manuscript, it is something that spoke to his lifelong interests in civic nationalism and urban boosters. It was also a project—the story of Cincinnati's King Records and the local attempts to memorialize its history—that examined activism in his adopted hometown and the focus of so much of his own work. King Records was founded by Syd Nathan in 1943 and was headquartered at 1540 Brewster Avenue in Cincinnati's Evanston neighborhood. King completely transformed the way in which music was recorded and marketed to the public in the decades after World War II. The styles of music King recorded and promoted ranged from country and bluegrass to soul, jazz, doo-wop, gospel, and funk, to rockabilly and rock 'n' roll. Eventually, King artists inadvertently influenced a new generation of music pioneers in the earliest days of hip-hop. It was where the music legend James Brown recorded a series of hits, including "Mother Popcorn," "Cold Sweat," "Funky Drummer," and "Say It Loud—I'm Black and I'm Proud, Pt. 1." The Godfather of Soul was King's brightest star, but he was far from the only influential musician to pass through the doors of the King Studios. At various points between 1943 and 1971, King's stable of talent included the R&B star Hank Ballard, bluegrass pioneers the Stanley Brothers, bluesman Freddie King, and funk impresario Bootsy Collins, among others. In addition to its notable contributions to American music and culture, the company served as a model for integration. King moved to integrate its personnel in 1947 and is believed to be the first company in Cincinnati to do so. Certainly, the King story is worthy of local and even national recognition. Unfortunately, apart from music aficionados and Cincinnati residents in the know, few are aware of the important role King played in the development of rock 'n' roll and the impact the label had on American culture at large.[17]

The effort to raise awareness and preserve the legacy of King Records with some sort of public display dates to the 1990s. Former mayor and Cincinnati city councilman Dwight Tillery (a onetime Evanston resident) vowed to do something to publicly memorialize the contributions the label made to American music and culture, by honoring a previous pledge to erect a plaque on Brewster Avenue: "The plaque could . . . happen. As chairman of the finance committee, I could have some fun with it. We could get the big companies involved." *Cincinnati Enquirer* reporter Cliff Radel, who interviewed Tillery, asserted simply, "Pay tribute to King. It's long overdue."[18]

Tillery and Radel were not the only urban boosters interested in promoting the King story as a point of civic pride. In 1993, community activists announced a new plan. A coalition of artists and community members envisioned purchasing the King studios site from a local convenience store chain and converting the space (at the time a warehouse) into a recording studio, community center, and educational hub. Tillery was again instrumental in pushing the plan forward, and he imagined more than a simple plaque to mark the spot where King once stood. As he stated in 1994, "We could get a plaque put up, but a plaque means nothing. What if somebody tears down the building? If somehow we could commemorate King's history, and at the same time give the kids a way to express themselves, we could possibly do something." The Evanston Community Council was also in favor of the plan, hoping that it would not only provide a creative outlet for at-risk youth in the neighborhood but also serve as a linchpin for economic revitalization in the community.[19] The push to honor the King legacy in the early to mid-1990s sparked several projects aimed at convincing Cincinnatians theirs was a rich story worth sharing with the world. The artists, activists, and urban boosters promoting King memorialization plans instinctively understood one of Miller's fundamental lessons. What happens at the neighborhood level can dramatically affect urban life and have broader implications for the cultural landscape writ large. It was a lesson Miller and I pondered often, over cocktails during our digital salon sessions discussing the Great Migration and the Jazz Age.

By the end of 1994, the plan to honor King Records remained alive; activists now hoped to place the building on the National Register of Historic Places.[20] The *Cincinnati Enquirer* reported on the developing vision for the site with the headline "King-Sized Dreams: Making Former Cincinnati Recording Plant into Museum Would Revive an Era." Radel covered the nascent proposal and the hope that it would once again house a recording studio. Unfortunately, the building owners were unwilling to support a historic designation of the property, and without owner consent, no building can be listed on the National Register of Historic Places. The plan to honor King Records with a fitting tribute on Brewster Avenue stalled for more than a decade.

In 2008 city council members Alicia Reece and John Cranley revived the idea of a museum or historical marker to honor what Cranley called "one of Cincinnati's greatest exports."[21] In November 2008, a renewed push to save the building began. On November 26, Cincinnati's city council unanimously approved a resolution to restart the process of seeking a historic designation to protect the site. Councilman Cranley, who proved a dogged proponent of King site preservation efforts, introduced the motion. His support meant that activists interested in preserving the structure (including one of Cranley's top aides, Elliot Ruther) had an ally in a position to apply pressure on the building's owners in a way not attempted in the 1990s.[22] Increasingly, urban boosters promoting the King story shared office space at city hall.

The city council's resolution occurred in tandem with the erection of a historical marker at 1540 Brewster Avenue. On November 23, activists, community leaders, and artists converged in front of the building where King Records once churned out chart-topping hits to unveil a marker funded by the Rock and Roll Hall of Fame and Museum. The marker was part of an ongoing, nationwide "landmark series" (which designates sites across the country important to rock 'n' roll history as historic landmarks) and erected by the city of Cincinnati. A new nonprofit group called Cincinnati USA Music Heritage Foundation, organized by local activists and musicians in late 2007, including Elliot Ruther, Bootsy Collins, and his wife, Patti Collins, spearheaded the marker project. The plaque was erected as the city marked the sixty-fifth anniversary of King Records with several celebratory events, including a lecture series, panel discussion, and an exhibit at the Hamilton County Public Library.[23] At the unveiling ceremony for the plaque, Collins professed, "I'd just like to say my heart goes out to the ones . . . that opened the door for all of us to be able to stand here in front of this historical sacred place. Words can't describe how I'm feeling now. . . . In here under this one roof you got everything."[24] Collins eloquently imparted the significance of place to the King story. Zane Miller would have undoubtedly agreed, given his lifelong interest in the importance of place. While the principal goal of memorializing King Records with a historical marker in front of the building was achieved, the goal of protecting the site with a historic designation remained elusive.

In 2009 the Evanston Community Council, in partnership with neighboring Xavier University's Community Building Institute, announced a new effort evoking civic nationalism known as King Studios to provide an educational facility and museum dedicated to the local heritage of King Records. The organization's website explains: "Inspired by the legacy of historic King Records and fueled by the academic investment and economic development of nearby Xavier University, this one-of-a-kind facility will be located in Cincinnati's Evanston community, in the heart of the Montgomery Road business district. It will feature the dynamic integration of music and arts education, entrepreneurial training, and cultural history all under one roof." The plan is to eventually build a museum three blocks from the original King site in the Evanston business district, on the corner of Brewster Avenue and Montgomery Road.[25] According to Christopher Schadler, an urban planner and director of the King Studios Board, the grand vision for the eventual museum (with the official title the King Studios and Experiential Learning Center) is to provide a welcome center and educational facility in the heart of the business corridor and invite visitors to stroll three blocks along a guided path to the original King site and visit the space that once housed the label. To date, the property in the business district has been purchased, and two-thirds of the land is cleared, but the work of starting a capital campaign to build the structure has yet to begin.

In June 2015, John Cranley (elected mayor of Cincinnati in 2013) proposed Issue 22, a multimillion-dollar tax levy to place on the November ballot to revamp the city's park system. If approved, the measure would have not only funded improvements to existing parks but also provided money to purchase the original King Records site and convert it into a museum / cultural center. The Cincinnati Park Board would then manage the site in conjunction with Cincinnati USA Music Heritage Foundation. Unfortunately, the issue failed at the polls (as explained below) for reasons unrelated to the plans to save the King building.[26]

The King Records site is currently in a state of decay and disrepair due to decades of neglect. After the mayor announced his plans, Dynamic Industries (which specializes in medium and large part machining and fabrication and owns the property) applied for a demolition permit. At about the same time, the Bootsy Collins Foundation and Cincinnati USA Music Heritage Foundation submitted an application to the Cincinnati Historic Conservation Board asking that it declare the entire site a local historic landmark. The measure next required approval by the City Planning Commission, and finally the city council had to sign off on the plan before the designation could take effect and potentially save the building from demolition.[27] The designation effort would not place the building on the National Register of Historic Places; nor would it give the city ownership of the building; voters would have to approve the November tax levy to raise the money for the purchase of the site before the city could buy the property outright. The levy also assumed that the owners of the former King Records facility would be willing to sell their stake in the site.

On August 12, 2015, just months before the issue would go before the voters, Tim Burke, the attorney representing Dynamic Industries, spoke out against the proposed local historic landmark status for the King site. He did so at a Cincinnati Historic Conservation Board meeting, which reviews applications in place of the city's zoning examiner to determine if the property in question holds historical significance. Burke opposed the recommendation on the grounds that the building had not been used as a recording studio for decades (thus lacking a connection to its historical past), that the demolition application was filed before the application for historic designation was submitted, and that the local landmark ordinance itself was unconstitutional, violating his client's rights as a property owner.[28] Despite Burke's argument, the Cincinnati Historic Conservation Board forwarded its recommendation to approve landmark status to the City Planning Commission.

On August 21, Cincinnati's City Planning Commission met to decide the fate of the local historic landmark designation for the original King site. At the meeting, nearly a dozen community members, activists, urban boosters, and preservationists testified for an hour on the matter before the commission rendered its decision. Only one individual spoke out against the designation: Tim Burke, attorney for Dynamic Industries, who reiterated the arguments put forward at the Historic Conservation Board meeting.

Sam Stephens, the city's professional adviser on economic development, testified that aside from the cost to purchase the building from the current owners, it could take as much as $450,000 to $500,000 to stabilize the deteriorating structure. Liz Blume of the Community Building Institute at Xavier University professed, "I think Evanston is really lucky as a community to have such a resource in it. It's really a rich story that talks about racial reconciliation. It talks about innovation in music and we are very fortunate to be able to tell this story in Evanston." Blume was sympathetic to the concerns of the property owner but hoped a compromise could be brokered: "I think it's important that we work with the existing owner who does have property rights, but I think there's a way to accomplish what is being proposed so that the long-term redevelopment of the larger Dynamic Industries site gets preserved and the historic site gets preserved." James "Jimmy" Railey, one of James Brown's Famous Flames, echoed Blume's sentiments, declaring, "Music is the bridge to racism in Cincinnati. If you could jam it, didn't matter what color you were.... We can't let our heritage for our kids and grandkids to be wasted away." Before casting the conclusive vote, Commissioner Byron Stallworth asserted, "As an African-American, there are things that have happened in our history that we have not been able to preserve. In Cincinnati we had people of different races together changing the world. For that to be factual and document[ed] and something for our city to be proud of to trumpet around the world, I think it is important that we preserve it."[29] Blume, Railey, and Stallworth linked the struggle to save the building on Brewster Avenue with the broader struggle for racial inclusiveness in a deeply segregated city. Their vision of civic nationalism defined the King project as a unifying force, one that could bridge substantial divides between disparate Cincinnati communities. Miller articulated (again in Chapter 1 of this volume) similar beliefs in discussing the role of civic nationalism in American society as "an antiaristocratic, antimonarchical conception of citizenship and governance." In reference to the likes of Railey, Stallworth, and others, Miller continued, "The boosters' touting of these icons of local pride as regional and national treasures not only prompts a sense of their self-importance but also connects them to a civic enthusiasm bridging neighborhood, ethnic, racial, social class, religious, gender, sexual orientation, and political party divisions." Meanwhile, Burke's appeal for the protection of his client's property rights fell on deaf ears as the City Planning Commission unanimously approved the local historic landmark designation, forwarding the measure on to the city council.[30]

The Evanston Community Council continues to hope, as of this writing five and a half years after the park levy went down in defeat, that marketing the King story to the general public can help ongoing revitalization efforts by promoting cultural tourism in the neighborhood. The urban boosters on the Evanston Community Council understand that the history made on Brewster Avenue not only affected their neighborhood but had an outsized influence on American culture. In harnessing the power of the King story, activists are promoting their own vision of civic nationalism that hopes to repair some of the damage of past policies that adversely affected the neighborhood. The construction of Interstate 71 in the 1960s cut a wide path through the heart of the neighborhood, leading to an extended period of economic decline (in fact, King Records at the southern end of Brewster Avenue was spared the wrecking ball). The president of the Evanston Community Council, Anzora Adkins, informed the journalist Richard O. Jones, "We lost a lot of houses, businesses and churches. We lost our downtown. We had a walkable business district where the residents could shop, but all of that went out." Adkins and the Evanston Community Council worked closely with Xavier University and the King Studios project to bring the vision of a revitalized neighborhood to fruition. "You must have a goal, an objective and a vision. . . . You want to be able to do what is right, obey the rules, respect each other and work together. And you got to keep the faith," Adkins noted.[31] King Studios is the sort of project that Zane Miller would have championed with all of his renowned enthusiasm and vigor. It combines his lifelong interest in the importance of place with music, neighborhood activism, and boosterism. Since the construction of the King Studios and Experiential Learning Center is planned for a parcel of land three blocks from the original King site, revitalization efforts will continue regardless of the status of the original building. However, activists and community members continue to advocate for a protected designation for the building.

On October 5, 2015, Cincinnati City Council's Neighborhoods Committee approved the historic designation, and two days later the city council followed suit, voting unanimously to designate the site a local historic landmark and imposing an indefinite stay on the demolition permit. Mayor Cranley maintained that the city was in negotiations with Dynamic Industries and I. S. Mechanical Systems to obtain ownership of the entire King site in "good faith." Bowdeya Tweh, covering the proceedings for Cincinnati.com, explained the mayor's rationale:

Cranley, recalling his days on city council, said King Records preservation efforts date back to 2008 after council approved a motion to work toward designating the properties as historic. The motion, he said, was approved prior to the owner purchasing the property and the buyer should have known the designation could eventually happen. "We're only following through on a commitment made prior to the current ownership."[32]

With the city council on the record in its attempt to save the original building, it was next up to the voters to approve Issue 22, the tax levy providing funds for the purchase and maintenance of the site, though the city would only control the property if the owners agreed to its sale.

On November 3, 2015, 58 percent of Cincinnati voters rejected Issue 22. Mayor Cranley declared that the failure of Issue 22 was a message from the voters that the city "must live within its means." The following day the *Cincinnati Enquirer* placed the blame not on the cost of the levy ($35 per year for a property worth $100,000) or on antitax activism but squarely on the mayor's shoulders. The *Enquirer* noted that a diverse coalition of community organizations objected to the levy out of concerns over "process, project specifics—or lack thereof—and priorities." Mayor Cranley went out of his way to sell Issue 22 to voters in television and radio ads featuring his likeness, but he did not make a substantive argument that eased the concerns of many voters. Therefore, the *Enquirer* declared the mayor "should take the levy's rejection a little personally. As the *Enquirer* editorial board noted in its endorsement of Issue 22, he short-circuited both council and public input in rushing the park levy onto the ballot. . . . We're unlikely to see another city park levy any time soon, but as Cranley regroups, he needs to engage citizens even more *before* announcing where we're headed next as a city."[33] Instead of rallying citizens behind a shared sense of values, history, and purpose—appealing to a collective sense of civic nationalism and pride—Cranley's proposal fell well short at the polls.

Preservation plans continued, in spite of the failed ballot measure. On January 17, 2017, the city council's budget and finance committee adopted a measure announcing the city's expressed intent to purchase and preserve the site. Two days later, the city council unanimously approved a resolution to seize the building using the power of eminent domain.[34] What looked like a drawn-out legal battle between the property owner and the city ended on April 4, 2018; the Cincinnati City Council approved a land swap deal with Dynamic Industries that grants the company city-owned land adjacent to the King site in exchange for the historic building. The next step will be to secure funding to stabilize the building and eventually preserve the structure and return it to its original condition.[35] Though it took decades of determined persistence to put memorialization efforts on the public agenda, the struggle to preserve the legacy of King Records in Cincinnati continues, as a compelling vision for a public space honoring King's history has yet to materialize. If such a vision were to succeed in the coming years, Miller would surely argue that it must be one embracing a "metropolitan mode of thought" that prioritizes the King story as one crucial to the common welfare of the city.[36]

The Cincinnati School

I was in the early stages of the King Studios project when Miller passed away. I was just about to send him what I had written to that point and ask for advice when I received the news of his passing. It will always be a great personal regret that he never got to read what I had drafted. It is the sort of project he would have loved, and I am certain it would have sparked several nights of scholarly back-and-forth via email. Miller's enthusiasm for urban history never wavered, especially when it pertained to Cincinnati's civic life and identity. With the King case, we see Miller's interest in the metropolitan mode of thought on display—individuals dedicated to building a broader community that appeals to the common good, binding Cincinnatians of disparate backgrounds. Though much of the memorialization efforts revolve around the physical space on Brewster Avenue, for many activists there is also something existential at stake. In a city that saw the first major incidents of racial unrest of the twenty-first century and routinely ranks among the most segregated in the country, the King legacy represents a unifying story line in a racially divided metropolis. Consequently, effective public history initiatives that convey the significance of King Records and its history of racial inclusiveness have the potential to positively impact not only the Evanston neighborhood but also Cincinnati's collective sense of self. The historians Andrew Hurley and Dolores Hayden have demonstrated the importance of public history projects that work collaboratively with civic partners and community organizations at the grassroots level in St. Louis and Los Angeles, respectively. Those projects proved successful in crafting more inclusive narratives that account for issues of race, class, and gender in the often-contested terrain of urban environments. Activists in Cincinnati look to harness similar strategies and tell the King story in a way that moves beyond the usual narratives of record sales and chart-topping hits, to provide Cincinnatians a lens through which to view their city in a new light.[37]

We also see in the King story Miller's proverbial boosters once again championing a cause that speaks to the virtues of civic nationalism in the Queen City. When Bootsy Collins describes the King site as a "historical sacred place," he is promoting the space as Cincinnati's communal, cultural legacy. When Byron Stallworth declares, "In Cincinnati we had people of different races together changing the world. For that to be factual and document[ed] and something for our city to be proud of to trumpet around the world, I think it is important that we preserve it," he is advocating not only for Cincinnati's inclusion in broader discussions of racial reconciliation and reform, but he is also intervening in how those narratives are celebrated by civic leadership. When the Evanston Community Council endorses the King Studios and Experiential Learning Center as a potential economic engine spurring development in the long-neglected neighborhood, they are serving as advocates promoting the broader good. The King story was not championed by local powers that be during the label's most prolific period; the *Cincinnati Enquirer* and the *Cincinnati Post*, the two major papers in the city, rarely covered the day-to-day or even year-to-year accomplishments of the company. Syd Nathan's sister, Dorothy Halper, once declared, "The newspapers weren't interested. Nobody cared about King Records. The city wasn't proud of its association. I think people in other cities were more interested and impressed with the company." One of Nathan's original partners, Howard Kessel, bluntly stated, "They never wanted anything to do with us. To them, we were just making records for hillbillies and black people."[38] The boosters of the present like Collins, Stallworth, and the Evanston Community Council are atoning for the sins of boosters past. The current King Records boosters seek to celebrate outsiders willing to upset the status quo, whose legacy can drive a reassessment of dominant modes of thought in a racially divided metropolis.

At a roundtable discussion on Zane Miller's legacy and influence at the Eighth Biennial Urban History Association Conference (an organization founded by Miller and other like-minded scholars), John D. Fairfield spoke of the late scholar's significance to the field. Among many contributions, Fairfield noted that Miller founded the Cincinnati School of urban history. Fairfield explained that Miller studied at the University of Chicago under the renowned urbanist Richard C. Wade, and therefore, Miller was part of the Chicago School of social science scholarship, which in the first decades of the twentieth century pioneered using the actual city as a laboratory for research. The Laboratory in American Civilization, founded by Miller and Henry D. Shapiro at the University of Cincinnati in the 1970s, brought that model to the Queen City. Generations of Miller protégés produced scholarship that challenged dominant narratives about the city and its residents, leaving behind a rich historiography of Cincinnati's past.[39] Fittingly, several of Miller's mentees and members of the Cincinnati School attended the roundtable discussion, including Charles F. Casey-Leininger, Judith Spraul-Schmidt, Robert Fairbanks, Patricia Mooney-Melvin, and David Stradling. With my work on King Records, I am now a card-carrying member of the Cincinnati School. I am immensely proud to stand in that tradition and to be Zane Miller's last mentee; his influence on my scholarship and career cannot be overstated. I am even prouder to call him my friend.

NOTES

1. Zane L. Miller, "Re: Bob Burnham," personal email message, September 13, 2011.

2. For more information on these projects, see Charles Lester, "'You Just Can't Keep the Music unless You Move with It': The Great Migration and the Black Cultural Politics of Jazz in New Orleans and Chicago," in *Escape from New York: The New Negro Renaissance beyond Harlem*, ed. Davarian Baldwin and Minkah Makalani (Minneapolis: University of Minnesota Press, 2013), 313–334; Charles Lester, "'They've Taken It All Away. The Only Thing Here Is Me': The Struggle to Preserve the Legacy of King Records," *Public Historian* 39, no. 2 (May 2017): 58–81. Brief excerpts from these titles appear in the following pages.

3. Eric Arnesen, ed., *Black Protest and the Great Migration: A Brief History with Documents* (New York: Bedford / St. Martin's, 2003), 1.

4. James R. Grossman, *Land of Hope: Chicago, Black Southerners, and the Great Migration* (Chicago: University of Chicago Press, 1989).

5. Alain Locke ed., *The New Negro: Voices of the Harlem Renaissance* (New York: Albert & Charles Boni, 1925). For more on the New Negro movement and the range of activities and locations associated with this moment of Black activism, see Baldwin and Makalani, *Escape from New York*.

6. David Levering Lewis, *When Harlem Was in Vogue* (New York: Penguin Books, 1997); Nathan Irvin Huggins, *Harlem Renaissance* (New York: Oxford University Press, 1971).

7. Sidney Bechet, *Treat It Gentle: An Autobiography* (New York: Twayne, 1960), 95.

8. Robin D. G. Kelley, *Race Rebels: Culture, Politics, and the Black Working Class* (New York: Free Press, 1994), 4, 9–10.

9. Zane L. Miller, "Cheers! (But Is That All There Is, My Friend?)," review of Richard B. Stott, *Workers in the Metropolis: Class, Ethnicity, and Youth in Antebellum New York City*, in *Reviews in American History* 18 (December 1990): 485–492.

10. Here, I am borrowing the concepts of mobilizing and organizing as outlined by noted civil rights activist Bob Moses in the 1960s. Moses argues that mobilizing efforts relied on relatively short-term, large-scale public events, while organizing efforts focused on the long-term development of leaders composed of ordinary individuals. For more information on this distinction, see Charles M. Payne, *I've Got the Light of Freedom: The Organizing Tradition and the Mississippi Freedom Struggle* (Los Angeles: University of California Press, 1995), 3–4.

11. Zane L. Miller, "M.A. Paper," personal email message, April 11, 2009.

12. Zane L. Miller, "Re: bravo," personal email message, June 15, 2010.

13. Zane L. Miller, "Intro., Chs. 1 and 2," personal email message, June 7, 2013.

14. Zane L. Miller, "Re: FW Question," personal email message, October 3, 2015.

15. Amiri Baraka (LeRoi Jones), *Blues People: Negro Music in White America* (New York: Harper Collins, 1999), 95–96.

16. Zane L. Miller, "Bird," personal email message, October 23, 2013.

17. For more information on the King Records story and the ongoing memorialization efforts, see Jon Hartley Fox, *King of the Queen City: The Story of King Records* (Urbana: University of Illinois Press, 2009); Lester, "'They've Taken It All,'" *Public Historian*, 58–81.

18. Cliff Radel, "Tribute to King Remains Long Overdue," *Cincinnati Enquirer*, December 28, 1993.

19. Randy McNutt, "Music Fans Seek to Save History," *Cincinnati Enquirer*, April 28, 1994.

20. Cliff Radel, "It's Been on the Charts; Is the Register Next?" *Cincinnati Enquirer*, November 6, 1994. There has been a long and complicated struggle in

Cincinnati over historic preservation and community development, specifically in the city's Over-the-Rhine neighborhood. For more information on these developments, see Zane L. Miller and Bruce Tucker, *Changing Plans for America's Inner Cities: Cincinnati's Over-the-Rhine and Twentieth-Century Urbanism* (Columbus: Ohio State University Press, 1998); Christopher Swope, "Over the Rhine Again," *Preservation Magazine*, March/April 2007, 29–35; Colin Woodard, "How Cincinnati Salvaged the Nation's Most Dangerous Neighborhood," Politico, June 16, 2016, http://www.politico.com/magazine/story/2016/06/what-works-cincinnati-ohio-over-the-rhine-crime-neighborhood-turnaround-city-urban-revitalization-213969.

21. Fox, *King of the Queen City*, 192.

22. "City of Cincinnati Council Resolution 200801440," November 26, 2008, 1–2, Cincinnati USA Music Heritage Foundation Files.

23. Rick Bird, "King of Them All," Citybeat, November 19, 2008, http://www.citybeat.com/music/music-feature/article/13018508/the-king-of-them-all; Rick Bird; "King Records Celebration," Citybeat, November 12, 2009, http://citybeat.com/cincinnati/article-19187-king_records_celebration_(2008).html.

24. Bootsy Collins, King Records Marker Ceremony, tape #1, Monument B-Roll, November 23, 2008, Cincinnati USA Music Heritage Foundation video, Lightborne Communications.

25. King Studios (website), "About," accessed February 5, 2022, http://www.xavier.edu/communitybuilding/kingstudios/about.cfm.

26. Chris Wetterich, "Which Parks and Facilities Will Be Built, Overhauled as a Part of Cranley's Plan?," *Cincinnati Business Courier*, June 25, 2015.

27. Richard O. Jones, "Bootsy Collins Foundation, Mayor John Cranley Fighting to Save King Records Building in Cincinnati," WCPO.com, July 28, 2015, http://www.wcpo.com/news/insider/bootsy-collins-foundation-mayor-john-cranley-fighting-to-save-king-records-building-in-cincinnati.

28. Tim Burke in Richard O. Jones, "King Records: Attorney Argues City Must Issue Demolition Permit," WCPO.com, August 12, 2015, http://www.wcpo.com/news/insider/king-records-attorney-argues-city-must-issue-demolition-permit.

29. Richard O. Jones, "Support Grows for King Records Historic Preservation," WCPO.com, August 21, 2015, http://www.wcpo.com/news/local-news/hamilton-county/cincinnati/support- grows-for-king-records-historic-preservation.

30. Jones, "Support Grows"; Bowdeya Tweh, "Supporters: King Records Deserves Landmark Status," Cincinnati.com, August 21, 2015, http://www.cincinnati.com/story/money/2015/08/21/king-records-cincinnati/32120299/; James Railey's comments are from the author's notes of the proceedings of the Cincinnati City Planning Commission, August 21, 2015.

31. Richard O. Jones, "King Records Looms Large in Evanston Revitalization Plans, Regardless of Historic Status," WCPO.com, September 6, 2015, http://www.wcpo.com/news/insider/king-records-looms-large-in-evanston-revitalization-plans-regardless-of-historic-status.

32. Chris Wetterich, "King Records Building Status Heads to Full City Council Vote," *Cincinnati Business Courier*, October 5, 2015; Bowdeya Tweh, "King Records Now a City Landmark," Cincinnati.com, October 7, 2015, http://www.cincinnati.com/story/money/2015/10/06/facing-wrecking-ball-king-records-site-up-landmark-vote/73479642/.

33. Editorial Board, "Editorial: Parks Loss Holds Lesson for Cranley," *Cincinnati Enquirer*, November 4, 2015.

34. Jordan Burgess, "City Looks at Buying King Records Property for Preservation," WCPO.com, January 17, 2017, http://www.wcpo.com/news/local-news/hamilton-county/cincinnati/city-looks-at-buying-king-records-property-for-preservation; Sharon Coolidge, "City May Seize King Records Building," Cincinnati.com, January 19, 2017, http://www.cincinnati.com/story/news/politics/2017/01/19/city-may-seize-king-records-building/96765394/; WCPO Staff, "City Solicitor: 'Uncertain' if City Will Be Successful in Buying King Records," WCPO.com, January 17, 2017, http://www.wcpo.com/news/local-news/hamilton-county/cincinnati/city-solicitor-uncertain-if-city-will-be-successful-in-buying-king-records.

35. Paula Christian, "Cincinnati Leaders Approve Land Swap Deal to Save Historic King Records from Demolition," WCPO.com, April 3, 2018, https://www.wcpo.com/news/insider/cincinnati-leaders-approve-land-swap-deal-to-save-historic-king-records-from-demolition; FOX19 Digital Media Staff, "City Leaders Approve Property Exchange for Iconic King Records Site," FOX19.com, April 4, 2018, http://www.fox19.com/story/37883302/city-leaders-approve-property-exchange-for-iconic-king-records-site.

36. Zane L. Miller, *Suburb: Neighborhood and Community in Forest Park, Ohio, 1935–1976* (St. Martin, OH: Commonwealth Book Company, 2016; repr. of 1981 edition), xxxiv. For more on Miller's fascination with the metropolitan mode of thought and its implications for urban life, see John D. Fairfield, "'The *Metropolitan* Mode of Thought': Zane L. Miller and the History of Ideas," Chapter 4 in this volume.

37. In April 2001, civil unrest broke out for three consecutive days after the police shooting of Timothy Thomas, a nineteen-year-old unarmed African American. The shooting and subsequent unrest led to federal oversight of the Cincinnati Police Department and a new "Collaborative Agreement" between communities and the police. For more information on these developments, see Kevin Osborne, "Reflections of Riots and Race," Citybeat, April 6, 2011, http://www.citybeat.com/news/article/13012138/reflections-on-riots-race. It was not the first incident of racial unrest in the city. Violence broke out in Cincinnati's Avondale neighborhood in 1967 and again in 1968 after the assassination of Martin Luther King Jr. Although Avondale lies just a few miles from Evanston, it is unclear what impact the unrest had on King Records. For more on the history of racial unrest in Cincinnati, see John Kiesewetter, "Civil Unrest Woven into City's History," *Cincinnati Enquirer*, July 15, 2001. Cincinnati has ranked among the most segregated cities in the United States for decades. For a concise

overview of segregation, ghetto formation, and housing discrimination in Cincinnati, see Charles F. Casey-Leininger, "Making the Second Ghetto in Cincinnati: Avondale, 1925-70," in *Race and the City: Work, Community, and Protest in Cincinnati, 1820-1970*, ed. Henry Louis Taylor Jr. (Urbana: University of Illinois Press, 1993), 232-257. For a more recent analysis of segregation in Cincinnati, see Nick Swartsell, "That which Divides Us," Citybeat, August 26, 2015, http://www.citybeat.com/home/article/13001852/that-which-divides-us. A study published in 2011 by the University of Michigan's Social Science Data Analysis Network ranked Cincinnati among the top ten most segregated cities in the United States. For more information on the study, see William H. Frey, Brookings Institution, and University of Michigan Social Science Data Analysis Network's Analysis of 2005-9 American Community Survey and 2000 Decennial Census Tract Data, https://www.psc.isr.umich.edu/dis/census/segregation.html, accessed March 8, 2022. For more information on Hurley's work in St. Louis, see Andrew Hurley, *Beyond Preservation: Using Public History to Revitalize Inner Cities* (Philadelphia: Temple University Press, 2010), 55-177. For more information on Hayden's work in Los Angeles, see Dolores Hayden, *The Power of Place: Urban Landscapes as Public History* (Cambridge, MA: MIT Press, 1995), 82-247.

38. Fox, *King of the Queen City*, 52, 191.

39. John Fairfield, "Making Sense of the City: Zane L. Miller and American Urban History," roundtable discussion at the Eighth Biennial Urban History Association Conference, Chicago, October 14, 2016; for more on the Chicago School, see Robin F. Bachin, *Building the South Side: Urban Space and Civic Culture in Chicago, 1890-1919* (Chicago: University of Chicago Press, 2004), 106-109.

8

Working with Zane Miller

LARRY BENNETT

My first contact with Zane Miller was in the late 1980s. I was shopping around a book manuscript, and at that time Zane coedited, with his friend and colleague Henry Shapiro, the Ohio State University Press Urban Life and Urban Landscape series. That book series, of course, was the precursor to the ongoing Temple University Press Urban Life, Landscape, and Policy series. Zane was generally enthusiastic about my project, which would be published as *Fragments of Cities: The New American Downtowns and Neighborhoods*, though among the comments he sent me, I do recall his stern admonishment to read more closely the text of the 1949 U.S. Housing Act! In retrospect, I can confirm that he was right: I had generalized too much and needed to tether a portion of my argument more closely to the intent of that legislation and the particular programmatic means it specified. I also recall that Zane was a late adopter of the personal computer: his first set of comments—if my memory serves me, running to nearly ten pages—were typewritten and, as such, were probably both the last and longest typewritten communication I ever received.

A quarter century passed, and fortuitously, Alex Holzman, who had headed the Ohio State University Press in the 1980s, had moved to Temple. And I was once more shopping around a manuscript, which

I submitted to Temple for review. Among the readers Alex recruited was Zane, who for a second time was supportive of what was a very different project. This was a comprehensive, coedited volume on contemporary Chicago that, when published, was titled *The New Chicago: A Social and Cultural Analysis*. What I did not know at the time was that Ohio State had dropped the Urban Life and Urban Landscape series, and Alex Holzman was in discussion with Zane about Temple's initiating an urban studies series. Within a year of the publication of *The New Chicago*, Zane and David Stradling invited me to join them editing the Urban Life, Landscape, and Policy series. In a very loose sense, Zane, the narrative urban historian was "life"; David, the environmentally engaged historian, was "landscape"; and I—trained as a planner, posing for many years as a political scientist—was "policy."

Working with Zane for approximately the decade before his passing was one of the most interesting, exhilarating, and intense experiences of my life. As many of the readers of this volume know, Zane was an ecumenical urbanist, enthusiastic about everything from memoir to ethnography, in addition to narrative urban history. What this meant for David and me was a lot of intellectual "stretching" to come to terms with and evaluate in an informed way a wide variety of manuscripts. This sometimes meant we were put in awkward situations, both in reading and evaluating texts *and* in communicating with Zane about our judgments. Very early in our coediting venture, I remember reading a manuscript that had been written by a retired Cincinnati musician, an acquaintance of Zane's and, I'm willing to bet, an engaging raconteur. Nor was he an inept writer, but possibly unlike his conversational gambits, in his writing he had no gift for actually connecting life experience to the cities he had visited as he gigged across the United States. It is often hard to read between the lines of emails, but I do remember sensing Zane's deflation when he responded to my suggestion that this manuscript had "too far to go" to become a part of our series.

The flip side of Zane's ecumenicalism—and beyond that, his seeming to know every urban historian between Portland, Maine, and Portland, Oregon, including graduate students about to make a mark in the field—has been that the Temple series has never suffered from a lack of submissions. In many cases, Zane did more than simply pull in proposals and participate in our reviewing process. He often functioned as a "developmental editor," working closely with a prospective author as the latter refined ideas, research, and text. As a result, at times I felt that Zane may have crossed over to advocacy of particular projects, but over the years—and through the discussion of many book proposals—Zane induced from me a more careful attention to the intent of authors and more articulated criticism of works in progress. Through my association with Zane I became a better editor.

Zane Miller the ecumenical urbanist was also an enthusiastic urbanist and intellectual. Zane loved cities, and in our email exchanges that were nominally directed at discussing manuscripts, he would often slip into recollections of cities he had visited, researched, or simply found interesting. He was always collecting and assessing new ideas, and I can imagine what his copies of the *New York Review of Books*—once read and digested—looked like: deeply furrowed, marked up, and probably unfit for anyone else to read.

With Patty Mooney-Melvin, during Zane's final years I was working with him on a book project that began as a third iteration of *The Urbanization of Modern America* but morphed into something more ambitious. Part urban history text, but part—and by far the more important part—summation of Zane's thinking about the American city, portions of this never titled work in progress are included in this volume. The core idea that Zane was developing was *civic nationalism*, a term that he borrowed from the polymathic Canadian Michael Ignatieff, but which he recalibrated in a specifically American, urban fashion. Whereas Ignatieff, in *Blood and Belonging*, presents civic nationalism—"a community of equal, rights-bearing citizens, united in patriotic attachment to a shared set of political practices and values"—as the alternative to "ethnic nationalism," "the nation as Volk," Zane viewed civic nationalism (in its U.S. guise) as the product of the Enlightenment universalism shared by the likes of Jefferson, Madison, and Franklin; early republican institutional design via the Constitution and, in particular, through the federal division of authority between national and state governments; and decades of continent-spanning community building.[1] In this American context, Zane's civic nationalism bears an evident resemblance to the historian Gary Gerstle's use of the same term in *American Crucible*, but Zane's insistence on the central role of cities in propagating civic nationalism is all his own.[2] At a further remove, the engagement with social diversity that is the day-to-day content of Zane's sense of civic nationalism might be linked to the sociologist Elijah Anderson's notion of the "cosmopolitan canopy."[3]

Zane's distinctive conceptualization of civic nationalism can be compressed to the following basic proposition: American cities have been more than simply the receptors or sites of democratic practice; they have been producers of democracy. The production of democracy has occurred as an outgrowth of everyday urban "practice," the mental attitudes and social skills that are spawned by city living, as well as by the more formalized processes of mobilizing political influence and governing. Given this sense of their cultural role in the United States, Zane viewed cities not so much as important places in which American democracy played out but rather as the forge defining the essential features of American democracy: widespread participation, tolerance (Zane's preferred term was *comity*), and a commitment to social progress.

For Zane, civic nationalism was also a cultural norm under threat. While I do not think he supposed that "big processes," such as post–World War II suburbanization or escalating globalization, negated civic nationalism, he was very sensitive to how American democracy has drifted toward irresponsible rhetoric, polarization, and intolerance. And this, in part, he attributed to the reduced place of urban life in the lived experience of most Americans. Civic nationalism, nonetheless, could experience a renaissance, and for this reason I think Zane was especially interested in such recent cultural trends as the "comeback" of central cities. My further sense is that in his final work Zane wanted to contribute to the prospective rebirth of civic nationalism by tracing its development and specifying the many salutary effects of this underappreciated foundation of American culture.

One of the great ironies of contemporary academic life turns on our remarkable capacity to collaborate at a distance: Zane and I never met face-to-face; over the decade of working together on the Urban Life, Landscape, and Policy series, we had exactly one phone conversation! Nevertheless, he was a pivotal figure in my development as a scholar and, indeed, as a human being. Zane Miller's unusual amalgam of attributes—intense commitment to work, unwavering curiosity, and resolute collegiality—made him a rare and inspiring figure.

NOTES

1. Michael Ignatieff, *Blood and Belonging: Journey into the New Nationalism* (New York: Farrar, Straus and Giroux, 1994), 6–7.
2. Gary Gerstle, *American Crucible: Race and Nation in the Twentieth Century*, 2nd ed. (Princeton, NJ: Princeton University Press, 2017).
3. Elijah Anderson, *The Cosmopolitan Canopy: Race and Civility in Everyday Life* (New York: Norton, 2011).

Appendix

A Zane L. Miller Timeline and Selective Bibliography

May 19, 1934	Zane Miller is born in Lima, Ohio.
	He attends public schools in Lima and in Peru, Indiana, graduating from Lima's South High School in 1952.
1956, 1958	Zane earns his BA and MS degrees from Miami University (Ohio).
	While at Miami University, he plays saxophone in the Campus Owls. Prior to graduate school, he marries Janet Smith, a Miami University graduate and teacher in Lima, and he teaches at Central Junior High School, also in Lima.
1959	Zane studies German language at the Deutsche Sprachkurse für Ausländer at the University of Vienna.
	Before beginning graduate studies at the University of Chicago, Zane teaches at Carl Sandburg High School in Orland Park, Illinois.
1961	"Senator Nathaniel Macon and the Public Domain, 1815–1828," Zane's first professional academic publication, appears in the *North Carolina Historical Review*.
	He is the Henry Milton Wolfe Fellow at the University of Chicago during 1961–1963 and a Social Science Research Council Graduate Training Fellow during 1963–1964.
1964–1965	Zane is appointed instructor in history at Northwestern University, Evanston, Illinois.
1965	Zane joins the University of Cincinnati History Department as instructor in history.

1966	Zane earns his Ph.D. from the University of Chicago. His dissertation title: "George B. Cox and the Municipal Reformers."
	He is appointed as an assistant professor at the University of Cincinnati.
1968	*Boss Cox's Cincinnati: Urban Politics in the Progressive Era* is published by Oxford University Press.
1968	Zane is selected a National Endowment for the Humanities Fellow.
1968	Zane joins a group of neighborhood residents and academics examining the urban redevelopment of Cincinnati's West End, the Queensgate II project. His work with this group over the next several years results in the publication in 1982 of *The Planning Partnership: Participants' Views of Urban Renewal*, coedited with Thomas H. Jenkins (Sage).
1969	Zane is promoted to associate professor of history, University of Cincinnati.
1970	Zane is appointed curator of the Metropolitan Studies Collection, Archival Collections of the University of Cincinnati.
1970	*Physician to the West: Selected Writings of Daniel Drake on Science and Society*, coedited with Henry D. Shapiro, is published by the University Press of Kentucky.
1971	Henry Jebsen, whose dissertation was supervised by Zane, is awarded his Ph.D. in history. Zane will supervise sixteen more doctoral dissertations during his tenure at the University of Cincinnati.
1972	Zane chairs the Hamilton County (Ohio) McGovern for President Committee.
1973	Zane, with his colleague and friend the intellectual historian Henry Shapiro, founds the Laboratory in American Civilization, an undergraduate research seminar emphasizing the collection and examination of primary sources. They will lead this seminar for more than two decades. In 1975 Miller and Shapiro share the University of Cincinnati's Robert Low Award for Innovation in Undergraduate Education.
1973	*The Urbanization of Modern America: A Brief History* is published by Harcourt, Brace, Jovanovich. The second, revised edition, coauthored with Patricia Mooney-Melvin, appears in 1986.
1973–1977	Zane serves on the Cincinnati Bicentennial Celebration Commission.
1973–1986	Zane serves on the editorial board of the *Great Lakes Review*.
1974	Zane is promoted to professor of history, University of Cincinnati.
1974–1980	Zane serves on the City of Cincinnati Architectural Board of Review.

1975	Zane receives the President's Distinguished Faculty Achievement Award, University of Cincinnati.
1977	Zane is the Newberry Library State and Community History Fellow in Chicago, Illinois.
1977–1991	Zane serves on the Editorial Board of the *Journal of Urban History*.
1978 (February)	"Scarcity, Abundance, and American Urban History" is published in the *Journal of Urban History*.
1978 (August)	"Teaching and Learning History by Doing: The Laboratory in American Civilization," coauthored with Henry D. Shapiro, is published in the *History Teacher*.
1980	At the annual meeting of the American Historical Society, a group of urban historians, including Zane, convene and agree to form the Urban History Association.
1981	Zane is a visiting scholar of African and Afro-American Studies Curriculum, at the University of North Carolina.
1981	With Henry Shapiro, Zane is appointed codirector of the new Center for Neighborhood and Community Studies, Institute for Policy Research, University of Cincinnati.
	Among the programs sponsored by the Center for Neighborhood and Community Studies was the Frontiers of Urban Research Seminar, bringing together Ph.D. students and faculty from a variety of University of Cincinnati departments.
1981	*Suburb: Neighborhood and Community in Forest Park, Ohio, 1935–1976* is published by University of Tennessee Press.
	Citing *Suburb*, in 1982 Zane receives the Ohio Academy of History's Publication Award (commending an active member of the academy for the outstanding publication in the field of history issued in the preceding year).
1981	"The Role and Concept of Neighborhood in American Cities" is published in Robert Fisher and Peter Romanofsky, eds., *Community Organization for Social Change: A Historical Perspective* (Greenwood Press).
1981–1986	Zane serves on the Ohio Historic Site Preservation Advisory Board.
1981–1991	Zane serves on the Cincinnati Historic Conservation Board.
1983	Zane receives the University of Cincinnati's George Rieveschl Jr. Award for Creative and/or Scholarly Works.
1987	*American Urbanism: A Historiographical Review*, coedited with Howard Gillette Jr., is published by Greenwood Press.
1987	Zane and Henry Shapiro are founding coeditors of Ohio State University's Urban Life and Urban Landscape book series.
	Between 1988 and 2007 forty-three titles were issued in the Urban Life and Urban Landscape series.

1988	Zane serves as coeditor, with Gene D. Lewis, of the Greater Cincinnati Bicentennial History Series, University of Illinois Press.
	The volumes published in this series included Robert B. Fairbanks's *Making Better Citizens: Housing Reform and the Community Development Strategy in Cincinnati, 1890–1960* (1988); *Ethnic Diversity and Civic Identity: Patterns of Conflict and Cohesion in Cincinnati since 1820*, edited by Henry D. Shapiro and Jonathan D. Sarna (1992); *Race in the City: Work, Community and Protest in Cincinnati, 1820–1970*, edited by Henry Louis Taylor Jr. (1993); and Steven C. Tracy, *Going to Cincinnati: A History of the Blues in the Queen City* (1993).
1991	Zane serves as president of the Urban History Association, succeeding Richard C. Wade, his longtime friend and dissertation supervisor at the University of Chicago.
1992	With University of Cincinnati colleague Roger Daniels, Zane organizes the Cincinnati Seminar on the City, a forum bringing together academic researchers, community leaders, and neighborhood residents to discuss their city.
1996	Zane is awarded the Oscar Schmidt Award for Public Service by the University of Cincinnati.
1998	*Changing Plans for America's Inner Cities: Cincinnati's Over-the-Rhine and Twentieth-Century Urbanism*, coauthored with Bruce Tucker, is published by the Ohio State University Press.
1999	Zane retires from the University of Cincinnati and is appointed Charles Phelps Taft Professor Emeritus of American History.
	With donations from former students, colleagues, and friends, the University of Cincinnati's Department of History establishes the Zane L. Miller Prize for graduate students. In 2010, a successor initiative, the Zane L. Miller Fund for Research in American Urban History, is created to support graduate students specializing in urban history.
2001	*Visions of Place: The City, Neighborhoods, Suburbs, and Cincinnati's Clifton, 1850–2000* is published by the Ohio State University Press.
2004	"The Death of the City: Cultural Individualism, Hyperdiversity, and the Devolution of National Urban Policy" is published in Hamilton Cravens, ed., *The Social Sciences Go to Washington: The Politics of Knowledge in the Postmodern Age* (Rutgers University Press).
2007	Zane is founding coeditor, with David Stradling and Larry Bennett, of Temple University Press's Urban Life, Landscape, and Policy book series.

	Between 2007 and 2016, twenty titles were issued in the Urban Life, Landscape, and Policy series.
2013	Zane endows the Zane L. Miller Professorship in American Urban History at the University of Cincinnati.
March 15, 2016	Zane Miller passes away in Pensacola, Florida.

Contributors

LARRY BENNETT is Professor Emeritus of Political Science at DePaul University.

ROBERT B. FAIRBANKS is Professor Emeritus of History at the University of Texas at Arlington.

JOHN D. FAIRFIELD is Professor of History at Xavier University in Cincinnati.

CHARLES LESTER is a faculty member in the Honors Tutorial College at Ohio University.

ZANE L. MILLER (1934–2016) was the Charles P. Taft Professor of History Emeritus at the University of Cincinnati.

PATRICIA MOONEY-MELVIN is Associate Professor of History at Loyola University Chicago.

DAVID STRADLING is the Zane L. Miller Professor of History at the University of Cincinnati.

Index

Page locators in italics refer to figures

"accidental cities," 93
Adkins, Anzora, 172
African Americans, 179n37; flight from cities, 68–69; and Great Migration, 59, 158–162; and mass migrations, 163–164; segregation in Cincinnati, 73–75, 171, 174, 179–180n37; segregation of, 5, 25, 30, 73–75, 80. *See also* jazz
airports, 94–96, 102, 114
American Bar Association, 49
American Crucible (Gerstle), 183
American Federation of Musicians, 158
American Revolution, 4, 14, 18, 39–40
Anderson, Elijah, 184
annexation, 104–105, 107–108, 113, 122–123n71
Appalachia, 59, 61–62
Appalachia on Our Mind: The Southern Mountains and Mountaineers in the American Consciousness, 1870–1920 (Shapiro), 61–62

Arlington, Texas, 90, 92–101; as agricultural community, 95; chamber of commerce, 97, 98, 111; city plans, 94, 111–113, 124–125n104; and Cold War defense sector, 96–97; diversity of, 114; industrial park, 99–100; intentional growth, 92–95, 97–99, 110–111; in postcivic era, 114–115; refunding program, 97–98; sports teams attracted to, 94, 100–101; as tourist town, 94, 100, 114, 121n50
Arlington Journal, 97, 98, 110
Articles of Confederation, 24
Atlanta, 22
austerity budgets, 25–26

bankruptcies, 25–26
Baraka, Amiri, 163–164
Barcelona, 28
Bechet, Sidney, 159
Bednarek, Janet, 72

Berlin, 35
"bettabilitarianism," 82
Biennial Urban History Association Conference (Eighth), 176
biography, sculptural, 131
blight, fears of, 29, 67, 73–74
Blood and Belonging (Ignatieff), 183
Bluestone, Daniel, 133, 135–136, 143
Blume, Liz, 170–171
Bodnar, John, 143, 144
Bogart, Michele, 143
Boorstin, Daniel, 41n13
boosterism, 4–5, 16–18, 104; and jazz tourism, 158, 165, 167, 171–172; and small cities, 93–94; of Vandergriff, 98–99. *See also* city builders
Bootsy Collins Foundation, 169
Boss Cox's Cincinnati: Urban Politics in the Progressive Era (Miller), 55–58, 75, 128, 130, 146
"bosses," 23, 29, 41n9, 56
Boyer, Paul, 134
Brown, James, 166, 171
Burgess, Ernest W., 129
Burke, Tim, 170
Burnham, Daniel, 70
Burnham, Robert, 156–157
Bush-Gore campaign, 80

Cabaret (musical), 35
Caldwell, Robert W., 111–113, 124n104
Caldwell and Associates, 111–113, 124n104
Carter, Jimmy, 66
chambers of commerce: Arlington, Texas, 97, 98, 111; Mesa, Arizona, 94, 101–103
Changing Plans for America's Inner Cities: Cincinnati's Over-the-Rhine and Twentieth-Century Urbanism (Miller and Tucker), 70–72, 76, 78, 80–81
charters of incorporation, city, 24, 58, 97
Chicago, Illinois, 127; ethnic composition of, 135; Haymarket Riot (1886), 139, 150n63; Humboldt Park, 141–142; as jazz center, 158; Lincoln Park, 136–142, 145, 150n60; park system, 136–142, 145, 150n60; Puerto Rican community, 146; West Park system, 141–142; World's Columbian Exposition (1893), 131. *See also* German immigrants
Chicago Citizens of German Descent, 140
Chicago Daily Tribune, 139
Chicago school, 4, 128, 145, 176
Cincinnati, Ohio, 3–4; Avondale-Corryville districts, 73–74; Charter Party, 58; Cincinnati Metropolitan Plan (1948), 58–59; City Council's Neighborhoods Committee, 172; City Planning Commission, 170; Clifton, 73–76, 87n45, 87n48, 90, 116; Cox machine, 57–58; earnings tax, 67; Evanston, 166–176; Forest Park, 62–64, 66–70, 85n25, 90, 116, 128; German immigrants, 136, 137; King Records, 165–174; Over-the-Rhine, 70–72, 86–87n40, 90, 116, 178n20; racial unrest, 174, 179n37; and rock 'n' roll history, 157; segregation, 73–75, 171, 174, 178–179, 180n37
Cincinnati Enquirer, 173
Cincinnati Historic Conservation Board, 169–170
Cincinnati Park Board, 169
Cincinnati school, 3–4, 7n2, 116, 174–176
Cincinnati Seminar on the City, 77
Cincinnati USA Music Heritage Foundation, 168, 169
cities: "accidental," 93; Black and white flight from, 68–69; capital, 15, 45, 110; charters of incorporation, 24, 58, 97; civic capacity of, 5, 18, 22, 27, 55–56, 79, 160, 183–184; death of the city, specter of, 23, 25; definition of, 18; destruction by war, 22; early modern North American, 14–16; European, 12–13, 22–23, 26,

31; federal-state-city compromise, 25; home rule, 24, 26, 29, 58, 113, 125n111; and ideas, 11–12; jazz centers, 157–165; lower tier, 29, 32; nineteenth-century despair about, 23, 35; and nineteenth-century reformers, 128–129; observed from two angles, across three eras, 18–21; Old World, 12–13, 19; as organisms, 57–58, 65, 128–129; as policy agencies, 11; in postcivic era, 114–117; as producers of democracy, 184; resiliency of, 5–6, 22–42, 56; "second cities," 15–16, 22, 26, 28–29, 31; as sources of energy, will, and means, 12; as sources of ideas, 11–12; state laws governing, 24; tripartite system of rule, 24–25; "world of," 27. *See also* Southwest, cities in
"Cities, American Civic Nationalism, and Fundamentalism" (Miller), 6, 43–52
city builders, 11–12, 16–18, 91–92, 94–95, 107, 113; and small cities, 91–95, 108–113. *See also* boosterism
city-improving specialty, 17
city planning, 68–69, 91, 111. *See also* Arlington, Texas; Chicago, Illinois; Cincinnati, Ohio; Mesa, Arizona
city-states, 5, 23–29, 40n1; medieval Europe, 23–24, 26; as sovereign powers, 23
civic art, 131. *See also* statuary
civic associations, 10, 23, 26–27, 33; leagues, idea of, 27–29; special-interest, 66, 69
civic capacity, 5, 18, 22, 27, 55–56, 79, 160, 183–184
civic illiteracy, 49–50
civic nationalism, 10–16; as antiaristocratic and antimonarchical, 10–11, 45; challenges to, 5–6, 31, 35, 37, 47–51; and civic illiteracy, 49–50; defined, 10–11, 183; founders' role in, 22, 43–48, 51n2, 183; and jazz, 158, 165, 168–169, 171–172; as prior to

ethnic nationalism, 32; prospective rebirth of, 184. *See also* boosterism; Constitution of the United States (1787); cultural individualism; federalism; nationalism
civic pride, 5, 16–17, 165, 167, 171
civic temperament, 20–21, 81
civics education, 49–50
civility, 80, 89n62
civil rights movement, 25, 161
Civil War, 22, 24, 31, 47
Clifton, Cincinnati, 73–76, 87n45, 87n48, 90, 116
Clifton Town Meeting (CTM), 73–75
Clinton, Bill, 36, 80
Clinton, Hillary Rodham, 36
cognitive dissonance, 57, 61–62, 81
cognitive units, 84n17
Cold War, 96–97
Collins, Bootsy, 168, 175
Collins, Patti, 168
colonial American thinkers, 10–14
Coming of Age in Samoa (Mead), 33
comity, compact with, 27, 49, 79–82, 86n36, 184. *See also* tolerance
Community Building Institute (Xavier University), 168–169
community of advocacy, 64–67, 115
community of limited liability, 65–66, 74, 83n4, 85n27, 87n48
consensus, 81, 86n36, 89n62
Constitution of the United States (1787), 14–15, 20, 32–33, 39; Tenth Amendment, 24; Thirteenth, Fourteenth, and Fifteenth Amendments, 24; first ten amendments (1791), 15, 33; Philadelphia Constitutional convention, 45; territorial and state governments established by, 45–46
Conzen, Kathleen Neils, 138
"cosmopolitan canopy," 184
Cox, George B., 57–58
Cranley, John, 167–168, 169, 172–173
cultural individualism, 4–5, 56–57, 71, 117n5, 118n12; emergence of, 19;

inward-turning tendency, 66–67, 69, 75, 115; in journalism, 33–37; and segregationist urban policies, 25; and social engineering, 77–78
cultural pessimism, 6, 50–51
culture of narcissism, 66

Dallas, Texas, 91, 97
Dallas–Fort Worth Metroplex, 92, 112–113
Dallas–Fort Worth (DFW) Turnpike, 100–101
Davis, Susan G., 134
death of the city, specter of, 23, 25
Declaration of Independence (1776), 14, 20, 32, 43, 46–47; psychological, 39
decongestion, 25, 29
democracy, 15, 20–21, 33; cities as producers of, 184; and city-states, 23; liberal, 39, 42n18
Department of Housing and Urban Development, 108
determinism, 37–38, 60–61, 72, 78, 82, 161
Detroit, Michigan, 25–26
Developers (real estate), 97, 105, 108, 110, 131
Dewes, Francis J., 141
Dewey, John, 77, 82
Dobbert, Guido, 137
Dobson, Cliff, 108
dominant modes of thought, 5, 10, 65, 90, 176
Drake, Daniel, 62
drug abuse, 30
Dynamic Industries, 169–174

Eisenhower administration, 25
Ellington, Duke, 35
embargo of 1807, 47
empire of liberty, 14, 44–45
Engels, Friedrich, 47
Englesman, Franz, 142
Eurocities, 27
European cities, 12–13, 22–23, 26, 31

Evanston (Cincinnati), 166–176
Evanston Community Council, 167–169, 171–172, 175–176
evils, list of, 29–30
"Evolution of a Major City" (Springer), 113
Experience and Nature (Dewey), 77
expressway legislation, 25

Fairfield, John, 176
Fair Housing Act (1968), 30
Fear and Loathing in Las Vegas: A Savage Journey into the Heart of the American Dream (Thompson), 36–37
federalism, 11, 15, 44–45, 46, 183; and city sovereignty, 23–24, 26–27; federal-state-city compromise, 25; territorial and state governments, 45–46
Finley, Charles, 103–104
Forest Park, Cincinnati, 62–64, 66–70, 85n25, 90, 116, 128
For the City as a Whole (Fairbanks), 91
Fort Worth Cats, 100
Foucault, Michel, 69
founders, (the), 43–48, 183; "civilizing" project of, 44; Roman empire, interest in, 22, 43–44, 51n2
Fragments of Cities: The New American Downtowns and Neighborhoods (Bennett), 181
France, 50
freedom, 142; Schiller's representation of, 139–140
"From Istanbul to Philadelphia: Ideas and the Urban Origins of the United States" (Miller), 4–5, 9–21
Fromm, Erich, 35
fundamentalism: market, 77–78, 80; religious, 6, 50–51

Gall, John, 140
Gandhi, Mahatma, 48
Geertz, Clifford, 69
General Motors (GM), 98, 99, 124n98

German immigrants, 131–142; Chicago, 136–142; Cincinnati, 136, 137; ethnic identity, shaping of, 137–140, 144; festive ritual repertoire, 138–139. See also Chicago, Illinois; immigration
Germany, 48–49
Gerstle, Gary, 183
ghettos, 30, 75; slum clearance, 65, 71, 72, 78, 80, 91
"global integration," 28
Globalization and World Cities Project, 28
Goodman, Ellen, 85–86n28
Görling, Felix, 141
Great Migration, 59, 158–162
Great Southwest Corporation, 99–100
Greene, Richard, 114–115
Groth, Paul, 130
Gruen, Victor, 108–110, 112
guilds, 23

Halper, Dorothy, 175
Hanseatic League, 26, 27
Harlem Renaissance, 158, 159
Harrison, Carter H., 139–140
Hawkes, George, 98
Hayden, Dolores, 175
Haymarket Riot of May 4, 1886, 139, 150n63
Hindenburg, Paul von, 49
hinterlands ("provinces"), 15–16, 18, 27, 44, 92
Hirsch, Arnold, 71–72
historical periods, 5, 10, 12, 116, 118n12, 128–130. See also symptomatic history; urban history
Hitler, Adolf, 48–49
Hofstadter, Richard, 79, 81, 89n64
Holli, Melvin G., 137
Holmes, Oliver Wendell, Jr., 82
Holzman, Alex, 181–182
home rule, 24, 26, 29, 58, 113, 125n111
hopefulness, 30–33, 55–56, 79
Housing Act of 1949, 181
Housing Act of 1954, 108

housing reform, 91. See also slum clearance
human agency, 4, 9, 91
Humboldt, Alexander von, 141–142
Humboldt Park (Chicago), 141–142
Hurley, Andrew, 175

ideas, 3–5, 9–10; antiaristocratic and antimonarchical, 10–11; cities as sources of, 11–12; dominant modes of thought, 5, 10, 65, 90, 176; and space, 128. See also civic nationalism; metropolitan mode of thought; mode of thought; symptomatic history; taxonomies of social reality
identity, 127–128; German ethnic, shaping of, 137–140, 144; statues as celebration of, 133
Ignatieff, Michael, 32, 50–51, 183
immigration: African, Asian, and Latin American immigrants, 146; assimilation and empowerment, relationship between, 135; Chicago's ethnic composition, 135; cultures of assent and descent, 142–144, 146; fear of the "foreign," 134, 142; German immigrants, 131–142; and host society acceptance, 142–143; and pluralism, 136, 144–145. See also German immigrants
impersonal social forces, 4, 9, 91
"in-city suburb," 73–74. See also Clifton (Cincinnati)
India, 48
Indigenous urban societies, 12
industrial parks, 99–100, 102
inter-core-city coordination, 27
interdependence, 4, 19, 24, 57, 59–60, 65, 73, 128–129
inward-turning tendency, 66–67, 69, 75, 115
isolationism, neighborhood, 75
Israel, 48
Istanbul, 12, 16, 22
"Is that all there is?" song, 34–35

Italy, 48
It Takes a Village (Clinton), 36

jazz: and boosterism, 158, 165, 167, 171–172; cities as centers for, 157–165; and Great Migration, 160; and King Records, 165–174; New Orleans brand, 161–162; political activism associated with, 157–161
Jazz Age, 156, 159, 162, 165
Jefferson, Thomas, 14, 44, 47
Johnson, Lyndon, 30
Jones, Albert, 97
Jones, Richard O., 172
journalists, 33–37, 41–42n17

Kelley, Robin D. G., 161
Kessel, Howard, 175
King Records, 165–174; ballot measure, 173; King Studios and Experiential Learning Center, 168–169, 172, 175
Kyoto Protocol (2006), 81

Laboratory in American Civilization (University of Cincinnati), 59–60, 62, 82, 176
landmark series (of rock 'n' roll sites), 168
land use, 57, 106, 110
Lasch, Christopher, 88n60
Las Vegas, 36–37
Lebanon, 48
Lefebvre, Henri, 145
legislatures, 14; territorial and state, 45–46; two-house, 49
Lewis, David Levering, 159
liberation history, 9, 78–79, 84n17
Lilla, Mark, 50
Lincoln, Abraham, 31, 39, 43
Lincoln Park (Chicago), 136–142, 145, 150n60
Lower East Side, Manhattan, 35
lower tier cities, 29, 32
Lush Life (Price), 35
lush lifers, 35, 38

Major League Baseball, 101, 103–104
Making Better Citizens (Fairbanks), 91
"Manifesto of the Communist Party" (Marx and Engels), 47
Marcus, Alan I., 79–80
Maricopa County Planning and Zoning Commission, 105–106
Marx, Karl, 47
Maslow, Abraham, 38–39, 42n18
McDonald, Terence, 68, 69
Mead, Margaret, 33
medievalist urban reformers, 23–24, 26; neomedievalists, 26–30, 40n5
Mesa, Arizona, 90, 92–94, 101–110; as agricultural community, 94, 95; chamber of commerce, 94, 101–103; city plans, 94, 105–107, 108–110; civic leaders, 107; defense systems industries, 102, 110; diversity of, 114; financial problems, 115; HoHoKams organization, 103–104; intentional growth of, 102, 106–107, 109, 110–111; lack of civic-mindedness, 115; options within, 109; suburban ranch classification, 107–108; tax structure, 105; as tourist town, 102–103, 106, 109–110, 114
metropolises, 57–59, 65–67, 86n28; city building within, 93–113
metropolitan mode of thought, 55–89; and change over time, 60, 69–72, 130; community of advocacy, shift to, 64–67; community of limited liability as successor to, 65–66, 74, 83n4, 85n27, 87n48; demise of, 4, 56–59, 64–67, 73–74; as "irretrievably past," 67, 77; preserving, 76–79; and symptomatic history, 60–64, 66–71; and taxonomies of reality, 57, 60–64, 68–71. *See also* ideas
Midwest, 93
Miller, Zane, 55–56; activist bent in work of, 5; as American pragmatist, 77, 79–82; "community of limited liability" concept of, 65–66; as

"decadent liberal," 81; emails sent by, 155–156, 162–163, 165; jazz, love of, 5, 156–157; legacy of, 76–79; liberation history, theory of, 9, 78–79, 84n17; metropolitan mode of thought, concept of, 55–60; "radically historical approach," 60, 63, 85n20; relationships as central to approach of, 156–157; as scholar, mentor, and friend, 155–185; timeline and selective biography, 187–191; Works: *Boss Cox's Cincinnati: Urban Politics in the Progressive Era*, 55–58, 75, 128, 130, 146; *Changing Plans for America's Inner Cities: Cincinnati's Over-the-Rhine and Twentieth-Century Urbanism*, 70–72, 76, 78, 80–81; "Cities, American Civic Nationalism, and Fundamentalism," 6, 43–52; "From Istanbul to Philadelphia: Ideas and the Urban Origins of the United States," 4–5, 9–21; "The Resiliency of Cities and the Uncertain Future of American Civic Nationalism," 5, 22–42; *Reviews in American History* article, 161; *Suburb: Neighborhood and Community in Forest Park, Ohio, 1935–1976*, 62–70, 77, 128; *Urbanism as a Way of Life: The City and American Civic Nationalism*, 56, 78–79; *The Urbanization of Modern America: A Brief History*, 183; *Visions of Place: The City, Neighborhoods, Suburbs, and Cincinnati's Clifton, 1850–2000*, 73–76. *See also* civic nationalism; metropolitan mode of thought; taxonomies of social reality

Mills, C. Wright, 85n26

mode of thought, 128; and change over time, 60, 69–72, 130. *See also* ideas; metropolitan mode of thought

Mooney-Melvin, Patricia, 183

Mormons, 94, 95

Moses, Bob, 177n10

Motivation and Personality (Maslow), 38–39

multicentered metropolis, 92

municipal and industrial revolutions, 47

Muslims, 28, 48

Mussolini, Benito, 48

Nathan, Syd, 166, 175

nationalism, 48; battle between types of, 32; civic nationalism as alternative to, 4; ethnic, 33, 183; and federalism, 15; post-Civil War, 61. *See also* civic nationalism

National Literacy Act, 49

National Register of Historic Places, 167, 170

nation-states, 18, 23, 26–27, 44, 160

needs, hierarchy of, 38–39

Nehru, Jawaharlal, 48

neighborhood organization movement, 60

neomedievalism, 26–30, 40n5

The New Chicago: A Social and Cultural Analysis (Bennett), 182

New Orleans, 161–162

New York City, 15, 20, 22; fiscal crisis, 25–26; as jazz center, 158

New York magazine, 42n17

Nixon, Richard, 30

nostalgia, 6, 50, 132

Obama, Barack Hussein, 33

Obama administration, 30

Ohio State University Press Urban Life and Urban Landscape series, 181, 182

Old World cities, 12–13, 19

Olmsted, Frederick Law, 70

Ottoman Empire, 12–13

"outer-city neighborhood," 73–76, 90

outsiders, 4–5, 10, 157, 164–165, 176

Over-the-Rhine, Cincinnati, 70–72, 86–87n40, 90, 116, 178n20

Index

Page, Max, 80
Palestine, 48
parks, 127–152; changing conceptions of, 131–134; Chicago, 136–142, 145, 150n60; as civic arenas, 131; industrial parks, 99–100, 102; Six Flags Over Texas amusement park, 94, 100, 121n50
patriotism, 5, 14, 43, 45, 134, 143, 183
Patterson, Dwight, 103
Philadelphia, Pennsylvania, 14, 16, 26, 31, 45
Phoenix, Arizona, 92, 95, 102, 110
Pitstick, Bill, 99
Plan of Chicago (Burnham), 70
pluralism, 15–17, 21, 24, 32, 79; cultural, 50, 57, 59, 71–72, 75, 145; and immigrant communities, 136, 144–145
political economy, 37, 44
postcivic era, 114–117
poststructuralism, 60–61
pragmatism, 77, 79–82, 88n60
Price, Richard, 35
The Private City (Warner), 55
privatism, 55–56, 85–86n28
problems, 10, 60–66, 75–76; city role in problem-solving, 20, 55, 79, 81, 86n36; as interdependent, 128–129; shifts in thinking about, 29–30, 90–91, 115–117, 132–133, 145
public interest, 4, 34–35, 37, 39, 67, 72, 74–76, 78, 80, 91, 115; defined, 56
Putin, Vladimir, 32

Race Rebels (Kelley), 161
racism: music as bridge to counter, 171; segregation, 5, 25, 30, 73–75, 80, 171, 174, 179–180n37
Radel, Cliff, 166–167
Railey, James "Jimmy," 171
Rapp, William, 140
Rau, Ernst, 140
Reaves, John, 100
Reece, Alicia, 167–168
reformers, 134; medievalist, 23–24, 26; neomedievalists, 26–30, 40n5; nineteenth-century, 24, 128–129
religion, 11, 44, 48; fundamentalism, 6, 50–51
Reno, Nevada, 51–52n4
republican vision, 43–45, 142, 183
"The Resiliency of Cities and the Uncertain Future of American Civic Nationalism" (Miller), 5, 22–42
Reuter, Fritz, 142
Revenue Sharing Program (federal government), 105
Rock and Roll Hall of Fame and Museum, 168
rock 'n' roll history, 168
Roman empire, founders' interest in, 22, 43–44, 51n2
Rosenthal, Julius, 139
rural regions, 44, 46–47
Russia, 32
Ruther, Elliot, 168
Ryan, Mary, 144, 145

Schadler, Christopher, 169
Schiller, Johann Christoph Friedrich von, 138–142, 151n67
Schiller Monument Committee, 139
Schuyler, David, 132
Schwabenverein (German ethnic club), 138, 151n67
sculpture, public, 127
"second cities," 15–16, 22, 26, 28–29, 31
segregation, 5, 25, 30, 80; in Cincinnati, 73–75, 171, 174, 179–180n37
self-actualization, 38, 42n18
Shapiro, Henry D., 59–62, 82, 84n17, 90, 176, 181
Sheehy, Gail, 33–38, 41–42n17
Short, Bob, 101
Six Flags Over Texas amusement park, 94, 100, 121n50
slavery, 13–14, 44
slum clearance, 65, 71, 72, 78, 80, 91
Smith, Scott, 104
social engineering, 77–78, 80

Index / 203

socialist movements, 47–48
social reality: taxonomies of, 3–5, 18, 60–64, 66, 68–72, 76, 78, 90–91; validated through use of space, 134
society, interdependence of, 4, 19, 24, 57, 59–60, 65, 73, 129
Southwest cities, 90–126; airport locations, 94–95; annexation laws, 104–105, 107–108, 113, 122–123n71; decentralization, 111–114; intentional growth, 92–95; and postwar migration, 95; Superstition Freeway (U.S. 60), 108, 109, 110; urban sprawl, 92, 95, 98, 114. *See also* Arlington, Texas; Mesa, Arizona
space, 127–152; character shaped by, 133; civic, 130–136, 141, 145–146; claiming, and civic engagement, 144–146; collective gatherings in, 134, 139–140; as interpretive tool, 130; landscapes as intersection of people and place, 130–131; and statuary, 127, 130–146
sports teams, 94, 100–101, 103
Springer, Marvin, 113
Stallworth, Byron, 171, 175
State and Local Fiscal Act of 1972, 105
statuary, 127, 130–146; as celebration of identity, 133; as civic art with a purpose, 131; claiming space and civic engagement, 144–146; and cultures of assent and descent, 142–144, 146; dedication ceremonies, 139–141, 142, 143; essential attributes of, 133; ethnic, 134; and host society acceptance, 142–143; monument drives, 141; as "petrified ethnics," 127, 130, 135; sculptural biography, 131; settings for, 133–134
Stephens, Sam, 170
Stradling, David, 76, 163, 182
Strayhorn, Billy, 35, 38
structuralism, 60–61
structure, 63
suburbanization, 23, 25, 59, 85n25, 118n10; and community of advocacy, 64–67; community of limited liability, 65–66, 74, 83n4, 85n27, 87n48; "in-city suburb," 73–74. *See also* Arlington, Texas; Mesa, Arizona; Southwest cities
Suburb: Neighborhood and Community in Forest Park, Ohio, 1935–1976 (Miller), 62–70, 77, 128
Superstition Freeway (U.S. 60), 108, 109, 110
symptomatic history, 3–4, 60–64, 66–67, 90, 92; critiques of, 68–72, 86nn35–36; defined, 63

Taft, Lorado, 127, 131, 132, 145
taxes, 46
taxonomies of social reality, 3–5, 18, 60–64, 66, 76, 78; Appalachian example, 61; applied to smaller cities, 90–91; and change over time, 60, 69–72, 130; critiques of, 68–71
Teaford, Jon C., 68
Temple University Press Urban Life, Landscape, and Policy series, 162, 181–183
Tenth Amendment, 24
Texas A&M University, 96
Texas and Pacific Railroad, 95
Texas Rangers, 94
Thatcher, Margaret, 34
Thomas, Timothy, 179n37
Thompson, Hunter, 36–38
Tillery, Dwight, 166–167
tolerance, 127–128. *See also* comity, compact with
tripartite system of rule, 24–25
Tucker, Bruce, 70–72, 76, 78, 80–81
Tweh, Bowdeya, 172–173

unincorporated land, 106–107, 113, 125n111
United Kingdom, 48
United States: campaigns for national conformity, 145; as city-building civilization, 12, 43–44; founders of, 22, 24, 43–44, 51n2; urban origins

of, 9–21. *See also* civic nationalism; Constitution of the United States (1787); founders; specific cities
University of Cincinnati, 73, 76, 155; Laboratory in American Civilization, 59–60, 62, 82, 176
Upton, Dell, 130
urban crisis, idea of, 20, 23, 81
The Urban Frontier (Wade), 6
urban hierarchy, 14–16, 22, 26
Urban History Association, 77
urban occupational specialists, 17–18
urbanism, 4, 19, 31, 47, 56
Urbanism as a Way of Life: The City and American Civic Nationalism (Miller, unfinished), 56, 78–79
urbanization, 11–13, 19–20
The Urbanization of Modern America: A Brief History (Miller, Mooney-Melvin, and Bennett), 183
urban sprawl, 92, 95, 98, 114
urban sweepstakes, 18, 22, 26, 27, 29, 51–52n4
U.S. Conference of Mayors' Climate Protection Agreement, 81

Vandergriff, Tom, 98–99, 100–101, 111, 121n50, 124n98
Vatican City, 28
Victor Gruen and Associates, 108–110, 112
Visions of Place: The City, Neighborhoods, Suburbs, and Cincinnati's Clifton, 1850–2000 (Miller), 73–76
Vocke, William, 142
volunteering, 56

Wade, Richard C., 6, 176
walking city, 57
Wallace, Michael, 144
warfare, 22, 26, 28
Warner, Sam Bass, 55
The War on Slums in the Southwest (Fairbanks), 91
"war on terror," 23
Washburne, Hempstead, 141
Washington, DC, 15, 45
Weltschmerz (world weariness), 35
Whyte, William H., 85n27
"world of cities," 27
World War II era, 72, 77–78; and Southwest cities, 104–105
Wright, Chauncey, 82
Wrigley, Phil, 103
Wynne, Angus, Jr., 99–100, 121n50

Xavier University, 168–169, 172

zoning regulations, 59, 71, 73–74, 104–106, 109, 111, 124n104, 170

Also in the series *Urban Life, Landscape, and Policy*:

Robert Gioielli, *Environmental Activism and the Urban Crisis: Baltimore, St. Louis, Chicago*

Robert B. Fairbanks, *The War on Slums in the Southwest: Public Housing and Slum Clearance in Texas, Arizona, and New Mexico, 1936–1965*

Carlton Wade Basmajian, *Atlanta Unbound: Enabling Sprawl through Policy and Planning*

Scott Larson, *"Building Like Moses with Jacobs in Mind": Contemporary Planning in New York City*

Gary Rivlin, *Fire on the Prairie: Harold Washington, Chicago Politics, and the Roots of the Obama Presidency*

William Issel, *Church and State in the City: Catholics and Politics in Twentieth-Century San Francisco*

Jerome Hodos, *Second Cities: Globalization and Local Politics in Manchester and Philadelphia*

Julia L. Foulkes, *To the City: Urban Photographs of the New Deal*

William Issel, *For Both Cross and Flag: Catholic Action, Anti-Catholicism, and National Security Politics in World War II San Francisco*

Lisa Hoffman, *Patriotic Professionalism in Urban China: Fostering Talent*

John D. Fairfield, *The Public and Its Possibilities: Triumphs and Tragedies in the American City*

Andrew Hurley, *Beyond Preservation: Using Public History to Revitalize Inner Cities*